ETHICS
CAN

To Marc
To making a greater
ethical difference
Cynthia
10.9.2014

ENDORSEMENTS

The title of this book, "*Ethics Can*", lives up to its promise. In addition to dealing with more recent issues such as cybercrime, social media and supply chain, the content is an illustration of how ethics permeates every aspect of the workplace. The book is packed with practical examples, and each chapter contains useful questions for workplace discussions and recommended reading. That the author eats, sleeps and breathes ethics shines through. If you are uncertain about how to take ethics from concept to implementation, read this book. And keep it for regular future reference.

Ansie Ramalho, Chief Executive Officer
The Institute of Directors, Southern Africa

Cynthia Schoeman is at the forefront of promoting business ethics in South Africa. Drawing on her extensive knowledge and experience, she has written an exceptional book. It offers a clear and systematic treatment of business ethics, and is laced with valuable insights and practical suggestions.

Rabbi Gideon Pogrund (MA (Cantab))
Business Ethics Consultant

Cynthia is an accomplished ethics professional and writer and I have had the pleasure to deal with her and attend several of her presentations on quite a few occasions in the past. As soon as you start engaging with Cynthia, you realise that she has a passion for ethics and the expertise to influence and be a catalyst for change.

What a pleasure to finally read a book about the practical implementation of ethics in organisations which makes perfect sense. As an ethics practitioner of nine years I had to find my own way around the corporate landscape addressing ethics in business. My life would have been made much easier if I could have an ethics 'bible' like this with me to guide me, support me, and in fact tell me what ethics in business is all about. We sometime s tend to focus too much on theory and then get bogged down in philosophy without knowing how to determine and implement the solutions.

Cynthia has a relaxed and cheeky writing style, making learning about ethics an absolute pleasure. It is sometimes difficult to present a good business case for ethics as it usually involves a loss in short-term profits and a focus on long-term sustainability. Cynthia makes an effective and succinct case and brings it home with workable examples.

The chapter on ethical leadership is especially close to my heart. Cynthia focuses on all the relevant aspects of an ethics programme as well as the case studies and tools to assist with implementation. This is a highly recommended publication for any ethics practitioner and I will be one of the first to invest in Cynthia's book.

Driekie Havenga, Nedbank Ethics Officer

ETHICS
CAN

Managing Workplace Ethics

by

Cynthia Schoeman

KNOWRES
PUBLISHING

2014

First published in 2014

ISBN: 978-1-86922-491-2
ISBN: 978-1-86922-492-9 PDF eBook

Published by Knowres Publishing (Pty) Ltd
P O Box 3954
Randburg
2125
Republic of South Africa

Tel: (011) 706-6009
Fax: (011) 706 1127
E-mail: orders@knowres.co.za
Website: www.kr.co.za

Printed and bound: Mega Digital (Pty) Ltd, Parow Industria, Cape Town
Typesetting, layout and design: Cia Joubert, cia@knowres.co.za
Cover design: Cia Joubert, cia@knowres.co.za
Editing and proofreading: Adrienne Pretorius, Gemini Editing Services, pretorii@mweb.co.za
Project management: Cia Joubert, cia@knowres.co.za
Index created with: TExtract, www.Texyz.com

DEDICATION

To Edward and Benjamin.

May you grow up in a society where ethics too has grown and developed.

ACKNOWLEDGEMENTS

Special thanks to my twin sister, Sandra, for her invaluable help.

My thanks also to Knowledge Resources for agreeing to publish a book on ethics, and to Cia Joubert for all her assistance and for the cover design. Thank you too to Adrienne Pretorius for such professional editing.

TABLE OF CONTENTS

ABOUT THE AUTHOR

Cynthia Schoeman BA (Unisa), MBA (Wits Business School)

Cynthia Schoeman is the founder and MD of Ethics Monitoring & Management Services (Pty) Ltd and is based in Johannesburg, South Africa.

Cynthia established the company with the aim of promoting the proactive management of workplace ethics and of providing practical support to organisations in order to improve their ethical status. She has worked in the field of ethics for more than a decade to build greater awareness of workplace ethics and to promote the more effective management of ethics. She has developed a web-based ethics survey, the Ethics Monitor, which serves as a valuable tool to measure, monitor, manage and accurately report on organisational ethics.

She is the author of *An Employee's Guide to Workplace Ethics,* which is a concise guide providing an overview of ethics in the workplace, as well as a book which addresses workplace ethics more fully: *Ethics: Giving a Damn, Making a Difference,* published in 2012. She writes a quarterly ethics newsletter, *Setting the Example*, and her articles are published frequently in business journals and the press.

Cynthia is a regular speaker at conferences and seminars on a range of topics in the field of workplace ethics. She is often interviewed as an ethics expert, including by CNBC Africa, Carte Blanche, eNCA, ClassicFM and SAfm.

She has lectured and facilitated workshops on workplace ethics for more than 10 years with a wide variety of audiences, from students to senior executives. She is part of the external faculty of Duke Corporate Education, Wits Business School, the Gordon Institute of Business Science and the University of Stellenbosch Business School Executive Development. In the field of ethics training, Cynthia designs and delivers customised corporate workshops and in-company courses, including web-based and e-learning ethics programmes.

INTRODUCTION

This is a book about ethics in the workplace.

The title of the book, I'm sure, warrants an explanation. The book already had another title – a very long one, and one that lacked the pizzazz of the title of my first ethics book, *Ethics: Giving a Damn, Making a Difference*. However, catching up on business reading over coffee in March 2014 changed that.

I happened to read the *Bloomberg Businessweek* 2014 Design Issue which included input from the many people who took part in their second annual design conference. A particularly noteworthy exchange was captured with Neville Brody, a British graphic designer and brand strategist, who is the head of Brody Associates and dean of the School of Communication at the Royal College of Art in London. Asked to fill in the blank, "Design can _____", he replied, "That's the full sentence. Design can. Ensuring that the world's population has access to water, food, sanitation, a roof over their heads – all of that is design." Maybe the better question is "What can't design do?" (Bloomberg Businessweek, 2014).

This echoes the "Yes We Can" slogan used by Barack Obama in his 2008 presidential campaign to motivate and drive change for the better, which saw him elected as the American President in 2009.

I'm still grappling with the vast extent of Neville Brody's claim about design and it will be for history to judge whether President Obama's motto did translate into major positive change. However, I immediately saw the applicability of the "blank space" exercise to ethics. "Ethics can" is also the full sentence.

Ethics can build trust; it can create pleasant, productive workplaces that are characterised by high levels of fairness, respect, accountability and responsibility; it can foster sound relationships with internal and external stakeholders; it can position the organisation as an employee of choice, attracting and retaining the best talent; it can boost the organisation's reputation and brand equity; it can create a high degree of customer and investor confidence; and it can and should be a key differentiator that accords ethical organisations a unique source of competitive advantage. In short, I believe that ethics can make all the difference.

The book covers six themes:

- Understanding workplace ethics beyond just what is right and wrong.

- Does ethics make good business sense? Can you motivate an ethical business focus well enough?

- Establishing whose role is ethics, which explores the role of leadership, the social and ethics committee, and HR.

- Managing workplace ethics, which outlines a comprehensive ethics management system and includes a detailed focus on topical workplace issues.

- The crucial tasks of measuring, monitoring and reporting on ethics and ethical performance.

- Ethical decisions and dilemmas, which examines how to make those really tough ethical decisions.

The book also includes various practical exercises, checklists and guidelines, suggested workplace discussions, case studies and commentaries, and further reading.

The themes and topics are applicable to organisations in all sectors and across all industries. While the burning issues or the emphasis may differ, the fundamentals, such as ethical leadership and a sound ethics management system, are necessary in all organisations.

The book comprises a collection of separate, stand-alone articles that have been grouped thematically based on the issues and challenges that are most pertinent in the workplace. Instead of necessarily having to read the book from cover to cover, the structure is intended to allow the topics to be read individually, as and when those issues arise or based on the reader's specific interest or area or responsibility. This serves one of the aims of book, which is to be a quick and easy reference of best practice guidelines. Where some articles overlap slightly, the content has not been repeated, but is cross-referenced to where the topic is explored more fully.

I wrote this book for a number of reasons. For all those who strive to maintain or improve ethics in their workplaces, it is intended to provide them with practical support to help them manage ethics even better. For those who are not yet fully convinced about ethics and its relevance, I hope this book will be persuasive. For organisations, the book can serve as a very useful resource. It can form part of a training programme and be given to executives, leaders and managers who have the responsibility of managing the ethics of their followers – or, in fact, to any employee who is interested in knowing more about ethics since the more widespread the knowledge and understanding of ethics is, the more it becomes the norm in terms of behaviour. But, above all else, I wrote this to share my knowledge and understanding in a clear and accessible manner so that it can contribute to building a great community of people who are both committed and competent to make a difference as regards workplace ethics – and because that difference is so sorely needed.

July 2014

CHAPTER 1

UNDERSTANDING WORKPLACE ETHICS

INTRODUCTION

This chapter addresses the basic features of ethics in order to provide a clear description of what ethics in the workplace is and what it constitutes. Although the contents of the book are designed to be read on a topic-by-topic basis, it would be ideal to read this chapter first as it is intended to serve as a foundation for the chapters that follow.

In addition to the basics – Ethics 101 – the chapter focuses on the context of workplace ethics and aims to add insight into the position of ethics in relation to other related concepts and issues. It also tackles the topic of actions that are ethical but illegal and unethical but legal, discusses the question of whether business ethics is an oxymoron, and explores whether ethics is constantly applicable.

The chapter includes guidelines for a workplace discussion, a practical exercise to evaluate the effectiveness of the organisation's rules and regulations, and a recommended case study together with supporting commentary.

1.1   WORKPLACE ETHICS 101: THE BASICS

Workplace ethics is not a new or unknown concept. Virtually every employee, manager and leader has some insight into ethics, whether it is into what ethics is, what being ethical is or looks like, or what being unethical entails. But in order to manage ethics more effectively and to build an ethical culture, it is ideal for leaders and employees to share a common understanding of what ethics is and what it involves.

Understanding ethics

Defining ethics is arguably complicated by the vast number of definitions. A search for "definition of ethics" on Google Scholar currently delivers more than 1 800 000 results. While this wealth of research and knowledge is relevant for academia, it is not valuable in the workplace. A clear, concise, practical definition of workplace ethics is preferable as it is easier to understand and share with others.

A description of ethics as "the right thing to do" meets these criteria and is accurate inasmuch as ethics is essentially concerned with what is right or good: one of its core features is that ethics centres on matters that have a right – wrong or good – bad dimension. An equally good variation of that, which is often attributed to Aldo Leopold, the American conservationist and wildlife biologist, is that "ethics is doing the right thing when no one is watching".

Another key feature of ethics is that it does not apply only to oneself – it also applies to others. This includes employees as well as external stakeholders, not just shareholders. In this regard, Peter Singer, an Australian philosopher and academic, acknowledges that "the notion of ethics carries with it the idea of something bigger than the individual. If I am to defend my conduct on ethical grounds, I cannot point only to the benefits it brings me. I must address myself to a larger audience" (Singer, 1993:10).

How ethics is recognised and judged is mostly derived from words and actions, for instance, by a company's decisions or a person's behaviour, and by whether those decisions or actions are considered to be good/right or bad/wrong in relation to the impact on others. Theft and fraud are obvious examples of unethical behaviour, as is failure to adhere to laws and codes of conduct. Ethics is also evaluated in terms of differences between proclaimed and actual behaviour – specifically between what is said and what is done. In fact, in *Business Ethics for Dummies*, Norman Bowie and Meg Schneider define ethics in these terms as "the code of moral standards by which people judge the actions and behaviours of themselves and others. Business ethics brings those moral standards into the workplace" (2011:10).

Lord John Moulton, an English jurist writing in the early 1900s, also focused on human actions and the drivers of those actions in his definition of ethics. He recognised three domains of human action, which can be viewed as functioning on a continuum. At one end Moulton recognised that human action is shaped by the law, prompting action that amounts to "obedience to the enforceable" (Kidder, 1995:66-67). At the other end of the continuum, Moulton recognised the domain of free choice, where individuals can decide for themselves how to act. This freedom covers actions that are considered to carry no adverse consequences for others. Examples include the freedoms common to many Western democracies, such as freedom of speech or religion.

Moulton's recognition of a middle domain, however, added significantly to the topic of ethics. In a speech he delivered to the Authors' Club in London (published posthumously in 1924 in *The Atlantic Monthly*), he described this domain as one that is subject to a personal inner voice unenforceable by others:

In that domain there is no law which inexorably determines our course of action, and yet we feel we are not free to choose as we would ... It grades from a consciousness of duty nearly as strong as positive law, to a feeling that the matter is all but a question of personal choice ... It is the domain of obedience to the unenforceable. That obedience is the obedience of a man to that which he cannot be forced to obey. He is the enforcer of the law upon himself (Kidder, 1995:66-67).

This introduces the aspect of what would commonly be referred to as "conscience" as a driver of behaviour. Its importance rests on it being self-imposed, as opposed to externally imposed (as is the case for rules and regulations), which makes it much more effective and impactful.

Since ethics centres on what is right or good as opposed to what is wrong or bad, it follows that ethics involves choices. It is these choices that shape whether behaviour is ethical or unethical. Added to this is another pertinent fact, namely that, within the workplace, employees almost always already know what is right and wrong – irrespective of what behavioural choices they make. While there are some circumstances when there is not an easy or obvious "right" answer (which topic is addressed in Chapter 6), in the majority of cases misconduct is the result of a conscious, deliberate choice. For example, the employee who steals the petty cash or solicits a bribe knows that his/her behaviour is wrong.

Ethical choices are thus reflected in words, actions, decisions and behaviour relative to oneself and others, which collectively reveals the ethical status of the individual or organisation.

Knowing what drives or shapes those choices – ethical or otherwise – is clearly also imperative. In the workplace (and elsewhere) those choices are mostly determined by values, by relevant laws, rules and regulations, by the norms or culture of the organisation and, crucially, by the leadership. Influencing behaviour into being more ethical therefore rests on these factors, and understanding them is necessary for the achievement of ethical behaviour or an ethical outcome.

Therefore, as ethics or being ethical is evaluated by the moral choices that are made and by what the person or the organisation does and says, so too is ethics gauged in terms of these factors that shape ethical choices. Being ethical in the workplace entails being committed to and living the organisation's values **and** abiding by applicable legislation, rules and policies. In an ethical environment, being ethical also involves conforming to the norms of the company's culture and striving to reflect the leadership example of ethical conduct.

 **Definition** Workplace ethics means doing what is good and right relative to oneself, the organisation and its stakeholders and abiding by the organisation's values and by applicable laws and rules.

Values and rules

In the workplace, values are generally captured in a value statement or code of values, and rules (encompassing laws, rules and regulations) are normally set out in a code of conduct.

Given that values and rules play a significant role in shaping behaviour, it is important that they are directly related to each other: that is, the code of conduct and its supporting policies should translate the organisation's values into workplace behaviours and actions. A policy aimed at preventing fraud, bribery and corruption should therefore echo and reinforce the values of honesty and integrity.

The crucial issue to understand in relation to values and rules is that they entrain or bring about quite different actions. Living in accordance with values requires action, that something positive is **done**. On the other hand, complying with rules necessitates inaction in the sense of **not** doing something. For example, honesty means that one is transparent and forthcoming about all the known facts, whereas abiding by a fraud and corruption policy means not performing any acts of fraud or corruption. This difference between action and inaction is fundamental to an understanding of ethics and the management of ethics.

This distinction can also be viewed in terms of acts of commission versus omission. These terms are typically used in relation to misconduct. For instance, lying is an act of commission when one deliberately tells an untruth, but it can also be an act of omission when one purposefully excludes pertinent information. In an unethical context, the moral distinction between commissions and omissions generally classifies acts of commission as worse than acts of omission.

If, however, the terminology of commissions and omissions is applied to values and rules, acts of commission can be viewed as deliberate, positive actions in pursuit of giving effect to a moral value or achieving an ethical outcome: in other words, acts of commission can be equated with doing something positive and ethical. In this context, acts of omission would be deemed to be deliberate inaction: they could be equated with not doing something unethical. In terms of this perspective, both acts of commission and acts of omission are desirable, although greater value would normally be placed on acts of commission.

Moral and business values

Moral values such as honesty, integrity, fairness and respect are included in the value statement in most organisations. Among their values, many organisations also acknowledge criteria such as innovation, valuing their people and customer service. While these are valid organisational goals or operational practices, they are business values rather than moral ones. The distinction is important because, for example, being the least innovative person in the company does not make one unethical.

Do values change? Should they change?

The difference between moral and business values is also relevant from the perspective of change. Altered circumstances could justify that business values change over time. For example, innovation could over time become less of a priority than customer service. However, moral values should remain constantly applicable – unless that change entails improvement.

A good example of such a positive change occurred in December 2013 when Andrew Witty, CEO of British drug maker GlaxoSmithKline, announced that the company would no longer pay doctors to promote its products and would stop tying compensation of sales representatives to the number of prescriptions doctors write. This effectively ends two common industry practices that have long been criticised on the grounds of conflict of interest. In a telephone interview Witty said the proposed changes were part of an effort "to try and make sure we stay in step with how the world is changing" and to explore "different ways, more effective ways of operating than perhaps the ways we as an industry have been operating over the last 30, 40 years" (Thomas, 2013).[1]

But if the change suggests that the value is no longer applicable, by definition the value can be viewed as temporary. By way of a test, consider which of the following values are changeable in the sense of being only temporarily applicable: fairness? honesty? respect? The answer, of course, is that moral values should be practised all the time. The constancy of an organisation's values reflects one of the key roles that values can and should fulfil in a business, namely that of providing a foundation or touchstone that guides behaviour and serves as an anchor in times of change.

Are values different for different people?

This claim that organisational values should be constant is often refuted on the grounds that values are different for different people. It is true that people and groups can hold divergent views on ethics, and personal values can differ widely as they are affected by a variety of factors including upbringing, culture and education. Consequently, employees' values can differ from those of the organisation, which compromises the ideal goal of aligned personal and organisational values.

However, although there may be differences, it is not only appropriate but essential that in the workplace the organisation espouses a set of values that reflects what is acceptable in that environment. An employee may have grown up in circumstances that condoned dishonesty or been part of a community where respect was exercised relative only to certain people. Such a background does not make this sort of behaviour acceptable at work. The values in the

---

1   This positive news is likely to be significantly diminished by bribery scandals the company is facing in China and Iraq and, more recently, for bribing doctors in Poland (Neate, 2014).

workplace are not a means for accommodating the full spectrum of values – from impeccable to appalling – among employees and stakeholders. The values serve, instead, to define the criteria and standards by which an organisation strives to operate.

It is important, therefore, that the organisation ensures that the company's values reflect what is expected of all employees in that environment and in the context of the employer–employee relationship. Similarly, leaders and managers should continually work towards aligning employees behind the company's values. They should acknowledge those with good values and poor values should be acted against, whether in terms of legislation or the organisation's code of ethics, code of conduct or policies.

General Electric's view on shared values represents quite a blunt approach: "We encourage the sharing of these values because we believe they are both fair and effective, but we realise they are not for everyone. ... Individuals whose values do not coincide with these expressed preferences will more likely flourish better outside General Electric Company" (Tichy & Sherman, 1993:172–173).

However, what **can** differ is the way the values manifest themselves in practice. A good example is the value of respect. While respect would undoubtedly enjoy overwhelming support from most organisations and individuals, people differ in the way they express it. Is it respectful to look at one's superior directly when being addressed, or should one lower one's eyes? Is it respectful for a man to precede a woman through a door or to let her walk through first? The answer depends on factors that include the prevailing culture. The key issue is to expose and explore the differences as a route to achieving agreement on what is appropriate within the context, goals and environment of the organisation. When determining what constitutes respectful behaviour towards customers, for instance, it is important to ask what those customers consider respectful and then to define it appropriately in the company's values and code of conduct.

Values: the criteria for effectiveness

It is also important that the values (and rules) the company chooses to live by are fair to all stakeholders and designed to be effective for the organisation. The effectiveness of values rests upon the following

1 *Whether values are lived, shared and understood:* A gap between what is said and what is done is destructive in an organisation, eroding trust and respect and undermining its ethical standards. For values to be lived and shared, employees need to understand what the company's moral and business values mean for them in their specific work context.

2 *What is valued most:* What a company claims to value is judged not simply in terms of words, but in terms of the actions, behaviours, decisions, policies, procedures and systems that employees, clients and other stakeholders experience.

3   *How values are arrived at, implemented and maintained:* The way in which the code of values is created, developed and implemented is crucial to its initial success or failure. The ideal is a broad, consultative process including as many members of staff as possible. The way in which the code of values is subsequently enforced and maintained is also crucial to its long-term success or failure.

4   *Whether the roles played by values are understood and leveraged:* Values can, and should, fulfil two important roles in an organisation. They should guide and shape decisions, behaviour and strategy, and they should provide a stable foundation in times of change (Schoeman, 2012).

Laws, rules and regulations

The rules and regulations that an organisation adopts are likely to be derived from and related to, among other factors, applicable local and international laws, industry or professional codes of ethics or codes of conduct, and the nature of the organisation's business. Generally these rules would be written up in a code of conduct and/or in supporting policies. It follows that the rules should align with the issues and topics addressed in a code of conduct and supporting policies. (A list is included in the article in Part III of Chapter 3, Checklist: Issues to be addressed in a code of conduct.)

Rules: the criteria for effectiveness

To reduce unethical behaviour in practice, to pave the way for employee buy-in to rules, and to enhance the successful enforcement of rules, an organisation needs to formulate rules and regulations that are perceived to be fair and that are effective. The opposite effect is well illustrated in John Irving's book, *The Cider House Rules*. The name of the book derives from the rules that are pinned to the wall in the cider house that is occupied by the itinerant fruit pickers. They observe that the rules have been made by Olive Worthington, the owner of the orchard, without any consultation with them and without considering their circumstances. Consequently they feel free to ignore the rules. As Big Dot Taft says, "Every year Olive writes them up, and every year nobody pays no attention" (Irving, 1994:354).

The effectiveness would depend upon the extent to which the rules and regulations are:

1   Fair to all employees and affected stakeholders

2   Consistently applied to all (management and employees alike)

3   Clear about the consequences of non-compliance

4   Formulated in a transparent and understandable way so that they are understood by all employees and affected stakeholders

5   Easily accessible to all employees and others affected by them

6   Relevant and comprehensive enough in the context of the organisation, its industry and the nature of its operation

7   Reviewed regularly – for example, at least once a year – to keep up to date with legislation and other relevant changes.

A practical exercise using these criteria is included in this chapter to enable companies to evaluate the effectiveness of their rules and regulations.

Values or rules?

Organisations mostly devote more time and effort to formulating and enforcing rules than to articulating and inculcating values. But, if these two drivers of behaviour are compared, it is clear that values and rules are neither focused on the same intended outcome, nor do they achieve the same results.

Rules aim primarily to achieve compliance, while values aim primarily for commitment – which represents a big difference, not least as regards sustainability. A code of conduct follows a rules-based approach that strives for compliance: "You may not smoke in any part of the office or the parking garage". And the enforcement or implementation of rules is, by definition, reactive. A code of values, on the other hand, relies far more on achieving willing commitment: "We treat all our stakeholders with respect".

This difference is pertinent to the question of whether organisations should focus on values or rules or both. Viewed in terms of which of the two offers the more sustainable course of action, if the goal is just short-term compliance, rules should be sufficient. But if a longer-term impact on behaviour is needed, then the focus will have to include both. As regards which is the easiest option, most organisations tend to consider rules a simpler, more direct mechanism to shape behaviour than a value-based approach. Yet, while rules are necessary, they are certainly not sufficient to achieve ethical behaviour. Organisations also need values. And they need values more because ethical behaviour can be achieved with sound values and very few rules, but not *vice versa*.

Culture

Organisational culture is influenced by, among other factors, the leadership, values and rules of the organisation. The nature of the business and the industry can also affect culture. Thus the culture in an advertising agency would differ profoundly from that in a nuclear power plant, and the culture in financial services would be different from that in the construction industry. In turn, the culture of the organisation influences ethical choices and behaviour. This can have positive and negative outcomes, such as whether respectful behaviour is commonly practised, or the use of bad language is widely accepted as the norm.

In addition to this role as one of the drivers of behaviour, the widely accepted definition of culture as "the way things are done around here" reveals another dimension of culture, namely, that it also acts as a reflection of behaviour: it mirrors the norms and standards of the actions and conduct both among employees and relative to external stakeholders. Culture, therefore, serves as a regular communication channel to "show" employees what is considered acceptable and unacceptable in the workplace. Since many of the messages take the form of non-verbal communication, its impact is often strengthened because actions generally do speak more loudly than words.

It is clearly important to understand how ethical or unethical the culture is. A practical exercise is included later which assesses the ethics of the company's culture. This is a simple paper-based exercise that is well suited to small and medium-sized companies which can administer it themselves.

Clearly an ethical culture is very desirable, not least because the optimal outcome of an ethical culture is trust, which delivers great value and multiple benefits to the organisation and its people. Therefore, instead of the focus being on culture as a driver of behaviour (such as values and rules are), it is much more impactful to focus on how to create an ethical culture. It is this emphasis that is addressed in the articles on culture in this book.

Leadership

While values and rules are critical to maintaining and improving an organisation's ethical status, leadership is widely recognised as the most influential factor in shaping behaviour – whether good or bad – and in setting and entrenching the organisation's ethical standards. In the workplace, as elsewhere, leaders should be good role models and, as such, enhancing and uplifting the ethics of their organisation is a primary role and responsibility of their position. It is therefore a particular focus area of this book, and a number of articles are focused on different aspects of leadership and ethics, particularly Part I of Chapter 3.

Behaviour, ethical maturity and ethical boundaries

Behaviour can range from very ethical to extremely unethical. Unethical behaviour is generally well understood. While the reality of misconduct is recognised by all organisations, the motives and how it is conducted or orchestrated are not necessarily understood.

There are many obvious examples that are familiar, such as bribery, fraud, corruption, dishonesty, theft, sexual harassment, conflicts of interest, insider trading, breaches of confidentiality, infringing intellectual property rights, improper use of company property and facilities, and more. The risk associated with these and other areas of misconduct warrant that organisations pay attention to both the known sources and the new and emerging sources of unethical practices. Part II of Chapter 4 focuses on select areas of misconduct: collusion, cybercrime and counterfeiting.

Given the desire for ethical behaviour and the need to influence behaviour towards being more ethical, two concepts are particularly useful because they link the key features of ethics: ethical maturity associates behaviour with its drivers, and ethical boundaries connect conduct to others.

The concept of ethical maturity reflects what drives ethical conduct. It extends from low to high ethical maturity, where low ethical maturity indicates a situation where ethical conduct is primarily achieved via the application of laws, rules and regulations, thereby achieving an outcome of externally-directed compliance. The problem with this situation is encapsulated in the saying, "When the cat's away, the mice will play". It means, in effect, that when the enforcement of rules declines – such as lowered levels of supervision or erratic checks and balances – behaviour can revert to being less ethical.

High ethical maturity, in contrast, reflects a commitment to values where behaviour is shaped largely by shared values. This indicates a very different situation where employees act ethically because they choose to do so, rather than because they have to do so. Given the greater worth of committed value-driven behaviour, organisations clearly need to focus on increasing the level of ethical maturity.

The concept of an ethical boundary centres on the nature and impact of behaviour and decisions on others and is measured by the degree of inclusiveness or exclusiveness. If the organisation operates within a very exclusive ethical boundary it means that they are primarily focused on themselves and their own interests to the exclusion of, for example, the interests of other stakeholders or of social and environmental responsibilities. A strongly inclusive ethical boundary, on the other hand, would encompass the interests of relevant stakeholders and pursue a triple bottom line (which adds social and environmental responsibility to a financial bottom line).

While an exclusive approach reflects being self-centred, it does not necessarily imply that the organisation is being unethical. However, the growing expectation that businesses should make more of a contribution than just a financial one to the society of which they are a part is increasingly casting these organisations as poor corporate citizens.[2]

From knowing and understanding to doing

While knowing and understanding ethics is a valuable and indispensable foundation, the difficult part of ethics does not lie in knowing what it is or is not. The difficult part is living it and behaving accordingly. To realise this, it is crucial

---

2   This concept is discussed more extensively in the article "Ethics without borders" in Chapter 4.

that the benefits of being ethical are fully appreciated, that the roles and responsibilities relative to ethics are well understood, and that ethics is effectively managed. This forms the focus of the majority of the sections in the rest of the book.

1.2 PRACTICAL EXERCISE: ASSESSING THE EFFECTIVENESS OF THE ORGANISATION'S RULES AND REGULATIONS

The effectiveness of the rules and regulations can be assessed by getting employees to evaluate them in terms of the questions listed below. The scale ranges from "not at all" or "rarely" as the most negative response, to "some of the time" or "to some extent" as an average response, and to "almost all of the time" or "a lot" as the most positive response.

This exercise is best suited to smaller companies which can administer it themselves.

Apart from revealing the degree of effectiveness of the rules, the value of the exercise also lies in considering the reasons for the results, for example, why the values are not considered fair to all, or why they are seen as not being applied consistently. Based on that insight, action should be taken to rectify the criteria that do not apply or that rarely apply and to improve those that apply only to some extent or some of the time.

Table 1.1: Assessing the effectiveness of the organisation's rules and regulations

Are the company's rules (as contained in its code of conduct and/or policies):	No, not at all, or rarely	Some of the time, or to some extent	Yes, almost all of the time, or a lot
1 Fair to all employees and affected stakeholders?			
2 Consistently applied to all, for example, to management and employees alike?			
3 Clear as regards the consequences of non-compliance?			
4 Written in a transparent and understandable way so that they are understood by all employees and affected stakeholders?			

Are the company's rules (as contained in its code of conduct and/or policies):	No, not at all, or rarely	Some of the time, or to some extent	Yes, almost all of the time, or a lot
5 Easily accessible to all employees and others affected by them?			
6 Relevant and comprehensive enough in the context of the organisation, its industry and the nature of its operation?			
7 Up to date, for example, as regards current legislation or other changes?			

1.3 ETHICAL BUT ILLEGAL AND UNETHICAL BUT LEGAL

The statement that ethical behaviour is "doing the right thing when no one else is watching" is often attributed to Aldo Leopold, the American wildlife biologist and conservationist. But mostly this saying excludes what can be regarded as the punch line: ethical behaviour is doing the right thing when no one else is watching – **even when doing the wrong thing is legal**. It would be ideal if what was considered ethical was mirrored by what was regarded as legal and if unethical conduct was always illegal. Unfortunately, the two do not always coincide.

The classic example in South Africa was the apartheid policy. Many actions under that banner may have been technically legal at the time, such as discrimination. However, they certainly were not ethical, not least because they compromised the moral values of fairness and respect. Abortion is often a very emotive example. It is legal in many countries, including South Africa, but many people consider it completely unethical.

In the workplace, many actions are recognised as both unethical and illegal, such as theft and fraud, but what about actions that are less clearly defined, such as being disrespectful to a subordinate? Many organisations include showing respect for others in their value statement. But disrespectful behaviour – such as swearing, shouting or humiliating someone, particularly in front of others – may not necessarily constitute acting outside the law (unless, in South Africa, the disrespect takes the form of a racial slur).

Fairness is also a prized value in many organisations. Acting unfairly can be illegal when, for example, you appoint or promote someone on the grounds of favouritism or because of a family or personal relationship, rather than because this is the best person for the job. It is also unfair to withhold credit due to others for a job well done and rather claim it for yourself. But that is not necessarily illegal.

Prior to the promulgation of the Competition Act 89 of 1998 collusion was more of an ethical issue than a legal one. However, further legislation has filled this gap and clearly defines what constitutes illegal collusive behaviour – and there are many convictions to emphasise the change.

Interestingly, the argument of doing what is right rather than what is lawful has been applied to Edward Snowden's actions. An American computer professional and former contractor for the American National Security Agency (NSA), in May 2013 Snowdon disclosed thousands of classified documents to several media outlets, which revealed the existence of numerous global surveillance programmes. He has just been included in *Time* magazine's April 2014 list of the 100 most influential people. He was nominated in the category of Pioneers by Daniel Domscheit-Berg, a German technology activist and a former spokesman for WikiLeaks, who stated that Snowdon showed "a sense of great responsibility" (Domscheit-Berg, 2014).

These examples are, however, eclipsed by two especially pertinent examples of the apparent conflict between ethics and legality, namely bribery and taxation. For bribery the question centres on whether actions that are accepted in one country minimise their being unethical elsewhere, and for taxation whether staying within the letter of the law constitutes being ethical.

Bribery

Bribery is widely accepted as offering, giving, receiving or soliciting something of value to influence the actions or decisions of a public official or other person. The bribe may take many forms: money, a gift, an advantage, or a promise or undertaking to induce or influence the action, non-action, vote or influence of a person in an official or public capacity. Bribery is also defined in terms such as "supply side", which constitutes "active" bribery when a bribe is offered, and "demand side", which involves "passive" bribery when a bribe is solicited. Also included in the scope of bribery are direct and indirect actions, for example, the use of intermediaries, and bribes that benefit third parties.

Bribery is regarded as both illegal and unethical in many countries, including South Africa. The increasing recognition of the extremely negative consequences of bribery has resulted in increased legislation over time.[3] However, although bribery is generally viewed as applying to both local and foreign public officials, the extension of legislation beyond local public officials is quite limited. A study conducted by the Organisation for Economic Co-operation and Development (OECD) and African Development Bank (AfDB) found that only four out of the 20 African countries studied had adopted specific criminal provisions for foreign public officials, namely Madagascar, South Africa, Tanzania and Zambia (OECD/AfDB, 2012).

As an exception to the application of the law, Michael Judin, senior partner at Attorneys Goldman Judin Inc. and a member of the King III Committee (the King Committee on Corporate Governance), points out that payments would generally be found to be acceptable when "they are made under fear of the loss of life, limb or liberty, where the briber is likely to have available to him the common law defence of duress. This is even more likely where the person making the payment was in a vulnerable position" (Judin, 2012).

An issue that can appear to make it unclear as to what is or is not ethical is the labelling of payments under many different names. A commission earned on sales is generally considered acceptable, but what about the "commission" paid for a lucrative contract? What about facilitation payments, or, as they are also sometimes known, "grease" payments: small payments demanded by officials to provide a service that they are obligated to perform at no cost? Are introductory fees, agency fees or handling fees ethical or unethical?

Some countries, such as the United States of America, make specific exemptions in their legislation for facilitation payments. While their Foreign Corrupt Practices Act (FCPA) bans bribes, it allows the payment of small sums to ease transactions in countries in which they are seen as customary. Stephen Clayton, a California lawyer specialising in international anti-corruption and the FCPA, emphatically opposes this. Writing for the FCPA Compliance and Ethics Blog, he states that:

> The FCPA contains an exception for low-level bribes euphemistically called "facilitation payments". Facilitation payments are bribes. This exception creates the illusion minor bribery of employees of foreign governments by US companies and their agents can be "legal". The exception for facilitation payments creates serious confusion for business people because it gives

---

3   In South Africa until 1992 bribery was a common law crime (that is, for which there is no actual legislation). The Corruption Act 94 of 1992 (now repealed) repealed both the common law crime of bribery and the previous Prevention of Corruption Act 6 of 1958 and created a new offence called corruption, which included the common law crime of bribery and the offences created by the 1958 legislation. This is currently addressed by the Prevention and Combating of Corrupt Activities Act 12 of 2004. Similarly, until the United Kingdom Bribery Act came into force on 1 July 2011, the British Parliament had not found it necessary to pass a law banning bribery.

them the impression that some bribes are permitted under US law, but it can be difficult in practice to determine which bribes Congress considers tot [to] be "legal". The facilitating payments exception is offensive to normal ethical standards of corporate governance and should not exist (Clayton, 2012).

The question of ethics and legality is often further complicated when differing social and cultural norms are taken into account. However, the tendency to treat a bribe as acceptable because it is commonly practised in a particular country or an industry is flawed. Just because "everyone" is doing it does not make it right, nor does it invalidate applicable legislation. This view is recognised by the OECD Anti-Bribery Convention, which holds that "an offence is committed irrespective of, amongst other things, the value of the advantage, perception of local custom [or] the tolerance of such payment by local authorities" (OECD/ AfDB, 2012:11).

By way of practical guidance, Ansie Ramalho, Chief Executive of the Institute of Directors in Southern Africa (IoDSA), advocates that when there is no clear legal prohibition, the following should be considered

> "… the amount of the fee, the nature of the service and transparency. If the amount paid is excessive in comparison to the service rendered, it should raise a red flag. The next question that should be asked is whether the nature of the referral, introduction or service is such that it over-shadows valid considerations such as merit. And lastly, the litmus test is whether the payment of the fee can withstand the scrutiny of objective third parties (Ramalho, 2012).

The latter needs to take into account that the company that pays bribes in, for example, Russia or Nigeria may well find itself accused of misconduct by stakeholders in London and Washington.

Ultimately, the legal or ethical debate relative to bribery should be guided by what is ethical – which entails abiding by the highest ethical and moral standards, rather than subscribing to the lowest legal requirements.[4]

Tax

Benjamin Franklin, one of the Founding Fathers of the United States of America, was famously quoted as saying that nothing can be said to be certain, except death and taxes (Franklin, 1789). What he could have added as a further certainly is that taxpayers would always strive to pay as little tax as possible. This often manifests itself in terms of tax avoidance or tax evasion.

---

4   A Harvard Business Review case study referenced at the end of this chapter explores the question of bribery in a cross-cultural situation.

Tax avoidance generally refers to the use of legal methods to modify the financial situation of an organisation (or an individual) by means that are within the law in order to lower the amount of tax payable. Tax avoidance mechanisms involve, among many others, using tax deductions, transfer pricing, establishing an offshore company in a tax haven, or locating factories, distribution hubs and headquarters in low-tax jurisdictions. The extent of the problem relative to tax havens is addressed in the Oxfam paper released in January 2014, *Working for the Few*. The research acknowledges a growing network of global tax havens where large amounts of money are hidden from view and largely untaxed, thereby "denying national treasuries vital resources that could be used to benefit society". Oxfam research conservatively quantifies the amount held offshore at $18.5 trillion (Fuentes-Nieva & Galasso, 2014:18).

This practice differs from tax evasion, which is the term for efforts to evade the payment of taxes by illegal means. This can entail dishonesty or misrepresentation when, for example, taxpayers overstate deductions or under-declare income, profits or gains and when they deliberately misrepresent or conceal the true state of their affairs to the tax authorities in order to reduce their tax liability.

While there are many instances of tax evasion, tax avoidance is a more relevant issue, because being ethical and acting legally do not necessary coincide (whereas tax evasion implies unethical conduct that corresponds with acting illegally). Companies have long had very complicated tax structures and have employed multi-disciplinary experts who have used a range of increasingly sophisticated practices to exploit tax legislation. In fact, being "tax efficient" would generally be viewed as sound business practice. But this has been taken so far that, despite tax avoidance being legal, public opinion on the ethics of tax avoidance is changing.

This is evidenced by the public protest against global firms such as Starbucks, Google and Amazon for avoiding payment of tax on their British sales. In these cases, Starbucks had sales of £400 million in the United Kingdom in 2012, but paid no corporation tax; Amazon had sales of £3.35 billion in the United Kingdom in 2011 but reported a "tax expense" of only £1.8 million; and Google's United Kingdom operation paid just £6 million to the Treasury in 2011 on turnover in the United Kingdom of £395 million (Barford & Holt, 2013). Yet everything these companies did was legal.

The effect of public protests, social media campaigns and "tax naming and shaming" has been to erode customer loyalty and, more importantly, to damage those companies' reputations. The result was that on 6 December 2012 Kris Engskov, managing director of Starbucks in Britain and Ireland, announced that the company would pay around £10 million a year more in 2013–2014 tax than it is required to pay by law, adding that, "We've heard that loud and clear from our customers" (*The Economist*, 2012).

This apparent "victory" does not necessarily mean that tax avoidance will decline dramatically. But it does mean that there is likely to be even more scrutiny of companies' tax practices and avoidance tactics within countries in which they operate in and, for multinationals, via cross-border co-operation between governments. The organisation's expertise in exploiting legal loopholes is therefore increasingly likely to be regarded as unethical conduct. As to what being ethical really means: it means contributing fairly to the country in which the organisation operates.

In conclusion, it is important to recognise that when the only or primary criterion for evaluating behaviour is whether it complies with the law, it is likely to foster "lowest common denominator" behaviour. The law – and the company's rules, code of conduct and policies – cannot address each specific action or provide guidelines for every situation that may occur. To do so rests on ethics and being a good corporate citizen. And, therefore, corporations need to be very clear about their ethical standards to ensure that they avoid any such "misunderstandings".

1.4   BUSINESS ETHICS: AN OXYMORON?

Evidence of a lack of business ethics is not hard to find. Unethical business practices are a very visible feature of the corporate landscape, with ethical scandals regularly making news headlines. These ethical failures illustrate a range of costs and adverse consequences, among others, financial losses, fines, executives losing their positions, eroded reputations, and, in extreme cases, business closure.

Examples of the latter which still loom large after more than a decade are the collapse of WorldCom, one the United States of America's largest long-distance telephone companies, and the accounting scandal that saw the demise of Enron and Arthur Andersen. Enron was an energy, commodities and services company that had employed close to 22 000 people, while Arthur Andersen had once one of the "big five" international auditing firms. In the United Kingdom the 1995 failure of Barings Bank is still quoted, but it has arguably been eclipsed by the collapse of the *News of the World*. First published in 1843, the newspaper went on to become one of the biggest selling English language newspapers – until 2011, when extensive cellphone hacking led to its closure. In South Africa, unethical practices were at the centre of the demise of Wendy Machanik Properties, Auction Alliance, once regarded as South Africa's leading auction house, and First Strut, which had been the country's largest unlisted company.

These examples, and the many more that can be added, are often used to support the view that business and ethics are a contradiction in terms, a view that is sometimes extended to infer a lack of ethics in all businesses. A discussion of business ethics therefore tends to elicit a range of perceptions and opinions that can easily skip over a focus on it being "the right thing to do" and overlook the huge costs associated with ethical failure. Instead, a common response is either to question whether there really is such a thing as business ethics or to maintain that business ethics is an oxymoron.

Countering this view with the argument that media coverage is given only to scandals and not to ethical practices is valid. The media does give much more coverage to scandals. So too can the cumulative effect of having access to news from around the world in real time create a more severe picture, which is arguably true of business in general. But this does not take away from the fact that there is a lot of misconduct in business and that there should be less.

But even if the comment that business ethics is an oxymoron is used flippantly, it is a view that warrants being addressed because it can be harmful. Instead of leading to meaningful debate and a deeper understanding of business ethics, it can undermine the pursuit of an ethical culture and deflect the effective implementation of workplace ethics initiatives.

Accepting the outlook that business is generally not ethical can lead to complacency. This view would maintain that provided your organisation is better than the worst, you can consider yourselves okay. This outlook can also foster "lowest common denominator" behaviour, where the worst conduct is accepted as the standard and the norm. Within an organisation, either view seriously impedes the pursuit of an ethical culture.

The best response to and defence against such views is action, specifically action in support of building and maintaining an ethical organisation. In this regard, leadership is especially important since leaders exercise the most influential position to correct such negative perceptions. Adding to that a sound, proactive ethics management system would go a long way to creating an ethical workplace. It would also answer the question of whether there really is such a thing as business ethics, which should be, "for this business, yes".

1.5 PERSONAL VALUES VERSUS COMPANY VALUES

The importance of values within an organisation is specifically addressed in the article included earlier in this chapter, "Workplace ethics 101: the basics". In considering whether organisations should focus on values or rules, the article concluded not only that organisations definitely need values, but that they need values **more**, because ethical behaviour can be achieved with sound values and very few rules, but not *vice versa*.

The article also explored the question of whether values are different for different people and acknowledged that while personal values could differ, the organisation is entitled to require that its employees abide by the organisation's values within the workplace and the scope of the employer–employee relationship.

The argument against this is that everyone enjoys the right to their personal values. This is supported by the protection of individuals' rights in section 15 of the Bill of Rights in the South Africa Constitution, which states that "everyone has the right to freedom of conscience, religion, thought, belief and opinion" (1996:6). However, as discussed more fully in "Workplace ethics 101: the basics", this personal right does not eliminate the organisation's right to expect employees to conform to its values while at work – or prevent the organisation from taking action against those who contravene its values.

However, a more positive approach would be to focus on what can be done to realise the ideal goal of aligned personal and organisational values.

One solution to this potential disparity in values is that organisations recruit for the right values. While certain pre-employment integrity assessments deliver some value, most of these tests do not realise the intended purpose because the potential candidate would easily know the right or most ethical answer. If a recruiter offered the following four choices of when bribery would be acceptable, what would be the correct answer?

1   When the value of the business deal exceeds R1 million

2   When it has been approved by your line manager

3   Never

4   When it has occurred previously in the company

Clearly 3 is the correct response.

Even when applicants are asked to consider more complex scenarios, they are still likely to give the answer that they think the prospective employer wants to hear and that would secure them the job, rather than necessarily revealing their personal values.

Another approach to aligning values is to use training programmes to clarify and reinforce the company's values and what behaviours are and are not acceptable in the workplace. For this to be effective, a trap that must be avoided is the inclusion of material that focuses on employees' personal values and ethics. Have you paid your traffic fines? Have you inflated an insurance claim after a burglary or loss? If you were given extra change, would you admit it?

While these situations lend themselves to discussions on ethics (or the lack of ethics), they are not suitable topics for two reasons: firstly because they infringe on the employee's right to exercise their values as they choose in their private capacity, and secondly because that intrusion is likely to create a barrier to the employee's further learning or engagement with the training material. The barrier would probably be expressed as "what I do in my private life is my business" or "you're not my mother/father/... to tell me what to do in my private life". The counter-argument that employees' personal ethics are carried into the workplace is perfectly valid – but it still does not warrant this intrusion into their private conduct.

A helpful test as to when a company is entitled to intervene is to ask whether you could formally act against the employee for such behaviour. If, for example, you found out that one of your staff had stolen his/her neighbour's cellphone, would you be entitled to start a disciplinary process at work? As much as the behaviour is unquestionably unethical, it does not fall within the scope of the employer–employee relationship and therefore, as the person's boss, you would not be able to institute any disciplinary action – although you could and should report criminal activity to the appropriate authorities.

There is, however, an exception to the general position that employees are free to exercise their personal values outside the workplace.

For leaders and executives this does not apply to the same extent. Their behaviour is generally so closely linked to the company and its reputation that inappropriate behaviour in their personal capacity would risk negatively impacting on the company. While this exclusion could be viewed as eroding their right to privacy, in reality it is simply the cost of occupying a high-profile position in an organisation. Their seniority and position as role models almost inevitably leads to their being held to a higher standard of conduct. The consequent challenge that leaders need to be aware of and to manage is the fact that those standards are not limited to office hours. Responsible leadership therefore demands of them that they conduct themselves ethically at all times.

Examples of high-profile misdemeanours illustrate this well. Dominique Strauss-Kahn, a French economist, lawyer and politician who served as France's Minister of Finance, was appointed the head of the International Monetary Fund (IMF) in 2007. But when he was charged with sexually assaulting a hotel maid in New York, did he have an option to stay on as Managing Director of the IMF? Could the IMF afford to be linked to such behaviour? The accusation was made on 14 May 2011, and he resigned on 18 May 2011.

A local public sector example is the South African Police Service, which was significantly affected by two successive National Police Commissioners being removed from office because of unethical conduct. Jackie Selebi was appointed the National Police Commissioner in 2000 and was the president of Interpol. But in August 2010 he was found guilty of corruption and sentenced to 15 years' imprisonment (although he was released on medical parole just 229 days into his 15-year sentence). His successor, Bheki Cele, took on the role of National Police Commissioner in 2009. However, he was suspended from the position in October 2011 and fired in June 2012 based on the findings of a board of inquiry into his involvement in two police lease deals for buildings in Pretoria and Durban.

The influence of divergent personal ethics on the organisation can therefore be damaging. But the benefits of alignment are as noteworthy in the reverse.

Values therefore necessitate attention, and building greater alignment between personal and company values should be treated as an important goal relative to **all** employees. There are many initiatives that would promote this, but the most effective route is to ensure that values constitute a real facet of the organisation and that leaders at all levels in the organisation actively, visibly and consistently live the values.

1.6 PART-TIME ETHICS: ETHICS AND E-TOLLS

The ongoing applicability of the organisation's values has already been recognised as crucial. While business values may change, moral values should not change, unless to improve. The question can also be posed relative to laws and rules: should compliance be constant or can it vary? Are laws and rules applicable only some of the time or only under certain circumstances? The issue of e-toll provides a relevant (if somewhat emotive) example against which to test these questions.

The arguments against the introduction of e-tolls on Gauteng roads have been wide-ranging, including that there may have been better and more cost-effective ways to finance the upgrading of the roads. Although these arguments appear to be valid, the government nonetheless decided to go ahead with the implementation of e-tolling in December 2013. Despite noteworthy legal challenges, primarily by the Opposition to Urban Tolling Alliance (OUTA), it has been held to be a valid law passed by a democratic government.

However, the furore around e-tolls has not abated. Its introduction has been followed by a deluge of complaints from motorists against the South African National Roads Agency (Sanral) for faulty billing, inefficient handling of billing queries, problems with Internet payments, and poor customer service. There have also been reports of intimidation tactics: such as SMSes threatening customers that they will be handed over to debt collectors. OUTA has presented a 10 000-word complaint to the Public Protector, accusing Sanral of contravening constitutionally enshrined human rights. The Democratic Alliance took the matter to court to have the legislation used to implement e-tolls declared unconstitutional and invalid. However, the application was dismissed by the Western Cape High Court in March 2014 (Agency staff, 2014).

In a briefing to Parliament's transport portfolio committee on 18 February 2014, Transport Minister, Dipuo Peters, conceded that there were "teething problems" with the electronic tolling system. Her admission that it constitutes a "positive outcome of implementation of the system" that the problems associated with duplicate and cloned licence plates, unregistered vehicles and vehicles without number plates have been identified is not to her credit. Having implemented a gantry system that tracks usage via vehicles' number plates, to identify those problems only now tends to confirm the view that the system lacked proper planning and thought at the outset. Her solution to these various problems is simply to instruct Sanral to "sort out the billing challenges and sort it out now" (SAPA, 2014).

Given these circumstances, it is pertinent to view this very contentious issue in terms of ethics. Opponents of e-tolls are likely to claim that e-tolls and ethics are a contradiction in terms. However, ethics is especially relevant because this issue raises the question of whether ethics matters only sometimes. Phrased differently, when is it acceptable to behave unethically? The simple answer, "never", is not the norm. Rather, it is likely to be: when it suits me; when it is convenient; when it furthers my self-interest or well-being; when it builds my self-esteem; or when it prevents or avoids an unpleasant or difficult situation.

The question of when it is acceptable to behave unethically relative to e-tolls may elicit the same responses. Many motorists are not only refusing to buy e-tags, but also implying that they will refuse to pay the tolls. This response is being supported by organisations such as OUTA. Wayne Duvenage, who heads up OUTA, stated in a January 2014 article in the *Daily Maverick* that "the law must be rational and acceptable to the masses expected to apply and obey it". He continues to outline the situation "that sparks citizens to see nothing wrong with breaking the law to enforce their rights" (Duvenage, 2014). He is right to the extent that the law does not require anyone to buy an e-tag. But refusing to pay tolls when you have used the toll road and have been invoiced correctly does constitute breaking the law and is therefore considered unethical.

It would, of course, be ideal if all laws were acceptable to everyone all the time. But, in reality, many citizens may disagree with policies and laws passed by the government. While there are actions that those who oppose a law can pursue (such as legal protests), it does not include the "right" to choose which laws to obey or disobey. In a democracy obedience to the law is neither optional, nor can it be exercised sporadically.

Pierre de Vos, who holds the Chair in Constitutional Governance at the University of Cape Town, presents a sound argument against such selective obedience to the law in his blog *Constitutionally Speaking*, noting that non-payment amounts to a refusal to obey a validly passed law that does not infringe on the fundamental human rights of anyone. He adds that protestors need to recognise that disobeying the law promotes lawlessness: "They demand a right to be lawless in order to oppose e-tolls, while criticising others who are lawless" – others being, for example, strikers who break the law or mini-bus taxi drivers who refuse to obey traffic rules (de Vos, 2013).

He also acknowledges that exceptions may arise when the democratically elected government acts to undermine democracy. In such cases, he recognises that "ignoring the law is aimed at protecting democracy itself and would be morally justified". Although the impact of e-tolls may be negative for many people, they do not constitute such as an exception because they do not undermine our democracy (2013).

Therefore, even though e-tolls may prompt the question of whether ethics can be selective, the answer remains that being ethical entails continually and consistently abiding by the applicable values and rules – be they the values enshrined in the Constitution or the company's values, or the laws of the state or the organisation's rules and policies. Selective or part-time ethics is not ethical: It erodes one's ethical status and negatively influences others. Instead, it is the constancy of ethical behaviour that builds ethical individuals, organisations and countries.

1.7 WORKPLACE ETHICS IN CONTEXT

The ideal is that ethics in the workplace should be a clearly understood concept. But the focus given to related concepts and issues can tend to blur that clarity. This includes corporate governance, the triple bottom line, corporate social and environmental responsibility, sustainability, corporate citizenship, stakeholder capitalism and shareholder capitalism. Clarifying the relationships between these issues and ethics – that is, defining the context of ethics – promotes a better understanding of the place ethics occupies and its central role in business.

The feature of ethics that is closely related to these issues is that ethics applies to self and others. This has also been linked earlier in this chapter to ethical boundaries. A company's ethical boundary can range from inclusive to exclusive, where an inclusive ethical boundary includes the interests of self and others and an exclusive ethical boundary is largely focused on self-interest.

Ethics and corporate governance

Although ethics and corporate governance are often treated synonymously, it is desirable that their similarities and differences are understood.

Corporate governance in South Africa is largely defined by the King reports, which are inextricably associated with Mervyn King and the IoDSA. The King Committee on Corporate Governance was formed in 1992 and produced its first report, the *King Report on Corporate Governance in South Africa*, or *King I*, in 1994, followed by *King II* in 2002 and *King III* in 2009.

While all the King reports recognise ethics as central to corporate governance, this is most pronounced in *King III*. Chapter 1, entitled "Ethical leadership and corporate citizenship", acknowledges that "ethics (or integrity) is the foundation of, and reason for, corporate governance" (IoDSA, 2009:21). This chapter also expresses two principles that position ethics as integral to corporate governance: Principle 1.1, which states that: "The board should provide effective leadership based on an ethical foundation" (IoDSA, 2009:20); and Principle 1.3, which states that: "The board should ensure that the company's ethics are managed effectively" (IoDSA, 2009:24).

Ethics should therefore be recognised as the foundation upon which corporate governance rests. It is not a sub-set of corporate governance. On the contrary, corporate governance is a very important facet of ethics. Phrased differently, ethics encompasses the whole, of which corporate governance is a very important part.

The rationale for this view is that workplace ethics involves the actions of **all** employees, from the chairman to the most junior employee. Therefore, when an employee steals the petty cash, for example, it is not considered a corporate governance failure: it is a breach of ethics.

Corporate governance, however, focuses primarily on the actions of the organisation's directors, on their role in running the company, and on the variety of stakeholder interests that need to be considered in their decision making. This focus is evidenced by the fact that much of the content of *King III*, especially the principles, starts with the words "the board should" or "the directors should".

Despite this distinction, workplace ethics and corporate governance are integrally linked. Good corporate governance is unlikely in the absence of workplace ethics, and *vice versa*. And while good corporate governance is neither a guarantee nor a predictor of good ethics – as good ethics is not an assurance of good corporate governance – it is certainly a reliable indicator.

Ethics and the purpose of business

The second implication of ethical boundaries and of ethics applying to self and others encompasses a number of interconnected topics.

The business of business is business

The inclusion of the interest of others is at the heart of the expansion of the purpose and scope of business from the limited view of "the business of business is business", a phrase attributed to Milton Friedman, an American economist who taught at the University of Chicago for more than three decades and won the Nobel Prize in Economics in 1976. The idea that the sole purpose of a firm is to make money for its shareholders was largely shaped by an article he wrote, entitled "The Social Responsibility of Business is to Increase its Profits", which was published in the *New York Times* on 13 September 1970 (Friedman, 1970).

Moving from a single, economic bottom line

That thinking has moved on since then is well reflected in the headline of Steve Denning's piece in the *Forbes* magazine, aptly entitled "The Origin of the World's Dumbest Idea: Milton Friedman" (Denning, 2013). The role that business (especially in the form of global corporations) plays in society has been greatly expanded. Boosted by the power of communication information technology and globalisation, multinational companies have come to exercise power (and sometimes generate revenues) that can eclipse that of many national governments. This has changed the public's attitudes to business and their expectations of the private sector. Instead of pursuing only a single, financial bottom line for the benefit of the business and its shareholders, business is increasingly expected to pursue a triple bottom line, which comprises not only economic but also social and environmental dimensions. This has effectively expanded the scope of business beyond its own financial self-interest to include other interests in the form of social and environmental responsibility. It echoes that statement that "Profit is like health. You need it and the more the better. But it's not why you exist" (Peters & Waterman, 1995:103).

This idea is not as new as it may seem. French society has long recognised the concept of *noblesse oblige*, which means that rank (nobility) brings with it responsibilities. This emphasis is echoed in many areas of society, when one person or a group holds significant power or wields substantial influence over others: the parent over the child or the priest over the congregation. For business, however, the change to encompass the interests of others outside of its own interests is still relatively new.

Triple bottom line

The term that captures the expanded role of business best is the "triple bottom line", a phrase coined by John Elkington of SustainAbility. It focuses on economic prosperity, environmental quality and social justice (Elkington, 1999) and is aimed at achieving balanced, integrated economic, social and environmental performance. This directly relates to an ethical boundary, which should include not only the interest of stakeholders, but also social and environmental responsibilities.

These changes are evident in the shift from earlier times when issues such as training, health care, protecting the environment and poverty alleviation were primarily – and often exclusively   the preserve of government. Now these are increasingly becoming areas of business responsibility.

Corporate social responsibility and corporate social investment

The social and environmental dimension of the triple bottom line incorporates the concept of corporate social responsibility (CSR) and corporate social investment (CSI) (the latter generally regarded as the funding and investment that facilitates the CSR). It is also encompassed by the concept of an ethical boundary. While labelled social, this generally includes the company's actions to address the effects of their operation on the environment and on social welfare and, for some companies, to make a positive contribution to broader society in these domains.

Sustainability or sustainable development

Moving from the purpose of business as "the business of business is business" to a triple bottom line re-frames Friedman's view to a purpose where the business of business is about **sustainable** business. Sustainability and sustainable development are largely the overarching terms that are used currently. The most often-quoted definition of sustainable development is "development that meets the needs of the present without compromising the ability of future generations to meet their own needs", which was first used by the Brundtland Commission, formally known as the World Commission on Environment and Development (WCED), in its 1987 report, *Our Common Future* (WECD, 1987:16).

Corporate citizenship

The other term that embraces both the triple bottom line and sustainability is corporate citizenship. Good corporate citizenship "considers the rights and responsibilities of companies within a broader societal context, and is, therefore, concerned with the contribution a company makes through its social and environmental impacts as well as its economic contribution" (Freemantle & Rockey, 2004:8). Freemantle and Rockey see this impact affecting the following: managing the enterprise, workplace practices, third party interactions, environment and transformation (2004).

Stakeholder capitalism and shareholder capitalism

A triple bottom line approach, sustainability, and being a good corporate citizen can all be regarded as stakeholder capitalism, which acknowledges that companies are also responsible to their workers, local communities and the environment. This contrasts starkly with shareholder capitalism, which suggests that companies should exclusively pursue the interests of their shareholders. These two approaches illustrate the difference between a purpose that is exclusive, serving only a particular group, the shareholders, against a purpose that is inclusive, serving the range of stakeholders. While it cannot be said that all businesses favour an inclusive approach yet, the exclusive approach is increasingly losing legitimacy as the inclusive approach gains wider support and approval.

This support is found, for example, in the inclusion of the triple bottom line in *King II* and *King III*. And, already in 2004, the Johannesburg Stock Exchange (now the Johannesburg Securities Exchange) (JSE) launched the Socially Responsible Investment (SRI) Index, which measures, monitors and reports on the triple bottom line performance of companies in the JSE All Share Index.

Linking this all back to ethics

The significance of this shift is that business ethics has moved beyond a focus on values or a code of conduct to bring the further element of organisational purpose into the realm of workplace ethics. This is embodied in the triple bottom line, sustainability and corporate citizenship. Phrased differently, being ethical in business means that organisations need to adopt an approach that includes these concepts.

There are, of course, many organisations that still engage in the exclusive pursuit of maximising shareholder wealth above all else. However, this is increasingly being judged against a more broadly ethical approach that views success in terms of outcomes for others as well. As Charles Handy, the well-known management author, states so well in his classic article, "What's a Business For?", "to turn shareholders' needs into a purpose is … to mistake a necessary condition for a sufficient one" (Handy, 2002:51).

 *WORKPLACE DISCUSSION*

What constitutes ethics in your organisation?

Consider the following

1   What defines your organisation's ethics? Is it adequate? Is it well understood by employees?

2   How do you deal with counter-arguments, such as ethics being different for different people or different cultures?

3   Does your organisation have a clear understanding of ethics in relation to corporate citizenship, corporate governance, compliance and corporate social investment and responsibility?

RECOMMENDED CASE STUDY AND COMMENTARY

Xin, K & Haijie, W. 2011. Culture clash in the boardroom. *Harvard Business Review*, September. HBR Reprint R1109L.

"Should a German-Chinese joint venture follow the ethical rules of the parent company or the company of operation?"

CHAPTER 2

DOES ETHICS MAKE GOOD BUSINESS SENSE?

INTRODUCTION

Chapter 2 focuses on the questions of whether ethics make good business sense and, related to that, why workplace ethics matters.

It explores the different scenarios of ethics being viewed as a necessity and when it is treated as an illusion or a luxury. In support of the rationale for sound ethics, this chapter looks at the cost of corruption in the South African context. On the positive side of why ethics is important, the topic of valuing ethical capital is discussed, encompassing the concepts of ethical capital and the new ROI, the return on integrity. There is also a specific focus on why ethics should be a priority in trust-based businesses.

This chapter also contains a suggested topic for a workplace discussion and references a relevant case study and recommended reading.

2.1 WORKPLACE ETHICS: ILLUSION, LUXURY OR NECESSITY?

Before exploring the questions of whether ethics makes good business sense or why ethics matters, it is best to start with an accurate understanding of how ethics is actually regarded in the organisation. Although organisations may be well aware of ethical scandals and the negative consequences of ethical failure, it does not automatically translate into ethics being central to the organisation. Ethics in the workplace can amount to a mere illusion, be considered a luxury or, ideally, be viewed as a necessity.

Is ethics an illusion?

Ethics as an illusion is something that is talked about, but which does not really exist. The claim that "our employees are our most valuable asset" may be a standard inclusion in most company's annual reports, but that often does not reflect reality. In fact, Scott Adams, the author of Dilbert cartoons, lists it as first among "the most popular management lies of all time" (Adams, 1997:51).

A more serious aspect of ethics as an illusion is the many ethical failures where the perpetrators specifically set out to create a false impression or misleading image. This can range from the clerk who steals the petty cash to the procurement officer who solicits a bribe, both of whom will strive to project the perfect picture of innocence.

Regrettably, Black economic empowerment (BEE) sometimes also falls under the banner of being an illusion. While the pursuit of transformation is unquestionably the right things to do, when transformation turns to tokenism it results in BEE becoming an illusion. Added to that, it can be very damaging for the people involved, who, instead of being sought out for their ability or potential, are expected to fulfil largely symbolic roles.

There are, no doubt, many companies where ethics does not appear to exist or is exercised only minimally. Looking at the cost of the absence of ethics is an interesting way to argue against allowing ethics to be an illusion.

One such example is industrial group First Strut (Pty) Ltd. The collapse of First Strut in 2013 exposed a massive amount of fraud and related white-collar crimes, extending to all facets of the business. Current information points to Jeff Wiggill, the late Chairman, and Andy Bertulis, the CEO, having directed or been party to this conduct. After the company's collapse, several executives admitted to numerous cases when poor performance went unpunished, where employees took advantage of the company or even openly stole from it, and where no action was taken (de Wet, 2013). The lessons this illustrates are worth emphasising. If leaders display a lack of ethics, it weakens ethics amongst their staff and erodes their credibility and authority. It also reduces the leader's ability to discipline or guide employees. And if the employees aid the company's misconduct, it will not be able to discipline those employees when they too engage in unethical practices for their own gain.

Is ethics a luxury?

Ethics as a luxury is premised on the view that while in theory it is the right thing to do, companies simply cannot afford it. Competitiveness is often used as the main reason that organisations cannot afford to follow an ethical approach. This is allied with the views that in the competitive world of business only the fittest survive and that "winning isn't everything; it's the only thing". This all too easily leads to a "results at any cost" attitude, which can include unethical conduct in order to achieve desired results. This approach can also be accompanied by the perverse logic that unethical behaviour is a good business strategy as long as you do not get caught.

Ethics is also seen to undermine competitiveness in that complying with all the relevant legislation and doing what is right relative to your stakeholders would typically be considered to take more time and incur more costs – and thereby erode profitability. Under the banner of competitive advantage, this can translate into a range of unethical behaviours, such as industrial espionage to steal critical information from competitors to undermine them, false advertising to deceive or mislead customers, or omissions in product labelling to avoid legal compliance. This view that a business cannot be both ethical and successful often echoes the claim that business ethics is an oxymoron.

Again it is worth acknowledging the potential consequences. The sub-prime mortgage crisis that was a pivotal factor in the global financial crisis of 2008 is a prominent example that involved unethical practices in pursuit of financial returns. And there were good returns – until 2008. The global financial collapse saw the closure of a number of large organisations, and others are still being held to account for their conduct. JPMorgan Chase & Company, for instance, settled the latest in numerous legal claims, agreeing to pay the American government $614 million for defrauding federal agencies by underwriting sub-standard mortgage loans. This had involved approving thousands of insured loans that were not eligible for insurance (Ingram & Henry, 2014).

Another issue that is particularly worth exploring in the context of ethics as a luxury is safety. Being ethical would entail, for example, being honest and alerting all affected parties to a safety hazard in one's product as soon as it was discovered. While there are obvious business benefits for the company by cutting costs in safety areas such as quality control or material standards, the serious implications this can have for the users of those products makes it deeply unethical.

A recent case involving Toyota proves this point. On 19 March 2014 the American Justice Department announced a criminal fraud charge against Toyota for misleading customers about unintended acceleration complaints in its cars and imposed a fine of $1.2 billion, the largest in history against any automobile manufacturer. In a damning statement, United States Attorney Preet Bharara said, "In its zeal to staunch bad publicity in 2009 and 2010, Toyota misled regulators, misled customers, and even misstated the facts to Congress" (Muller, 2014).

Ethics can also appear to be a luxury when it negatively impacts on an organisation's access to work. This would apply to situations such as when work can be secured only by paying a bribe. Sayings such as "when in Rome do as the Romans do", or "if you can't beat them, join them" will be used to justify this type of behaviour or to rationalise doing what others are doing. But while this approach may deliver short-term gains, it risks also delivering far bigger long-term disadvantages. This includes not only public outrage, but also reputational damage and the erosion of stakeholder trust, which can cast a shadow over the organisation long after the financial or other costs have been settled.

This type of damage is illustrated by events unfolding at South African information technology company, Pinnacle Holdings, based on only the **allegation** of bribery. Executive director Takalani Tshivhase was arrested on 5 March 2014 on a charge of attempting to bribe a senior police official with R5 million to win a tender for the company. Despite the company's assurance of their ethical conduct, the cost via the market's response was high. The fall in share price over just two days wiped 43% off the company's market value, which amounted to a loss of R1.5 billion (Mantshantsha & Mungadze, 2014).

As these examples illustrate, choosing not to afford ethics does not deliver a sustainable benefit. On the contrary, it carries a cost. The only reason that the cost may not be paid is that the issue or misdemeanour may not yet have surfaced – which means it is only a tenuous advantage.

Paradoxically, the claim that only the fittest or strongest survive does not, in fact, support the view of ethics as a luxury if the full quotation upon which it rests is considered, namely that "It is not the strongest or the most intelligent who will survive but those who can best manage change" (Solis, 2012). This quote is often misattributed to Charles Darwin, the English naturalist who outlined the theory of evolution, but it was actually written by Leon Megginson, Professor of Management and Marketing at Louisiana State University, who was paraphrasing Darwin. The far stronger argument of the full quotation is therefore that those companies that embrace change – for example, in favour of an ethical approach – are, by making that change, more likely to become fitter and stronger.

Is ethics a necessity?

It goes without saying that this book supports the view that ethics is a necessity. There are a number of sound reasons that this is so.

Compliance

Compliance may not be an interesting reason for ethics being a necessity, but it is nonetheless one that needs to be taken into account. In the field of workplace ethics, compliance requirements for ethics stem in particular from the Companies Act 71 of 2008 and the 2009 *King Report on Corporate Governance in South Africa (Kind III)* (IoDSA, 2009).

The Companies Act mandates that all state-owned companies, listed public companies and larger private companies with a public interest score above 500 establish a social and ethics committee. The committee's role is to monitor the company's activities with regard to relevant legislation, other legal requirements and best practice in the areas of ethics (and stakeholder management), and to report to shareholders at the company's annual general meeting. (The role and duties of social and ethics committees relative to ethics are the focus of Part II of Chapter 3.)

While *King III* is a voluntary code that works on an "apply or explain" basis (that is, organisations are expected either to apply its provisions or explain why they have not done so), compliance with the *King Reports* has been a requirement for companies listed on the JSE since June 2010. In accordance with Chapter 1 of *King III*, this entails the assessment, monitoring, reporting and disclosure of an organisation's ethical performance. This is considered necessary "to provide the board and management with relevant and reliable information about the achievement of ethics objectives, the outcome of ethics initiatives and the quality of the company's ethics performance" and to provide external stakeholders "with relevant and reliable information about the quality of the company's ethics performance" (IoDSA, 2009:26–27).

The cost of ethical failure

While this is a negative reason, the cost of ethical failure – and avoiding or minimising that cost – are very real reasons why ethics should be a necessity.

The many high-profile ethical breaches reveal a wide range of costs. Guilty individuals have lost their positions and, sometimes, their freedom following jail sentences. Companies have faced huge financial costs in the form of fines or legal settlements. Costs to reputation have ranged from eroding an individual's credibility to reducing confidence in an organisation and negatively impacting on its share price. In some instances, the cost has also led to the closure of the business.

When this happens, the employees who lose their jobs also bear the cost. This illustrates a particularly nasty consequence common to many ethical failures, namely that the cost extends beyond the perpetrators to innocent victims who effectively "share" the costs.

This adds enormously to the public outrage, the publicity and the damage – and also illustrates each time how much ethics matters.

Ethics creates a trustworthy workplace

On the positive side, ethics is a necessity because it promotes ethical behaviour, reduces unethical activity, and creates a more trustworthy workplace.

In situations of high trust, organisations are likely to enjoy the advantages of better and faster decision making, greater consistency of responses and decisions, good confidence in top management action and more individual accountability with less need for policing. In an article fittingly entitled "The Most Valuable Business Commodity: Trust", David Williams, author of *The 7 Non Negotiables of Winning*, acknowledged that the trust we create matters most to our success. He sees trust as one of the primary "things in work, and in life, [that] are unmeasurable and without equal" (Williams, 2013).

These benefits are significant for the company and its people. They support operational excellence and create a more pleasant workplace for employees, which, in turn, is likely to improve performance and productivity.

Ethics improves stakeholder relationships

From the perspective of stakeholder relationships, ethics is also important. All the company's stakeholders – employees, customers, investors or unions – assess the ethical status of the organisation. They base their conclusion on a myriad of things, such as press reports, what the employees say about the company and its leaders, how stakeholder groups are treated, whether there is a gap between what is said and done, and whether the values are lived or just framed on the wall. Their conclusions about the ethical status of the organisation may rest on perception, but those perceptions represent the reality that will be acted upon.

All stakeholders can easily recognise the benefits of dealing with an ethical organisation and they would place greater value on relationships that are characterised by, for example, honesty, fairness and respect than on less trustworthy associations. A positive view lends itself to many benefits, while a negative view can be very damaging on many fronts.

The benefits of being recognised as an ethical organisation by external stakeholders include the ability to attract and retain top staff and board members, improved investor and market confidence, reduced cost of capital, easier access to capital, improved brand equity, and enhanced corporate reputation.

Ethics is a source of competitive advantage

Arguably, the ultimate reason that ethics should be treated as a necessity is because ethics can be a source of competitive advantage.

Competitive advantage is increasingly critical, but is frequently subject to a limited window of competitive opportunity. Advances in technology, for example, are vulnerable to the ease and speed with which they can be copied. A unique source of competitive advantage, which cannot be easily copied, would therefore have infinitely greater value – and workplace ethics offers just such a source. This derives from the fact that ethics is not easy to copy. To this can be added that ethics can also not be bought, sold, owned, traded or delegated. Instead, it must be lived every day.

Ironically, each fresh corporate scandal enhances the value of organisations seen to be ethical and makes them even more likely to be rewarded for their ethical stance.

Ethics makes good business sense

The reasons and arguments in favour of an ethical approach and against ethics being either an illusion or a luxury are both strong and sound, especially from the perspective of the organisational rewards an ethical approach delivers. In terms of a cost-benefit analysis, both the benefits and the costs are high, the difference being that the benefits aid and support the organisation, while the costs undermine it.

In short, therefore, it is an easy conclusion to draw that ethics really does make good business sense.

2.2 COUNTING THE COST OF CORRUPTION IN SOUTH AFRICA[ii1]

"All that I can say to this nation and this committee is [that] corruption in this country has reached crisis proportions," These are the words of the Public Protector, Adv. Thuli Madonsela, spoken at her annual report to Parliament in October 2013 (eNCA, 2013a).

Her view, unfortunately, is reflected in the many corruption scandals that continue to feature in our press. It is also supported by the country's level of corruption as measured by Transparency International's Corruption Perceptions Index (CPI) and Global Corruption Barometer, which confirm that the high levels of corruption are not a mere perception. The CPI is a global survey that annually measures the perceived level of public sector corruption on a scale of 0 to 100, where 0 is highly corrupt and 100 is "highly clean". South Africa has consistently scored in the lower, more corrupt half of the scale. In 2012 South Africa's score was 43 and it was ranked 69th out of 176 countries (Transparency International, 2012). In 2013 South Africa's results declined in score and ranking to 42 and 72nd out of 177 countries (Transparency International, 2013a).

Adding to this is Transparency International's Global Corruption Barometer, which surveyed 114 000 people in 107 countries in 2013 to assess people's experiences of bribery and corruption in the main institutions in their countries. In South Africa 47% of people reported paying a bribe in the previous 12 months – versus a global average of 27% – and the police were considered the most corrupt institution in the public sector (Transparency International, 2013b).

The PricewaterhouseCoopers (PwC) *Global Economic Crime Survey* offers further insight into economic crime. The 2013 survey was conducted among 5 128 senior respondents from over 93 countries, which included 134 organisations across 17 industries in South Africa. The findings reveal that asset misappropriation remains the most common form of economic crime, reported by 77% of respondents. It is followed by procurement fraud (59%), bribery and corruption (52%), human resources fraud (42%) and financial statement fraud (35%). More than half of CEOs surveyed (53%) reported being concerned about bribery and corruption and bribery and corruption have been the fastest growing economic crime category in South Africa since 2011. Regionally, economic crime is most pervasive in Africa, where 50% of respondents say they have been victims, followed by North America at 41%, Eastern Europe at 39%, Latin America and Western Europe, each at 35%, Asia Pacific at 32% and the Middle East at 21% (PwC, 2014).

It may be a naïve question to ask why this is happening. It is certainly not because those involved do not know what is right and wrong. Rather, at the level of the "petty" bribe to a traffic official, it can be seen as an avoidance strategy by the person paying the bribe, for example, to avoid a fine or, worse, being jailed for a more serious offence such as drunken driving. For bribes offered for tenders, the recipient's most obvious motivation is money and self-enrichment. So, someone avoids a fine and someone else gets rich. Is that really so bad? The costs and consequences of corruption answer this question best.

Quantifying the financial cost of corruption, Alec Hogg noted on Power Lunch on CNBC Africa that South Africa has lost R675 billion owing to corruption since 1994 (BizNews, 2013). A report produced by Peter Allwright of law firm Edward Nathan Sonnenbergs, based on figures from the Public Service Commission, says South Africa is fighting a losing battle against corruption, imposing a cost on taxpayers of nearly R1 billion in the 2011–2012 financial year. And, although 88% of people accused of financial misconduct in the public sector are found guilty, only 19% are dismissed. Allwright says most get off with a written warning and remain in government service and continue stealing (eNCA, 2013b).

Such levels of corruption bring with them many costs and negative repercussions. One such consequence is that corruption increases the cost of doing business but, crucially, without adding corresponding value. Instead of the full contract amount going towards the delivery of the product or service, only a portion is productively employed. This can erode quality and safety when, for example, sub-standard materials are used on building projects. When money meant for infrastructure and development is diverted to corrupt officials, it also undermines service delivery and the fight against poverty.

A further cost relates to leadership, specifically because leaders exert the most powerful influence on ethics, defining by their behaviour what is and is not acceptable. Therefore, when high profile leaders are involved in bribery, corruption or unethical and illegal action, their impact as role models is very damaging. It risks creating a culture that condones misconduct, illegal behaviour and the prioritisation of improper personal gain, and where "lowest common denominator" behaviour prevails, whether for employees in a company or citizens in a country.

This cost is confirmed by research into the link between unethical leadership and poor business performance by Robert B Cialdini, the Regents' Professor Emeritus of Psychology and Marketing at Arizona State University and author of *Influence:*

The Psychology of Persuasion. He found that cheating at the top generates huge hidden costs, even if the leaders think they are "getting away with it". His findings show that when leaders cheat, they make employees less productive; it drives away the company's best employees (with the added costs associated with high staff turnover); and it increases cheating by others within the company (that is, cheating begets cheating) (James, 2014).

There are many examples of corruption, such as the extensive fraud and corruption that was exposed following the collapse of the First Tech Group in 2013 and the collusive practices uncovered in the construction industry following the 2010 Soccer World Cup. Within the public sector, apart from corruption associated with government tenders, there are many other incidents with wide-ranging costs involving, for instance, nepotism and conflicts of interest.

While ethical failure affects people in all spheres of society, it is more noteworthy in the public sector – the reason being that it affects many more people than when it occurs in a company. When, for example, a country is perceived to be corrupt, it does not erode only the benefits of a sound ethical status, such as enhanced access to international investment and funding, favoured trading partner status, and good tourism revenues. It also negatively affects the businesses and institutions operating in the country and the population's quality of life. And when corruption is perceived to allow those in power to amass personal wealth without benefiting their people, it brings with it the added risk of serious social unrest.

Ivo Vegter, writing in the *Daily Maverick*, makes a further important distinction between private and public sector corruption that emphasises the greater cost of public sector corruption. In business the consequences of fraud and corruption are largely borne by the company's investors and clients, both of whom are free to remove their support for the company if they suspect corruption. In the public sector, however, the consequences of fraud and corruption are borne instead by taxpayers and citizens who are effectively its investors and clients. But if they are unhappy about corruption, taxpayers cannot choose to withhold their taxes or pay them to another entity they trust more. Nor can citizens choose to rely on a party other than the government for government services (Vegter, 2013).

These many costs should, ideally, be mitigated when corruption is uncovered and successfully prosecuted. It is a positive sign that our media is exposing many of these scandals. However, countering this is the apparent impunity of those who are politically and financially powerful and the low rate of successful convictions. This is echoed in the Public Service Commission's report on financial misconduct for the period 2011–2012. Among those found guilty of financial misconduct, only a small percentage lost their jobs: 11% in 2008–2009; 21% in 2009–2010; 23% in 2010–2011 and 24% in 2011–2012 (Public Service Commission, 2013:12).

There are many issues that would have to be addressed to turn back the tide of corruption.[1] Foremost among them is the need for a nationwide focus on transparency and accountability. But until that happens, the costs and negative consequences will continue to grow.

As to the question of whether corruption is really so bad, it is impossible to refute the enormous cost of bribery and corruption – which is a cost far higher than our country can or should afford.

2.3   VALUING ETHICAL CAPITAL AND THE NEW ROI

While regular ethical scandals continue to highlight the costs and negative consequences of ethical failure, there is not even close to an equal focus on the opposite, namely the rewards of being ethical.

The section earlier in this chapter on workplace ethics as an illusion, luxury or necessity specifically looked at why ethics is a necessity and why it makes good business sense. The reasons included compliance, the cost of ethical failure, the value of a trustworthy workplace, improved stakeholder relationships, and competitive advantage. While the value of ethics is implicit in these reasons, the topic warrants further attention.

Ethical capital

This centres on two issues, the first of which is ethical capital. The value that is generated by an ethical organisational culture – namely ethical capital – needs to be recognised and named. The benefits it delivers include, among many others, a high-trust working environment, the ability to attract and retain top staff and board members, increased customer loyalty, improved risk management, enhanced reputation and brand equity, and reduced cost of capital. Yet despite the obvious merit, ethical capital is not widely acknowledged as a source of value.

Apart from the benefits just mentioned, its value is well illustrated as part of an organisation's asset base.

Financial capital represents the most obvious element of an organisation's asset base to which, traditionally, tangible assets such as plant and machinery have contributed either positively or negatively. However, two factors brought into effect and gave priority to intangible assets as a new class of organisational assets, namely: the rise of the knowledge economy and the accompanying shift in emphasis from financial capital to people as a primary source of competitive advantage.

---

1   The article on tackling misconduct in Part I of Chapter 4 addresses this further.

I developed a model many years ago to illustrate the key components of an organisation's asset base, building on work by Hubert Saint-Onge, then vice president of People Knowledge & Strategy at The Mutual Group in Canada (Saint-Onge, 1997). I defined intangible assets as comprising the following (as illustrated in Figure 2.1):

1   *Employees' knowledge capital*, which encompasses their knowledge, skills, experience, creativity and innovation.

2   *Employees' relationship capital*, which encompasses their relationships with team-mates, colleagues, associates, suppliers and customers.

3   *Organisational capital*, which is vested in the organisation's leadership, culture, structure and systems.

4   *Customer capital and supplier capital*, which represent the value of an organisation's ongoing relationships with these stakeholders.

5   *Community capital*, which represents the value of an organisation's ongoing relationships with external stakeholders (other than customers and suppliers) on whom the organisation's operations have an impact. This particularly includes the residents local to the company's operations who may be affected by a range of positive or negative factors, such as better work opportunities, emissions or increased traffic.

6   *Ethical capital*, which is created by and directly proportional to ethical conduct, decisions and choices relative to employees and all of the organisation's external stakeholders.

As is the case with tangible assets, intangible assets can affect financial capital. A company's IT system going down can, for example, undermine customer capital. Similarly, a rude or inefficient employee can undermine supplier or customer capital and non-delivery on commitments to the local community can erode community capital.

The reverse is also true. Organisations can become more successful through having fair systems, helpful and respectful relationships, and committed employees who willingly share their knowledge and skills.

Similarly, ethics is an important intangible asset in the form of ethical capital. Ethics also adds overarching value to all the other areas of intangible assets. Sound workplace ethics and high ethical status contribute significantly to the value of employee capital, organisational capital, customer capital, supplier capital and community capital. In particular, ethics enhances the quality of the relationship capital the organisation enjoys with its people and with its external stakeholders. In contributing to the value of an organisation's intangible assets, ethics contributes, in turn, to its financial capital.

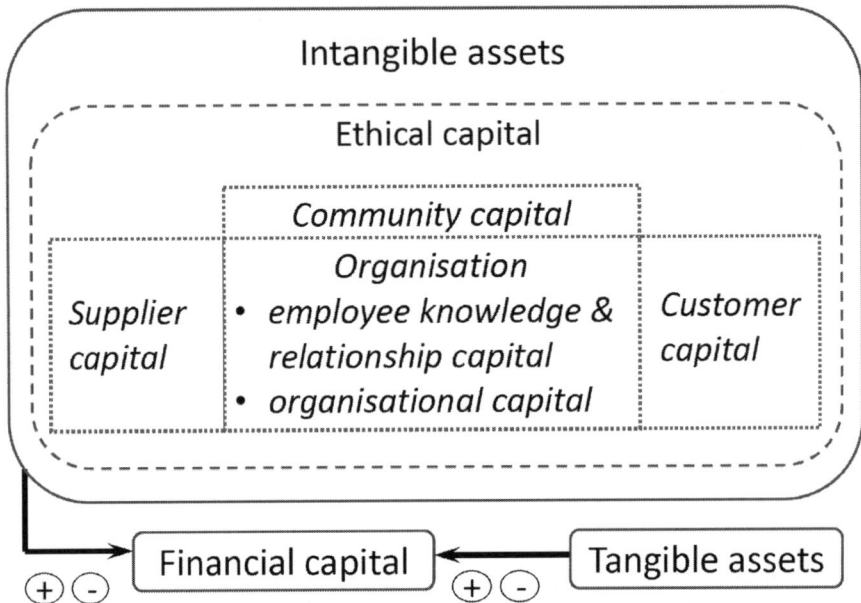

Figure 2.1: Intangible assets as a key component of an organisation's asset base

An organisation's asset base is represented here as consisting of financial capital to which tangible assets and intangible assets contribute either positively or negatively. Tangible assets include plant and machinery. Intangible assets include employees' knowledge and relationship capital, the company's organisational capital, customer and supplier capital, community capital and ethical capital. The interaction between the different elements is indicated by dashed and dotted lines to illustrate porous boundaries. Ethical capital stems from ethical behaviour exercised both within the organisation and relative to its external stakeholders. It also enhances the other sources of intangible assets by, for example, improving the quality of the relationship capital between the organisation and its people and its external stakeholders and by increasing their trust in the organisation.

Quantifying ethical capital

Although intangible assets, by their nature, are often not visible and can be difficult to measure, it should not diminish their value. In the case of an organisation's ethical capital, one way in which this can be quantified is in the form of an ethics rating via the use of a tool such as the Ethics Monitor, a web-based ethics survey. The rating ranges from AAA, the most ethical rating, indicating ethical conduct that applies to internal and external stakeholders and encompasses a triple bottom line, to a D rating, the worst rating, signifying unethical conduct in pursuit of self-gain.

An ethics rating and the supporting results produced by the Ethics Monitor serve as an effective way to enable organisations to manage their ethics more effectively and thereby reduce ethical risks and maximise ethical capital. And, much as credit ratings fulfil an important role in evaluating the credit worthiness of businesses and governments, so too can an ethics rating add significant value by allowing investors and other stakeholders to assess an organisation's ethical risks. Ethics ratings can also be used as a benchmark between multiple branches of a company or within industries, market sectors and regions.

For an organisation, an ethics rating further affords it the opportunity to receive recognition for creating a workplace with an ethical culture. By way of illustration, I have asked audiences at various conferences and workshops to identify just three companies operating in South Africa that have really distinguished themselves as being ethical. The minimal number of companies identified is a telling sign – not that there are no ethical companies in South Africa, but rather that very few organisations have been widely acknowledged for their sound ethical culture. The lack of such recognition represents a waste of ethical capital. Seeing that organisations rarely waste other sources of capital, it is prudent that companies quantify their ethics to ensure they can leverage its inherent benefits.

The new ROI

Aspiring to the highest ethics rating, AAA, necessitates more than good intentions and a recognition of the value of ethical capital. It warrants the ongoing commitment from leadership to a sound ethical culture, which includes the requirement that ethics is clearly identified as a high priority business goal and integrated as a core feature of the organisation's strategy. In the absence of this support, the value of the company's ethical capital is unlikely to be fully realised and the pursuit of ethics risks being overtaken by operational targets.

A valuable concept that can support this leadership pursuit of ethical capital and an ethical culture is the new ROI.

ROI, as the acronym for "return on investment", is central to most businesses. The investment of capital and resources is intended – and expected – to deliver a financial return. But there is another new ROI that centres on an investment in workplace ethics, namely the return on integrity. This represents the second reason (in addition to ethical capital) that the topic of the value of ethics warrants further attention.

As a return on investment would be measured in increased financial capital, so too can a return on integrity be measured in terms of improved ethical capital. The two ROIs are also similar as regards failure to deliver. Failure to deliver financial returns and failure to conduct a business ethically both risk eroding shareholder confidence and, ultimately, jeopardising the ongoing existence of the company. Unethical conduct can also reverse the benefits delivered by ethical capital. It can damage the organisation's reputation, diminish customer support, and incur financial costs in the form of fines or legal settlements.

Yet the attention afforded to ethics and the return on integrity is rarely comparable to that given to the return on investment.

Reaping the benefits of the new ROI and building the organisation's ethical capital will largely fall to leadership. This warrants their most committed attention not simply because ethics is a necessity, but because it is so valuable that it makes **great** business sense.

2.4 ETHICS SHOULD BE A PRIORITY IN TRUST-BASED BUSINESSES

While ethics is – or should be – important in all businesses, it is especially relevant for businesses that are trust-based. This includes companies in the financial services sector and professional practices such as auditing and legal practices. The services and advice offered by professionals in these fields require a high level of client trust as regards both expertise and integrity – which can exceed the level of trust required in many other businesses, for example, in the retail industry, where a customer's interaction may entail only a transactional purchase.

Earning and maintaining this trust is, therefore, crucial for the success of these types of businesses. But this trust has been eroded by many ethical failures.

The erosion of trust

Unethical auditing and accounting practices have featured in some of the biggest American scandals: Enron in 2001, WorldCom and Tyco in 2002, Freddie Mac in 2003, American Insurance Group (AIG) in 2005, and Lehman Brothers and Bernie Madoff in 2008. Auditors' responsibility for vouching that the business is a "going concern" was often contradicted by business closures in late 2008. Ethic is consequently a major issue in auditing organisations, focusing on concerns such as the degree of independence, unintentional bias, and conflicts of interest.

In the financial sector a number of incidents suggest that an ethical culture is often absent. Still noteworthy is Greg Smith's very public resignation as an executive from Goldman Sachs in March 2012 via an opinion piece in the *New York Times*. He described the company as "morally bankrupt" and having a "toxic culture" (2012). Just three months later, in June 2012, Barclays plc in the United Kingdom was fined a massive £290 million for rigging inter-bank lending rates. These events and others raise the question of whether the financial services industry has changed from the self-serving culture that was perceived to have contributed to the global financial crash in 2008.

Legal practices are just as vulnerable to low levels of trust that can be fuelled by misconduct. Misappropriating trust funds is a well-recognised risk area, although in South Africa the Attorneys Fidelity Fund (AFF) protects the public against loss as a result of the theft of trust funds by practitioners. But, while the AFF 2013 report reveals that there have been fewer claims in 2013 compared to the same period in 2012, there was an increase in the amounts being misappropriated (Sedutla, 2014). In some legal practices, the way in which candidate attorneys are treated represents less than ethical conduct. If the practice aspires to an ethical culture this should be addressed, not least to ensure that such undesirable conduct is not perpetuated.

An American poll that reveals further opinions about these industries is the annual Gallup poll to assess perceptions of honesty and ethics in different professions. The most recent poll, conducted in December 2013, found that nurses are considered the most honest and ethical, with 82% of respondents scoring them very high or high. (Interestingly, except for 2001, nurses have been at the top of this poll since 1999.) The honesty and ethics of lawyers and bankers, on the other hand, were found to be very high or high by only 20% and 27% of respondents respectively (Swift, 2013).

Building higher levels of trust rests on an ethical culture[2]

Building, rebuilding or maintaining trust should, therefore, be a priority. An optimal approach to realising this is to focus on creating an ethical workplace culture to serve as a guide for the business and its people's behaviours and decisions. While an ethical culture is not an absolute guarantee of high levels of trust, it is a non-negotiable prerequisite and the highest probability conduit.

Within organisations, trust is built when the company and its people are ethical (in other words, when the company has an ethical culture). This entails, for example, that the practitioner assigned to the matter has the necessary knowledge and experience and that he/she acts with integrity, in accordance with the law and in the best interest of the client. Providing honest and unbiased advice at all times is essential, as is client confidentiality. In addition, according to Vanessa Hall, the author of *The Truth about Trust in Business*, three things are essential to build trust, namely, managing people's expectations of you, your business, your products and your services; meeting people's needs; and keeping your promises (Hall, 2009:22).

Leadership's commitment to ethics is a primary factor in creating a trust-based workplace. Their behaviour effectively demonstrates to their employees, colleagues and clients what is and is not acceptable. Internally, this shapes the company's culture and reinforces – or undermines – trust and its ethical values.

A high level of transparency is a further factor. Since transparency is synonymous with openness and honesty and involves sharing all relevant information, it builds and maintains trust and an ethical culture (recognising that sharing "relevant" information should accommodate the need for client confidentiality).

---

2   Ethical culture is addressed in greater detail in the section "Ethics management system", in Part I of Chapter 4.

Promoting an ethical culture can also be furthered by using goals and measurement, for instance, to monitor sensitive issues in an attempt to reduce unethical behaviour. An example of this at an industry level is the AFF's tracking and reporting of claims against attorneys for the misappropriation of funds.

But internal business goals and measures can also have the effect of encouraging unethical behaviour. This is especially relevant for time-based billing. The focus on billable hours in many organisations – accounting, consulting and law firms – often includes financial targets. Delivering on those targets is clearly in the employees' best interests as it is likely to positively impact their rewards, whether a salary increase, a promotion or a bonus. This can easily lead to expanding the scope of work unnecessarily or, worse, to inflating or fabricating the billable hours. Although unethical, it can foster an "ends justify the means" view.

An interesting case was heard before the Wisconsin Supreme Court of an American lawyer who inflated his billable hours over a three-year period to qualify for bonuses from his law firm. After the firm had paid him each of the bonuses, but before the bills had been sent to the clients, the lawyer reduced or "wrote-down" his billable hours for those years. Two facts are pertinent to this action. It was done without notifying the firm, and the "write-down" reduced his billable hours to below the bonus threshold. The result was that he was fired from his job and the Court imposed a one-year suspension on him for falsifying billable time to obtain a bonus, even though no clients were ultimately harmed (Corsmeier, 2013)[3].

Leaders should, therefore, always consider what types of behaviour the company's goals and measures are likely to encourage and avoid ill-conceived goals that can lead to unintended negative consequences and foster an attitude of "results at any cost". In the case of time-based billing, this means that billable hours cannot be the only criterion for evaluating someone's performance or contribution to the practice.

Trust-based businesses should also pay attention to sustaining a high degree of ethical awareness in the workplace. Ethical awareness means that ethics needs to be a real part of the organisation, included throughout its operation, for example, from its strategy to its staff training. It should be evident in company communications, as an agenda item at senior meetings, and as a criterion for performance evaluations.

Regularly measuring and reporting on the company's ethics is important because it adds to ethical awareness and contributes to the creation of an ethical culture. The measurement and reporting of ethics and ethical performance is now mandated by the Companies Act 71 of 2008 and is a primary recommendation of *King III*. However, this has mostly not been translated into meaningful-enough interventions.

---

3   The case is: *In the Matter of Matthew C. Siderits, Case No. 2011AP259-D (1/4/13)*. The opinion is available at: http://www.wicourts.gov/sc/opinion/DisplayDocument.html?content=html&seqNo=91260 [Accessed 27 March 2014].

Ethics assessment is often limited to the opinion of the board and fails to produce accurate, credible and quantitative results that add value to the pursuit and management of ethics. However, if positioned as a "listening" exercise to bring to the surface all employees' experiences and views of ethics, an ethics assessment can foster significantly increased trust when the results are shared with employees and poor results are acted upon.

Similarly, ethics reporting does not often provide information that offers a clear picture of the company's ethical performance. When it does, reporting can also contribute to the creation and preservation of a high-trust ethical culture.

A noteworthy initiative in the area of ethics reporting that recognises the importance of trust in the legal profession was the September 2013 launch by the Law Society of South Africa and the AFF of Trustline: Promoting Trust in the Attorneys' Profession. Trustline provides a confidential and anonymous complaints line and tip-off service for members of the public to report alleged and suspected unethical, fraudulent, corrupt or dishonest behaviour by attorneys or their staff.

The commitment which the pursuit of a high-trust ethical culture requires is more than met by the rewards. Apart from enjoying clients' trust, it deepens and strengthens relationships, fosters client loyalty, and reduces the risk of ethical failure, fraud or corruption and the associated costs. More importantly, it should also create a valuable source of competitive advantage.

Given this correlation between ethics, trust and success, it should follow that building and maintaining an ethical culture is imperative. The only question that remains is why all trust-based organisations are not acting accordingly and visibly advocating and nurturing an ethical culture.

WORKPLACE DISCUSSION

Does ethics matter in your organisation?

Is ethics in your organisation viewed as a luxury you can't afford? Is it just an illusion (spoken about but not acted on), or is it recognised as a necessity? Is ethics valued to its full extent?

Consider the following:

- Do your people (especially the leadership) understand the potential benefits of ethical capital, the return on integrity and an ethical culture?

- Do they clearly understand the negative costs and consequences of ethical failure or a breach of ethics?

- What would an ethics cost-benefit analysis reveal in the short term and the long term?

RECOMMENDED CASE STUDY AND COMMENTARY

Eisenmann, C. 2009. When hackers turn to blackmail. *Harvard Business Review*, October. HBR Reprint R0910B.

"Lives are at stake when extortionists shut down a hospital's electronic medical records system."

FURTHER READING

Beard, A & Hornik, R. 2011. It's hard to be good. *Harvard Business Review*, 88–96, November. HBR Reprint R1111E.

"It's hard to be good. But it's worth it. Here are five companies whose success is built on responsible business practices."

Endnote

i   Acknowledgement: Original, abridged article first published in *HR Future* magazine.

CHAPTER 3
WHOSE ROLE IS ETHICS?

INTRODUCTION

This chapter addresses the question of whose role ethics is. It focuses on three functional areas within the organisation: leadership, the social and ethics committee, and human resources (HR). This focus does not ignore that other designations could fulfil significant roles as regard ethics, such as an ethics officer (who would probably exercise the overall responsibility for the management of ethics), the company secretary, or the compliance officer. In this chapter, these are all considered leadership roles.

The section on leadership includes discussions that explore whether a company can be ethical if its leaders are not; the ethical issues surrounding women leadership; and also ethical leadership in the public sector (with a focus on South Africa). It also addresses the important topic of the need for more ethical leaders.

Part II deals with the social and ethics committee, and reviews whether the committee is a cost or an added value. It also clarifies the roles and responsibilities of the committee relative to ethics.

In Part III, HR is recognised as fulfilling a crucial role in the advancement of ethics, and there are a number of articles that will provide useful support for HR professionals. These are ethics in relation to selection and recruitment and remuneration, ethics training, and the key features for drafting a sound code of ethics. Practical guidelines are included for writing a gift policy and a conflict of interest policy.

PART I: LEADERSHIP

3.1 CAN A COMPANY BE ETHICAL IF ITS LEADERS ARE NOT?[i]

Whether an organisation has a good or a bad reputation may stem from many different factors, but it is always related to the actual or perceived ethical status of a company. The difference between a good or bad reputation – as between having a positive or negative ethical status – is profound. A positive ethical status lends itself to many advantages while also minimising the risk of reputation damage and the many costs associated with ethical breaches. Realising these benefits is clearly very desirable.

Since leadership is widely recognised as one of the most influential factors shaping behaviour – whether towards being more or less ethical – leadership is a particularly important issue. This strong link between leadership and behaviour raises the crucial question of whether a company can be ethical if its leaders are not.

If the ethics of a company is viewed as separate from that of its leaders, it apparently supports a "yes" answer based on the rationale that the leader is not the organisation and that the organisation is larger than the leader. But, in practice, the ethical strength or failing of senior leadership does have an impact on the company.

Barclays was a high profile example in the 2012 London inter-bank offered rate (Libor) rigging scandal, which saw the resignation of its chairman, CEO and COO. The fallout was not only $464 million in fines (Vaughan & Finch, 2013). It also dictated that the new CEO, Antony Jenkins, place major emphasis on values and creating an ethical culture to rebuild stakeholder trust. When he took over in August 2012, he sent out a clear message to all staff that they either adopt the bank's new values or leave, and that bonuses and performance would be assessed against a new "Purpose and Values" blueprint (*The Telegraph*, 2013).

The reverse is also true when leadership ethics shapes the company positively. The founding of Infosys reflects such an example. When N R Narayana Murphy and six colleagues set up Infosys in 1981 in India, they agreed to create a value-based organisation with a vision statement to be India's most respected company. Quoted in a *Harvard Business Review* interview as to what he meant by that in practice, his reply was noteworthy:

> If you seek respect from customers, that means you must deliver what you promise. If you seek respect from your employees, you must treat them fairly and with dignity. If you seek respect from investors, you must operate with transparency and accountability. If you seek respect from vendor-partners, you must deal with them on merit. If you seek respect from governments, you must never violate any laws. If you seek respect from society, you will live in harmony with it and create goodwill. If we could do all that, I argued, we would attract customers, employees, vendors and investors; revenues, profits and market capitalisation would follow (Raman, 2011:81).

Both good and bad examples illustrate the immense value of ethical leadership. But the challenge that is most commonly raised is that there are often too few ethical leaders. This can prompt a response where the situation of poor ethics is simply accepted.

That may appear to be the only option relative to national leadership when a leader holds very long-term control of a country. Zimbabwe and Cameroon come to mind for entrenched leadership and poor ethics. Transparency International's Corruption Perceptions Index (CPI) assesses the extent of public sector corruption on a scale of 0 to 100, where 0 represents "very corrupt" and 100 is "highly clean". In 2013 Zimbabwe scored only 21 and Cameroon 25, very much in the lower corrupt end of the scale (Transparency International, 2013a). Corruption is seen to have increased in both countries according to the 2013 Global Corruption Barometer, with the percentage of people who reported paying a bribe in the previous 12-month period in almost the highest range of 50–74.9% (Transparency International, 2013b).

The leaders in these countries have been in power for a long time. Robert Mugabe came to power in 1980, as Zimbabwe's Prime Minister from 1980 to 1987 and as President from December 1987 to date. Paul Biya became Prime Minister in 1975 and took on the role of President of Cameroon in 1982, which role he still occupies. There may therefore appear to be few options to realise meaningful change in these instances.

Fortunately, this stasis does not apply as easily in the private sector. In business a preferable approach to the view that there are too few ethical leaders would be to look to the individual as another important source of ethical behaviour and, in doing so, also to promote the recognition that the pursuit of ethical behaviour need not be solely dependent on ethical leadership.

In recognition of the power of the individual to shape ethical behaviour, two basic features of ethics are pertinent. The first is that ethics centres on the individual's choice between good and bad and right and wrong. While leadership is a very strong influencing factor on behaviour and that choice, it is still only one factor. The individual's choice is equally shaped by personal values, by the norms of a groups to which he/she belongs (such as family, cultural groups or community groups), by the organisation's culture, and by applicable laws, rules and regulations.

The individual's ethical choice is also subject to the second feature of ethics, namely that people almost always know the difference between right and wrong. Even if a leader condones misconduct – for example, corruption related to tenders – it does not affect the classification of the behaviour as wrong. The employee still knows it is wrong. Thus, apart from situations of coercion or autocratic leadership, the individual is generally free to choose whether to follow a path of ethical or unethical conduct – and the power of this original choice should not be underestimated.[1]

The challenge of a lack of sufficient ethical leaders also warrants that a leadership assumption articulated by Peter Senge, author of *The Fifth Discipline*

---

[1]   The article on tackling misconduct in Part I of Chapter 4 addresses the issue of how to deal with making a moral choice in an organisation where less ethical conduct is practised.

and director of the Center for Organizational Learning at the MIT Sloan School of Management, is addressed. He acknowledges that "when things are going poorly, we blame the situation on incompetent leaders [and] when things become desperate we can easily find ourselves waiting for a great leader to rescue us" (in Jaworksi, 1996:2). Senge notes that this outward focus of looking for **someone else** to be the leader who raises the level of behaviour misses the bigger question, namely, what are we, individually and collectively, able to contribute? Organisations should reinforce these messages: that individuals taking personal responsibility for behaving ethically can make a difference in their sphere of influence and that they can and do contribute to ethics, because the ethical status of a company is made up of the behaviour of all the individuals. Each person's every act – ethical or unethical, positive or negative – either builds or erodes the ethical status of that group.

Regular lapses of leadership ethics should therefore not be the concluding point as regards leadership and ethics. Rather, companies should also strive to build a critical mass towards achieving an ethical tipping point where the behaviour of the majority of employees tips in favour of sound ethics.

3.2 WOMEN, LEADERSHIP AND ETHICS[ii]

There have been numerous studies that show that women are not equally represented in senior roles in the workplace or in the boardroom.

Lack of equal representation

Among both the 2013 Fortune 500 companies and the 2013 Fortune 1000 companies, women hold only 4.6% of CEO positions (Catalyst, 2014a). Catalyst, a non-profit organisation working in the Americas, Australia, Europe and India to expand opportunities for women, has tracked women's representation in the workplace over many years. Their analysis shows that as executive officers in Fortune 500 companies women's representation has stagnated over the last five years. In 2009 the percentage of executive officer positions held by women was 13.5%, in 2010, 14.4%, in 2011, 14.1%, in 2012, 14.3%, and in 2013, 14.6%. The statistics for Fortune 500 board seats held by women over the same five-year period increased only slightly: from 15.2% in 2009 to 16.9% in 2013 (Catalyst, 2014b).

In South Africa the 2012 Women in Leadership Census, undertaken by the Businesswomen's Association, found that while women make up 52% of the South African population, they account for just 5.5% of chairperson positions, 17.1% of directorships, 3.6% of CEO positions, and 21.4% of executive management positions.

While there are reports that display some progress, it generally does not reflect a constant upward trend. By way of example, gender transformation in the South African judiciary moved forward in May 2013 when President Jacob Zuma appointed five new female judges (Mail & Guardian, 2013). However, also in

May 2013, Lesotho's Constitutional Court upheld a section of the Chieftainship Act, which denies daughters the right to succeed to chieftainship (Mabuza, 2013).

The lack of equal representation at senior leadership levels is coupled to many workplace factors that impact women. These include stumbling blocks that often exist even in companies that support the need for gender transformation. The following issues are especially noteworthy as they cross the line of sound ethics.

Unfairness and discrimination

Virtually all businesses would accept that fairness and the absence of discrimination are fundamental to a productive and ethical working environment. However, this does not always apply to women.

An obvious example is that many companies still treat pregnancy as if it is a problem, discriminating against the recruitment or advancement of young women whom they think may be planning to have a family.

Another prominent issue for working mothers is the dilemma of balancing work and family, especially children. Both deserve her commitment and care – both are "right" choices – but often time does not accommodate both. In this instance, it can be argued that men also face the challenge of achieving a work-life balance, although mostly with lesser family demands. However, American statistics show that it is women who bear the brunt of the bias associated with being a working mother or a caregiver. This so-called "maternal wall bias" translates into a 79% reduction in a woman's chance of being hired if she has a child and a 50% less likelihood that she will be promoted than a childless woman (Williams & Cuddy, 2012:95–96). Joan Williams, Distinguished Professor of Law and Hastings Foundation Chair at the University of California, Hastings College of the Law, and Amy Cuddy, associate professor at Harvard Business School, reported that a newer field of employment law, family responsibility discrimination, is growing (in contrast to decreasing overall employment litigation) and juries are taking the side of women (Williams & Cuddy, 2012).

The COO of Facebook, Sheryl Sandberg, in her 2013 best-selling book, *Lean In: Women, Work and the Will to Lead*, acknowledges that men continue to treat women differently, even without meaning to hold them back, something she refers to as "benevolent sexism". But she also believes that women derail their own careers by "leaning back" during meetings, sitting in the corner and not at the table, by questioning their capacity to lead more often than men do and by pushing less often for promotions or pay rises (*The Economist*, 2013a:74). Supporting the issue of promotions, internal research by Hewlett-Packard found that women only apply for jobs for which they feel they are a 100% match, while men do so even when they meet no more than 60% of the requirements (*The Economist*, 2013a:74).

One of the most sensitive areas of unfairness and discrimination centres on remuneration. While the principle of equal pay for the same job is an example of a fair, ethical approach, numerous studies still show that women often earn less than men for the equivalent job. A Bloomberg study in 2012 of the top five executives in each company in Standard & Poor's (S & P) 500 Index focused on the gender pay gap. The study found that female executives earn an average of 18% less than their male counterparts in similar positions. Of the five best-paid executives at each of the S & P 500 companies, only 198 out of a total of 2 500 executives in the United States of America were women, that is, just 8% (Hymowitz & Daurat, 2013).

Another challenging source of unfairness and discrimination for women is that the rules of behaviour for getting to the top are not the same for men and women. Women also face gender stereotypes and backlash for showing too much ambition. For example, the same behaviour is often labelled quite differently: His "strong and decisive" is her "autocratic and dictatorial". Writing for the *Harvard Business Review* Blog Network, Marianne Cooper, the lead researcher for *Lean In*, references decades of social science research that has repeatedly found that women face distinct penalties for doing what they need to do, and what men are allowed to do, in order to get to the top. She notes that high-achieving women in particular experience a "backlash because their very success – and specifically the behaviours that created that success – violates our expectations about how women are 'supposed to behave', resulting in successful women leaders being considered either insufficiently feminine or too masculine" (Cooper, 2013).

Sexual harassment

Sexual harassment in the workplace – the unwanted physical, verbal or non-verbal conduct of a sexual nature – is another area of challenge for women. While in theory it is not limited to women, in practice they are the primary targets of this type of unethical conduct.

The problem with speaking out against this can be viewed in much the same light as whistleblowing. Despite there being legislative measures in place (for instance, the Protected Disclosures Act 26 of 2000) to protect employees from occupational disadvantage when reporting wrongdoing, many people are still reluctant to report unethical conduct because they feel vulnerable to a range of adverse consequences, whether dismissal, compromised promotion opportunities or reduced prospects for salary increases or bonuses. This is especially the case for a sensitive issue such as sexual harassment and even more so if the harassment is happening at a senior management level.

An added factor that limits workplace reporting is that instead of being seen as a loyal employee speaking out for the benefit of the organisation and other employees, the employee is sometimes treated with hostility as an informer or a trouble-maker. It can – and has – given rise to a situation where the institution "shoots the messenger" for bringing unwelcome news.

Research by the Helen Suzman Foundation into the problem of sexual offences in South Africa confirms that societal attitudes and perceptions about these offences are often not on the victim's side. The article notes that "ambiguous notions of consent often place the blame on the victim or obviate [sic] a perpetrator altogether. Victims often feel ashamed. There are many factors that discourage reporting these crimes. These include fears about perceptions and blame, negative associations and the intimidating process of making an official report" (Louw, 2013).

Addressing the problem

The challenges faced by women can be viewed as supporting the claim that there simply is not a level playing field at work for women – which is reinforced by that fact that gender transformation never applies to men. But understanding the extent of the disadvantage should, ideally, be combined with a focus on what can be done to improve the situation or avert the problems.

In South Africa the empowerment of women is addressed by various organisations. Notable among them is Business Engage, a Johannesburg-based organisation that has developed the Gender Mainstreaming Awards to encourage the private sector to buy in to achieving more meaningful representation of women in the mainstream of business.

Although Sandberg thinks women are partly responsible for their lack of leadership, she also acknowledges that corporate structures and cultures work against them too (*The Economist*, 2013a:74). Within organisations, changes can be achieved with leadership's support for and commitment to building an ethical corporate culture that does not tolerate any form of discrimination. Giving emphasis to the advancement of women can make a big difference, which necessitates that this is formally included in talent management and succession-planning discussions.

It is much easier if women facing obstacles such as these have support. Having a mentor is useful to provide advice, feedback and coaching, for example, to improve workplace performance. However, having a sponsor can help a great deal more since sponsors are regarded as people in positions of authority who use their influence intentionally to help others advance.

As to what else women can do, Kerry Hannon, a personal finance journalist writing a critique of Sandberg's book for *Forbes*, endorses the five steps Sandberg recommends:

1   "Be more open to taking career risks", tor example, accepting stretch assignments and new challenges on the job.

2   "Skip the people pleasing." Sandberg admits that she has faced this too: during her first formal review at Facebook, chief executive Mark Zuckerberg told her that her "desire to be liked by everyone" would hold her back.

3   "Visualise your career as a jungle gym, not a ladder", which takes into account that career growth need not be only vertical, it can also be lateral.

4   "Allow yourself to fantasize about your career", which implies that women should have a long-term dream and a shorter-term plan to pursue immediate workplace goals.

5   "Start a Lean-In circle" comprising a peer group of eight to 10 women who meet monthly to offer one another encouragement and development ideas (Hannon, 2013).

Finally, women should use workplace ethics as the over-arching issue against which unacceptable and unethical practices are raised. And, arguably most importantly, they should continually and actively promote sound ethics because when ethics shapes workplace behaviour, decisions and strategy, it offers the best bulwark against all forms of abuse and misconduct.

3.3   ETHICAL LEADERSHIP IN THE PUBLIC SECTOR

Leadership is, and has always been, extremely important in government, business and the many institutions in society. Its importance stems from leaders being able to exert a far greater influence than most other people by virtue of the greater authority, power and visibility and via the easier access to resources which their more senior role affords them. This influence is reflected in leaders being role model for others, often irrespective of whether the leaders intended to be one or not. In this capacity, leaders effectively "teach" others what is acceptable and desirable by what they say and do, and *vice versa*.

Leadership in the public sector is especially relevant as the influence of leaders extends beyond the employees and stakeholders of a single company or group of companies to a whole country. Whether their leadership is good or bad therefore has the potential to impact huge numbers of people.

Good versus bad leadership

Good leadership is always to be applauded, but it should be distinguished from effective leadership which would, for example, refer to leaders who achieve the organisation's goals. In the public sector, delivering on election promises would reflect a welcome level of effectiveness. However, good leadership should also imply moral leadership: leadership that upholds sound ethics. Sound ethics means that leaders commit to core moral values, such as honesty, integrity, fairness, respect, responsibility and accountability, and that they live by those values for the betterment of those over whom they have influence.

But the very power that enables political leaders to make a great contribution to helping others also facilitates the pursuit of self-gain. The focus on the betterment for self is a trap for politicians that is often at the heart of unethical leadership within the public sector.

In South Africa, breaches of ethics by government officials are regularly exposed in the media for misconduct ranging from fraud to corruption. The Nkandla saga looms large following the many findings implicating the President and other Ministers in the R246 million taxpayer-funded expenditure on President Jacob Zuma's personal homestead near Nkandla in KwaZulu-Natal, as exposed in the Public Protector's report (Public Protector, 2014a:4). There have also been cases where unethical political leaders have lost their positions, such as Sicelo Shiceka, the Minister of Co-operative Governance and Traditional Affairs, who was sacked in October 2011 following findings by the Public Protector that he had committed numerous violations of the Executive Ethics Code. In the same period, Public Works Minister, Gwen Mahlangu-Nkabinde, was fired for maladministration with regard to a police leasing saga, and the National Police Commissioner, General Bheki Cele, was fired in June 2012 for his part in that scandal.

More recently, in July 2013, the communications minister, Dina Pule, was fired for a range of offences, including that she used her office to benefit her boyfriend improperly, which afforded him a R6 million telecommunications indaba contract. This did not, however, prevent her from being nominated on the ANC's national list for the May 2014 election. Her position on the list even made it likely that she would return to Parliament, but for the fact that she chose to withdraw her name.

There are also examples of political leaders being given other posts that appear to reward them instead of holding them accountable for their actions. An example is the former Minister of Women, Youth, Children and People with Disabilities, Noluthando Mayende-Sibiya, who was fired and then posted as South Africa's ambassador to Egypt; and dismissed Labour Minister, Membathisi Mdladlana, who was sent to Burundi (Rossouw, 2011).

The message these redeployments and Dina Pule's nomination sends is that who you know outweighs what you do or do not do, be that misconduct or non-delivery. It also erodes the expectation of leadership accountability, which is a very dangerous outcome. When leaders are not seen to be answerable for their actions, it does not merely undermine a value that is essential for sound political and organisational health, it oils a slippery slope towards autocratic and arbitrary action. It is one of the largest risks relative to the Nkandla scandal: whether anyone will actually be held accountable.

This issue is echoed by the Institute for Justice and Reconciliation, a South African non-governmental organisation based in Cape Town, which emerged out of the Truth and Reconciliation process in 2000. The 2013 edition of its annual transformation audit, titled *Confronting Exclusion*, suggests that an "immediate, but only partial, remedy to the current state of affairs would be to prioritise transparency, accountability and leadership integrity within the system to restore trust in the bona fides of key institutions" (Hofmeyr & Nyoka, 2013).

Other evidence of the ethical status of public sector leaders is the perceived level of public sector corruption. While corruption in government may not necessarily exactly reflect the extent of unethical leadership, there would certainly be a correlation. South Africa's results in Transparency International's CPI are not great. South Africa has consistently scored in the lower, more corrupt half of the scale. In 2013 South Africa's results declined from the previous year to a score of 42 and a ranking of 72nd out of 177 countries (Transparency International, 2013a).

Understanding the contributory factors

In order to address this measure of unethical leadership, it is necessary to explore the contributing factors.

One such factor is the common tendency to rationalise or justify unethical behaviour. The perpetrator finds an excuse to rid him-/herself of the guilt and culpability. This "self-administered exoneration" unfortunately also tends to allow the repetition of such behaviour. A much-used justification in South Africa is the injustices of the past, which often manifests itself as a sense of entitlement. While the wrongs of the past are undisputed, this leads to a classic situation of compounding one wrong with another. Irrespective of the wrongs of the past, it still does not add up to a right. Rather, it sends a message that placing your own interests and gain above others is acceptable.

A further factor which is particular to South Africa arises from the ethical dilemma of a right versus right choice: when one must choose between two morally right options.[2] Four examples of right versus right dilemmas are the choices which exist between short term versus long term, individual versus community, justice versus mercy, and honesty versus loyalty (Kidder, 1995:18). These are often the most difficult ethical decisions a leader will need to make, far surpassing an easier right versus wrong situation.

The conflict between truth or honesty versus loyalty is specifically pertinent. It may not, at first sight, appear to be a difficult ethical dilemma because, for many people, honesty is the stronger value. It can, however, present a difficult choice when the bonds of loyalty among colleagues or comrades are very strong. When people have shared a profound experience – as those who were part of the struggle for freedom in South Africa did – it understandably builds extraordinary bonds of loyalty. This presents a choice of supporting a long-standing friend or comrade who is guilty of misconduct in the name of loyalty versus reporting him/her for a breach of ethics in the name of honesty. While the choice in favour of loyalty may be understandable, it nonetheless still serves to condone unethical behaviour.

---

2   This topic of right versus right ethical dilemmas is discussed in detail in Chapter 6.

Increasing ethical leadership

How, then, do we increase ethical leadership in our public sector?

Much as leadership development and ethics training may spring to mind as solutions, these actions will not necessarily resolve the problem. That is because almost all people already understand the difference between right and wrong and between ethical and unethical behaviour. A lack of understanding of the issue or even of the consequences of misconduct is not the problem or the challenge. Instead, ethical behaviour is the result of a choice and therefore the focus should be on how to influence that choice.

In an organisation, in addition to leadership, values, rules and group culture are key influencing factors. But given that leadership is widely recognised as the most effective way to influence people to be ethical, it raises the pivotal question: who influences the country's leaders?

South Africa already has good, comprehensive rules, regulations and laws – most notably the Constitution, 1996, which addresses almost all areas of misconduct. Therefore, the levers that remain to effect a change are the influence of fellow leaders in government or from the opposition; their commitment to sound values (such as accountability); and peer pressure from the culture surrounding them. Citizens can make some difference, too, for instance, by exercising their vote to choose leaders they consider to be ethical and using mechanisms for reporting and investigating unethical incidents, such as Corruption Watch, a non-profit organisation launched in January 2012 that uses public reports of corruption to fight corruption and hold leaders accountable; and the office of the Public Protector. But the effectiveness of these factors to shape ethical choices is not as effective in a strong majority government as in the private sector, where shareholders are far more able to hold the organisation's leadership to account.

Thus, the real impetus for ethical leadership ultimately rests on political will. This raises the fundamental question, "Who will guard the guardians?", which is attributed to the Roman poet Juvenal from the late 1st and early 2nd century AD. When government is largely its own guardian, the choice to be or not to be ethical leaders has profound consequences. James Madison, writing a commentary on the Constitution of the United States of America, captured this dilemma really well:

> If men were angels, no government would be necessary. If angels were to govern men, neither external nor internal controls on government would be necessary. In framing a government which is to be administered by men over men, the great difficulty lies in this: you must first enable the government to control the governed; and in the next place oblige it to control itself (Madison, 1941:337).

A standard that would reflect the extent of sound, ethical leadership and the legitimate use of official leadership power is captured in Robert Greenleaf's concept of servant leadership. He defined this as the behaviour of a leader who is focused firstly on serving others to ensure that "other people's highest priority needs are being served", rather than on primarily serving him-/herself (Greenleaf, 1977:13).

3.4 BE THE ETHICAL LEADER YOU WANT

The goal of achieving ethical behaviour in the workplace is shared by organisations across different sectors, industries and countries. As acknowledged in previous sections in this chapter, of the factors which shape behaviour, leaders are widely recognised as the most influential. As role models, they effectively set the ethical standards of the organisation by the values they demonstrate, by what they say and do, and by what they do not say and do not do.

Good leaders and bad leaders

Good leadership implies that the leader acts to entrench the organisation's values and code of conduct. It reflects what *King III* refers to as "responsible leaders" who "do business ethically rather than merely being satisfied with legal or regulatory compliance", and who are characterised by the ethical values of responsibility, accountability, fairness and transparency (IoDSA, 2009:20).

The winners of the Nobel Peace Prize offer a number of high-profile examples of good leaders: Desmond Tutu in 1984, the 14th Dalai Lama in 1989, Aung San Suu Kyi in 1991 and Nelson Mandela in 1993.

There are, however, many more examples of unethical leadership in the public and private sectors. Misconduct has resulted in jail sentences for businessmen such as Raj Rajaratnam, the founder of the Galleon Group, a New York-based hedge fund management firm, who was convicted of insider trading in October 2011 and is now serving an 11-year jail sentence. Bernard Madoff, the American financier whose Ponzi scheme defrauded thousands of investors of an estimated $18 billion, was sentenced in June 2009 to 150 years in prison, the maximum allowed; and in March 2014 five of his former employees were found guilty of conspiracy to conceal the massive Ponzi scheme (Rushe, 2014).

Unethical leaders intending or hoping to hide their behaviour are often unsuccessful in the face of technology and a press eager to investigate and expose wrongdoing.

In pursuit of more ethical leaders

Given the immense value and importance of ethical leadership, it follows that developing and nurturing more ethical leaders is very desirable. However, to realise this goal there are a number of restrictive assumptions that need to be avoided.

A primary assumption, arising out of leadership being associated with a small group of individuals at the top of an organisation, is that leadership exists only in certain people. This approach denies the recognition that leadership exists at all levels in an organisation. It also limits leadership to the few, as opposed to shared leadership, which benefits from many more sources of leadership.

This assumption also echoes the notion that leaders are born, not made, juxtaposing the opinion that leadership ability is largely determined by genetics and childhood conditioning against being able to develop leadership via experience, opportunity and teaching. While there may be "born" leaders, a focus on this ignores the reality that organisations cannot influence any of the factors that would generate more "born" leaders. Within the workplace, the only option that exists is to focus on developing more effective leaders.

An allied view is that only a few select people have leadership potential. This has as a consequence a limited development focus. Only a few potential leaders are developed, rather than developing the leadership potential in everyone.

A further assumption (already mentioned in the first section in this chapter) is Peter Senge's comment that "when things are going poorly, we blame the situation on incompetent leaders [and] when things become desperate we can easily find ourselves waiting for a great leader to rescue us" (in Jaworksi, 1996:2). This outward focus on someone else to be the ethical leader ignores focusing on what the other members of the organisation are able to contribute. It also has the effect of minimising personal responsibility for exercising ethical leadership when the opposite would be ideal: that is, if members of the organisation took greater responsibility for being ethical leaders and role models.

This point is specifically recognised by Peter Drucker, the renowned American management educator and author. He defined effective leadership as being not about "rank, privileges, titles or money" but about responsibility (Drucker, in Hesselbein, Goldsmith & Beckhard, 1996:xii). This applies equally to ethical leadership. Responsibility is key, as is the effect of setting an example.

Adding to the acceptance that leadership exists in everyone and that shared leadership is optimal is one further point relative to leadership and ethics. That centres on the distinction between ethical leadership and organisational leadership. Whereas traditional organisational leadership rests on an appointment by others – the CEO by the board or the departmental manager by the HR director – ethical leadership rests only on being ethical. It is a role that can be assumed and chosen by anyone without reference to others.

Paraphrasing a quotation attributed to Mahatma Gandhi that "we need to be the change we wish to see in the world" summarises the issue of ethics and leaders well, namely, that we need to be the ethical leader we want and wish to follow.

Towards being an ethical leader

The traditional approaches to developing leadership include leadership courses, leadership development programmes, executive coaching and succession-planning initiatives, all of which can add value. To enhance the impact of ethics, all these initiatives should be underpinned by the following behaviours, which are core to fostering more ethical leadership.

Understand and live your values

The crucial moral values in the workplace are honesty, integrity, fairness, respect, responsibility and accountability. Living these values entails a personal commitment to the values – not merely superficial compliance – which is evident in all the leader's decisions and actions.

Live the organisation's culture

Leaders who live the organisation's culture offer visible behavioural support for the way things should be done in the workplace. This makes no allowance for the leader who does not make the link between "what I do and what is being seen" and "what I say".

Comply with and support applicable legislation, rules and regulations

This takes into account that the law is only ever a minimum standard. It means that leaders should aspire to do more than the bare minimum, and it excludes a "tick-box" approach to compliance.

Follow the golden rule to do to others as you would like them to do to you

The philosophy of reversibility is a well-recognised approach and a principle at the centre of most religions which includes considering the effect of one's actions and decisions on others. (It does not include the variation of "doing unto others before they have a chance to do to you"!)

Lead to empower others, not just for self

Leadership that aims to empower others and to better enable them to be leaders represents the optimal leadership purpose. This contrasts with leadership which is primarily for personal gain. This leadership style is reflected in the works of both Robert Greenleaf and Peter Block. Greenleaf uses the term "servant leadership" and Block refers to "stewardship" to describe leadership that chooses serving, supporting, empowering and developing others above self-interest (Greenleaf, 1977; Block, 1993).

As good role models, leaders should enhance and uplift the ethics around them: in their teams, their departments, their businesses or their communities. Giving greater effect to this as a primary leadership role and responsibility is a good start towards developing more ethical leaders, both in number and quality.

PART II: THE SOCIAL AND ETHICS COMMITTEE

3.5 SOCIAL AND ETHICS COMMITTEE: A VALUE OR A COST?

In accordance with section 72 of the Companies Act 71 of 2008 (the Act) and regulation 43 of the Regulations promulgated under the Act, formation of a social and ethics committee is now a legal requirement in South Africa.

The Act mandates that every state-owned company, listed public company and any other company that scores more than 500 public interest points in any two of the previous five years must establish a social and ethics committee (the original deadline was by 1 May 2012). Since the public interest score is based on the number of employees, number of shareholders, annual turnover and third party liability, this generally excludes only small companies. Subsidiaries also do not need a social and ethics committee if the holding company's committee performs this role on their behalf.

The committee needs to be appointed by the board and should comprise no fewer than three directors or prescribed officers (senior managers or executives), at least one of whom has served as a non-executive director for the previous three financial years.

The functions which the Act assigns to the committee are to monitor the company's activities relative to social and economic development, good corporate citizenship, the environment, health and public safety, consumer relationships, and labour and employment. The committee is also required to draw matters to the attention of the board as required and to report to the shareholders at the company's annual general meeting.

But the crucial question is whether this is yet another initiative which adds costs (especially given the seniority of the committee members) without also adding value.

The answer lies in part in assessing the intention of the Act. This can be deduced from the naming of the committee, that is, to create a specific focus on the company's social and ethical behaviour. These outcomes – harmonious stakeholder relationships and a sound ethical culture – are positive for all businesses. Added to that, they also serve to avoid the cost of the opposite, such as financial and reputational damage when ethical breaches occur and losses incurred when relationships break down, for example, when employees go on strike.

The cost versus value question is also answered by analysing the outcome of the committee's functions. In effect, it enforces that the company acts as a good corporate citizen by following a triple bottom line approach that extends its focus beyond a single, economic bottom line to encompass social and environmental dimensions as well. Their social responsibilities amount to actively taking into account the interests of their stakeholders, including employees, consumers and communities. Their environmental role incorporates health, public safety and the impact of the company's activities, products and services. Their ethical duties include the prevention of unfair discrimination and the reduction of corruption.

This approach – good corporate citizenship and a triple bottom line – is widely recognised and supported, most notably by *King III*. The *King III* recommendations concerning stakeholders and ethics are also implicit in the social and ethics committee legislation.

This good corporate citizenship/triple bottom line approach also rests on a sound rationale. Globalisation and communication information technology, among other factors, have facilitated the massive growth of the power of business, epitomised by global, multinational businesses that often eclipse the power of national governments. This has given rise to a societal expectation that this vast influence should be balanced with responsibilities to deliver an economic outcome **and** to act as good citizens by also recognising their responsibilities to support the people, communities and environments with which they engage and on which they have an impact.

For those organisations that do not pursue a triple bottom line approach, this legal requirement will probably not be persuasive. Their social and ethics committees are likely to amount to an expensive exercise (given the seniority of the members and the cost of their time) aimed at a minimal "tick-box" approach.

But for organisations who strive to be good corporate citizens and who are prepared to embrace the associated responsibilities, their social and ethics committees should add value to the company.

There are two additional factors which these companies should take into account, which will further enhance the role of the committee.

Firstly, the social and ethics committee should include a member from the company's audit committee (or risk committee or compliance committee). This ensures that information is appropriately shared (for example, an ethics report) and avoids the potential duplication that can otherwise occur between these committees.

Secondly, organisations should guard against the social and ethics committee assuming the role of the sole custodian of ethics in the workplace. While the committee provides a formal "home" for ethics, which is to be welcomed as it is lacking in many organisations, they cannot and should not take on the employee's ethical responsibilities. Instead, the committee's success will rest on the extent to which they achieve buy-in from all members of the organisation to their role and contribution to the company's ethical status.

3.6 CLARIFYING THE ETHICS ROLES AND RESPONSIBILITIES OF THE SOCIAL AND ETHICS COMMITTEE

It is now more than two years since the mandate of the Act regarding the formation of social and ethics committees came into force. In theory, the question of what the responsibilities of the social and ethics committee are and what actions would fulfil those responsibilities should have been answered and acted upon already. However, as regards ethics, the Act is not as clear as would be ideal about the responsibilities or definitive about what actually needs to be done.

Rather than this lack of definition being an obstacle, it should be viewed as an opportunity to choose and customise how ethics is approached and what is done so that the committee's actions align best with the company's values, strategy and operations.

In terms of regulation 43(5) under the Act, the functions of the social and ethics committee are divided into monitoring and reporting responsibilities.

Duty to report

The committee's duty to report is clear enough: to draw matters to the attention of the board as required and to report to the shareholders at the company's annual general meeting. By way of sound guidelines for effective reporting, Chapter 9 of *King III*, "Integrated reporting and disclosure", advocates that reporting should be "timely, relevant, accurate, honest and accessible and comparable with past performance" (IoDSA, 2009:109). To that can be added that sound reporting should also be understandable and verifiable.[3]

Duty to monitor

The committee's monitoring responsibilities entail that they monitor the following areas of the company's activities relative to "relevant legislation, other legal requirements or prevailing codes of best practice" (South Africa, 2011:54, reg 43(5)):

1   Social and economic development

2   Good corporate citizenship

---

3   The information that should be shared to ensure sound ethics reporting is addressed in Chapter 5 in the section entitled "Business ethics reporting: what should you tell?"

3   Environment, health and safety

4   Consumer relations

5   Labour and employment.

The legislation and codes that are specified in the Act are the Employment Equity Act 55 of 1998, the Broad-Based Black Economic Empowerment Act 53 of 2003, the Consumer Protection Act 68 of 2008 (by inference), the United Nations Global Compact Principles, the Organisation for Economic Co-operation and Development (OECD) recommendations regarding corruption, and the International Labour Organisation (ILO) Protocol on decent work and working conditions. The Act also gives specific mention to the goals of reducing corruption, preventing unfair discrimination, and promoting equality.

The intention of these three pieces of legislation (the Employment Equity Act, the Broad-Based Black Economic Empowerment Act and the Consumer Protection Act) and the actions expected of businesses in support of these laws are generally well understood. There are also many more laws that relate to ethics that apply to the operation of a business, such as the Protected Disclosures Act 26 of 2000 and the Prevention and Combating of Corrupt Activities Act 12 of 2004. But here, too, there is generally sufficient clarity.

The governance codes to which the Act refers add a great deal of detail in terms of principles and recommendations. However, they do not serve to identify that much better the mandate of the social and ethics committee as regards ethics.

The 10 principles of the United Nations Global Compact

These principles outline behaviours relative to human rights, labour, the environment and anti-corruption. The principles that relate to ethics include that businesses should:

1   Support human rights and ensure that they are not complicit in human rights abuses.

2   Eliminate forced or compulsory labour, child labour and discrimination.

3   Promote greater environmental responsibility.

4   Work against corruption in all its forms, including extortion and bribery (United Nations Global Compact, 2000).

OECD recommendations on corruption

Compliance with the OECD recommendations regarding corruption is made somewhat complex by the large body of documentation relating to bribery and corruption. These include:

1   The December 2008 OECD and the African Development Bank (AfDB) Initiative to support business integrity and anti-bribery efforts in Africa (OECD, 2008)

2   The *OECD Convention on Combating Bribery of Foreign Public Officials in International Business Transactions*, which seeks to criminalise bribery of foreign public officials in international business transactions (OECD, 2009)

3   The 2006 report, *The OECD Fights Corruption*, which addresses combating "supply side" active bribery, fighting bribery through export credits, denying tax deductibility of bribes, and strengthening transparency and accountability in the public service (OECD, 2006)

4   Various recommendations (categorised as Legal Instruments on Corruption Prevention) on fighting corruption in the public sector that address, for example, conflict of interest, integrity in public procurement and combating bribery in foreign public officials.

International Labour Organisation Protocol

The ILO deals with labour issues pertaining to international standards and addresses a wide range of applicable labour issues. In addition to those that echo the UN Global Compact labour principles, they also recognise employment injury benefits, hours of work, holidays with pay, and sickness insurance.

Decent work country profile: South Africa, published by the ILO in 2012, provides an analysis on the ten internationally agreed thematic areas of decent work, namely: employment opportunities; adequate earnings and productive work; decent hours; combining work, family and personal life; work that should be abolished; stability and security of work; equal opportunity and treatment in employment; safe work environment; social security; and social dialogue, workers' and employers' representation; as well as proposals for monitoring indicators (ILO, 2012).

Defining the optimal goal of the social and ethics committee

This lack of clarity about what is required as regards monitoring ethics allows a latitude that should be used to define the organisation's own ethical goals and supporting actions (or strategy), with the proviso that they encompass the Act's focus on reducing corruption, preventing unfair discrimination, and promoting equality and that the organisation's actions fulfil the outcome of being a good corporate citizen.

The optimal ethical goal that includes these outcomes is the creation and maintenance of an ethical culture. This implies that ethics permeates "how things are done": that strategies, decisions and behaviour within the organisation and relative to external stakeholders are ethical. The company's values should be used as the core principles by which the company chooses to operate. These values should, in turn, shape the company's code of conduct to clarify what is acceptable and unacceptable conduct. Together with visible leadership support for ethics, which is crucial, this serves as a basis for creating an ethical culture. Other initiatives that strengthen an ethical culture include ethics training and the incorporation of ethics into operations and business systems, procedures and practices.[4]

Support for this approach is found in *King III*, which provides clear guidelines about ethics and corporate citizenship. (In fact, its status as a valuable guide and reference for good governance makes its exclusion from the Act as a code of best practice a noteworthy gap.) Chapter 1, entitled "Ethical leadership and corporate citizenship", expresses two principles regarding ethics: Principle 1.1, which states: "The board should provide effective leadership based on an ethical foundation" (IoDSA, 2009:20); and Principle 1.3, which states: "The board should ensure that the company's ethics are managed effectively" (IoDSA, 2009:24).

King III further advocates the assessment, monitoring, reporting and disclosure of an organisation's ethics performance via both an internal and external assessment. The internal assessment is recognised as being "necessary to provide the board and management with relevant and reliable information about the achievement of ethics objectives, the outcome of ethics initiatives and the quality of the company's ethics performance" (IoDSA, 2009:27). The external assessment is viewed as "necessary to provide internal and external stakeholders with relevant and reliable information about the quality of the company's ethics performance" (IoDSA, 2009:27). *King III* motivates the external assessment on the grounds that "the independent assurance of the company's ethics performance, supported by an assurance statement (as part of the integrated report) enhances the credibility of the information provided to stakeholders" (IoDSA, 2009:27).

These recommendations specifically align with the Act's requirement that the committee "monitor" the company's activities since this can be interpreted to mean that ethics should be checked or assessed in some way and that this should be done regularly over time.

In combination, therefore, identifying an ethical culture as the organisation's primary ethical goal and subscribing to ethical leadership, the effective management of ethics and the assessment, monitoring, reporting and disclosure of an organisation's ethical performance can be adopted as the responsibilities of the social and ethics committee in relation to ethics.

Ideally, organisations should also identify the methodologies in terms of which they will assess the realisation of those ethical goals. A web-based ethics survey, such as the Ethics Monitor, serves as a quick and easy tool to do an accurate and reliable external assessment. In support of the effective management

---

4 Building and maintaining an ethical culture is the focus of the first article in Part I of Chapter 4. It outlines an ethics management system to support this goal.

of ethics, the survey results provide a comprehensive ethics risk analysis (of ethical weaknesses and strengths) and identify and prioritise the necessary actions to improve ethics. Conducting an annual ethics survey meets *King III*'s recommendations and the Act's requirement as regards monitoring, allowing organisations to assess their ethical progress or regression over time. Since the Ethics Monitor survey is based on the confidential responses of all employees and executives, it also offers a credible, accurate measurement of ethics and an ethics rating for reporting purposes, thereby also meeting the recommendation for an assurance statement.

In conclusion, despite the lack of clarity in the Act as regards the responsibilities of the social and ethics committee, the inclusion of ethics in the naming of the committee conveys a clear message about the intended importance of ethics in the workplace. It remains for the social and ethics committee to give effect to this.

PART III: THE ROLE OF HR

3.7 HR FULFILS A CRUCIAL ROLE IN THE ADVANCEMENT OF ETHICS

The importance of ethics in the workplace is increasingly being acknowledged. As a result, many organisations have recognised the need to guard against major misconduct. A smaller number of organisations are going beyond just avoiding misconduct and are also striving to increase the level of ethical behaviour. For those organisations, the ultimate goal would be the creation of an ethical culture, where ethics permeates "the way things are done".

Realising this goal is, however, not an easy, one-step exercise. It is determined by a combination of initiatives and necessitates wide support within the company. This latter factor can be an obstacle to ethics being addressed in a co-ordinated manner and to the effectiveness of an ethics programme. Even when a company has a social and ethics committee and an ethics officer, championing and implementing facets of ethics can be shared among numerous roles: the CEO, the company secretary, the compliance officer, the risk officer, or the HR officer. However, of these players, HR is able to fulfil an important role to promote ethics within the three primary areas that contribute to an ethical culture, namely ethical standards, ethical awareness, and important elements of operational ethics.[5]

---

5   This content is also addressed as part of the ethics management system in Part I of Chapter 4 and via other separate articles in this chapter, such as those on ethics training and leadership.

Ethical standards

The principal purpose of the company's ethical standards is to provide a clear guide for behaviour. They should ideally be documented in a code of values, a code of conduct, and supporting policies, which together constitute a code of ethics. Since this is generally considered an HR function, HR is perfectly placed to ensure that this foundational aspect of ethics is up-to-date, reviewed annually and well understood within the organisation – and, consequently, to ensure that this is an effective facet of the organisation's ethics programme.

Ethical awareness

Ethical awareness is a very effective factor – often under-rated – that serves to promote ethical behaviour and reduce unethical behaviour. The best example of the latter is the effect of visible policing, for example, the private security vehicles that patrol some suburbs. Their presence may not result in many (or any) criminals actually being apprehended, but it serves to raise ethical awareness and, in so doing, acts as a deterrent to crime being committed in that area.

The same principle applies in a workplace with high levels of ethical awareness. This can be achieved by a variety of mechanisms of which the following are especially impactful.

Assessing, monitoring and reporting on ethical performance

The Companies Act 71 of 2008 social and ethics committee and *King III* (IoDSA, 2009) advocate that a company's ethical performance should be assessed, monitored, reported on and disclosed. These actions also serve to promote ethical awareness (among other benefits). HR is able to initiate this process or to make recommendations to drive the process forward so that it is conducted in a manner that adds value. For example, a tool such as the Ethics Monitor offers employees total confidentiality to share their experiences and perceptions and therefore serves as a very useful "listening" exercise to surface ethical and unethical issues in the workplace.

Ethics training

Training programmes and workshops can be important contributors to building and maintaining ethical awareness. HR needs to ensure that the training is not a mere "tick-box" compliance exercise undertaken once during on-boarding or induction processes. Instead it should fulfil a meaningful role to deepen employees' knowledge and understanding of workplace ethics and to build increased commitment to an ethical approach.

Leadership

In their capacity as role models, leaders are able to build ethical awareness very successfully. HR can again be involved to ensure ethics workshops are conducted with the company's leadership and top talent to emphasise the company's commitment to ethics and to better equip their leaders to be ethical role models.

Operational ethics

Integrating ethical standards into the company's operations is really important as it influences whether and how ethics is practiced. This has a proportional impact on ethical standards, ethical awareness and an ethical culture, either supporting and building or undermining and eroding them.

Within HR's domain, ethics can be incorporated into a range of practices, systems and procedures, such as: ethics hotlines; selection and recruitment checks; remuneration and promotion discussions and decisions; performance management systems and evaluation criteria; employee award programmes or employee-of-the-month nominations; and transparency in communications (for instance, about disciplinary incidents, which can discourage further unethical behaviour and promote ethical behaviour by the company's visible commitment to its values and rules).

Being successful at building an ethical culture brings with it many internal operational benefits, such as greater trust; better and faster decision making and consistency of responses; greater confidence in top management action; more individual accountability and less need for policing; and the avoidance of excessive regulation. Other benefits include being able to attract and retain top staff and board members; increased employee engagement and commitment; improved risk management; higher levels of investor and market confidence; and enhanced corporate reputation and brand equity.

Many of these benefits of sound ethics directly support HR's areas of responsibility and therefore represent a good reason why HR should support ethics. However, the greater reason is arguably that HR maximises their spheres of responsibility and influence to make a meaningful contribution to creating a more ethical workplace for their employees. As is always the case, the extent to which HR makes this difference will rest on their commitment to ethics and the level of their engagement in pursuing an ethical culture.

3.8   ETHICAL SELECTION AND RECRUITMENT

The benefits of workplace ethics are often well recognised within organisations. However, realising those benefits rests on the organisation being able to implement and integrate ethics into the organisation's culture, including its systems and processes. This is especially relevant for HR professionals as many of their roles and functions are particularly sensitive to ethics and can impact the goal of creating an ethical environment. Two related areas that warrant attention are selection and recruitment.

Recruitment and selection should be shaped by legislation, the company's policy, and its values (notably values such as fairness and integrity), which together would represent best practice. However, when these parameters are compromised, it can amount to conduct that is both unethical and illegal. This can include conduct such as unfairness, discrimination, nepotism, or not following due process.

HR practitioners should be familiar with the requirement that the selection of candidates should be based on merit and that there can be no discrimination in selection or recruitment, whether on the grounds of race, religion, gender, sexual orientation or marital status (amongst other criteria). The job can give preference to certain candidates – for example, in pursuit of transformation and the greater inclusion of previously disadvantaged candidates – but only when that is in accordance with the law and when this provision has been clearly included in the job specification.

Nepotism and cronyism, on the other hand, entail favouritism or giving preferential treatment without regard for merit to relatives (nepotism) and to friends and close associates (cronyism). In terms of misconduct, this would generally be categorised as a conflict of interest since it represents a situation where the recruiter has placed his/her interests (with regard to the recruitment of a family member or friend) above the interests of the company to recruit the best candidate for the job.

Misconduct can also occur when the correct procedure is not followed. An example of the lack of due process was found to have occurred at the South African Broadcasting Corporation (SABC). In February 2014 the Public Protector, Adv. Thuli Madonsela, released her report on the SABC, aptly entitled *When Governance and Ethics Fail*. Among the many negative findings, the report confirmed that the appointment of Gugu Duda as Chief Financial Officer was grossly irregular and the actions involved constituted improper conduct, maladministration and abuse of power. Themba Phiri, the Acting Deputy Director General of the Department of Communications, and Hlaudi Motsoeneng, the SABC's acting Chief Operations Officer, were found to have arranged the appointment of Duda long after the recruitment and selection process had been closed (Public Protector, 2014b).

HR also needs to be alert to inaccurate information in applicants' resumés. This can include the job history being falsified, the inclusion of fraudulent qualifications, or invalid personal documentation. Danie Strydom, chief executive of QVS, one of the largest qualifications verification services in South Africa, states that on average about 13% of the degrees that are submitted to them for verification turn out fraudulent to some extent (such as higher symbols, subjects added, or outright fakes) (IOL, 2013). False qualifications carry the added risk that once employed applicants may not be capable of performing their duties.

To avoid this, all qualifications should be checked for all applicants. Actions taken by the University of South Africa (Unisa) illustrate best practice: they pursued criminal prosecutions for all those who handed in false qualifications to gain access to the university, which amounted to 94 cases of qualifications fraud (mainly of fraudulent matric certificates) from 2010 to 2013 (IOL, 2013). HR checks should also extend to verifying work history and other information such as the validity of drivers' licences for employees whose work requires them to drive, or work permits for foreign nationals.

As the applicant is expected to be honest and open about relevant personal information and work experience, so too should HR exercise the highest level of honesty and transparency. This includes bringing relevant issues about the company to the attention of the candidate, especially **information that is not publicly known but** which could materially affect the new employee.

Recruiters also need to take in account any agreements the company has with other organisations such as its suppliers or customers as regards recruiting each other's employees. This is most likely to apply to highly skilled staff or people with a skill set that is in short supply. Contravening the agreement can be very damaging for the company's relationship with that stakeholder. Transparency among all parties and following the agreed procedure are imperative to avoid the company being accused of poaching staff.

Recruitment lends itself to a greater threat of misconduct when, for example, economic times are tough and there is a shortage of employment. In extreme cases, instead of selecting the candidate based on the stated job criteria, recruiters are "selling" jobs. By way of example, staff members at Gwanda Provincial Hospital in Zimbabwe have suggested that there is massive corruption in the recruitment of student nurses at the Gwanda School of Nursing, with prospective students allegedly paying between $400 and $600 to get a place at the school (Bulawayo24, 2014).

In all these circumstances HR's ethics is vital – and it delivers noteworthy rewards. HR practitioners can serve as role models for the ethics of the company and can create a sound ethical introduction for new employees to the organisation.

3.9 ETHICS AND REMUNERATION

Remuneration is generally one of the most sensitive issues in the workplace. Employees are often not satisfied with their remuneration because it is perceived to be too low and many more are dissatisfied with what senior executives earn because it is seen as being too high. Increased wage demands are at the centre of the strike in the South Africa platinum sector, which started in January 2014, making it the longest strike in the industry's history (Williams, 2014). There is also the issue of unequal pay for women, which was addressed in an earlier section in this chapter ("Women, leadership and ethics").

This warrants that remuneration is managed ethically, in line with all applicable legislation and the company's policies and values, and that the necessary structures and processes are put in place to ensure this.

Remuneration committee

In most medium to large organisations remuneration, and specifically the remuneration policy, would be the responsibility of the remuneration committee. A remuneration committee is generally a board committee established by the organisation's board of directors that serves to monitor and strengthen the objectivity and credibility of the organisation's remuneration and bonus system and thereby keep it ethical.

At an operational level, remuneration also includes the HR or payroll department. They would provide recommendations to the remuneration committee, as would senior management.

The main purpose of the remuneration committee is to ensure the adoption of remuneration policies that aim to attract, retain and motivate top talent and senior executives, are aligned with and support the company's strategy, drive performance in the long and the short term, and comply with relevant legislation and corporate governance best practice.

The remuneration committee would normally have the responsibility for setting remuneration for the chairman, all executive directors and senior management. In some cases this extends to all employees. The committee's responsibilities and duties would typically include the review of the remuneration policy relative to applicable employees, the regular review of current industry practices, and the review of fringe benefits and retirement and termination payments, as well as making recommendations to the board about these matters.

Remuneration policy

As regards best practice for a remuneration policy, the IoDSA Remuneration Committee Forum produced a Position Paper in December 2013 that provides comprehensive guidelines for drafting a remuneration policy (RemCo, 2013). The paper addresses the following:

1   What is a remuneration policy?
2   The requirement for a remuneration policy.
3   The context for the remuneration policy.
4   Composition of a remuneration policy.
5   Who sets the remuneration policy?
6   What employee levels should the policy address?
7   How should the remuneration policy be disclosed?
8   Guidelines for evaluation of a remuneration policy
9   Reviewing the effectiveness of the policy.
10 Engaging with shareholders on the remuneration policy.
11 Where should the remuneration details be disclosed? (RemCo, 2013)

Ethics and remuneration

While structures and systems such as a remuneration committee, a remuneration policy and the organisation's compliance with legislation, its policies and its values should avoid dissatisfaction, in reality it is not always the case. Accordingly, to avoid remuneration decisions being seen to be unfair, discriminatory or based on favouritism, the organisation should be as transparent as possible about its processes and decisions. When necessary and where possible the company should engage with its employees to address and, ideally, to resolve their grievances – or at least to reach a mutually acceptable compromise.

However, wage disputes, especially those involving unions, are often much more complicated and cannot be addressed with a few recommendations, no matter how sound they may be. This is viewed as a specialist topic that has not been addressed in this section.

The issue of executive remuneration is also a very contentious topic. International media headlines continue to be dominated by executive pay rises and bonus schemes that are in stark contrast to workers' wage demands.

A British campaign group established to monitor executive pay and set out a road map towards better business and economic success, the High Pay Centre, suggests top executives earned more in just over two days than the average United Kingdom worker takes home annually. The study reported that executive pay increased by 74% over the past decade, while wages for ordinary workers remained flat. Quoted on Sky News, High Pay Centre director Deborah Hargreaves said: "When top bosses take home more in two-and-a-half days than the average worker earns in a year, there is clearly something wrong with the way pay is set for both bosses and workers" (Sky News, 2014).

Attention is being given to these inequities, for example, to allow shareholders a greater say in the remuneration policy. From a corporate governance perspective, Principle 2.27 of King III recommends that "shareholders should approve the company's remuneration policy" (IoDSA, 2009:52). This has been written into law for shareholders in South African banks, who have been given a greater say in the design of remuneration policies governing the pay of top executives and directors. In August 2013 Parliament's Finance Committee included a clause in the Banks Amendment Bill that would require the remuneration committee of the board of directors to consult with shareholders about the bank's remuneration policies. The insertion does not, however, specify how and when this consultation should take place (*Legalbrief Today*, 2013).

This has also happened in Switzerland. In March 2013 when Swiss voters had the opportunity to vote on what was called the "people's initiative against fat-cat pay", 64% voted in favour of a measure that requires listed companies to offer shareholders a binding vote on senior managers' pay and appointments at each annual general meeting. When written, the law that will put this vote into practice will form part of the Swiss constitution (*The Economist*, 2013b:58).

By way of improvement, PwC's report, *Executive Directors' Remuneration – Practices and Trends Report: South Africa 2013*, found that nearly 40% of CEOs in financial services are changing the way they set executive rewards in response to shareholder and public reaction (Pickworth, 2014). Dr Mark Bussin, in his new book *Remuneration and Talent Management*, identifies a number of trends that are aimed at more ethical results: increased scrutiny of performance metrics selection, the introduction of more long-term incentives to encourage ethical behaviour and increase retention, more performance-based instruments, a decline in complex, opaque pay plans, the rise of indexed share remuneration and limits on share-based compensation. It is to be hoped that research such as this coupled with ongoing investor and stakeholder scrutiny will increasingly create more equitable remuneration systems (Bussin, 2014).

There are two other issues that are especially relevant to the subject of ethics and remuneration that warrant attention: monitoring the payroll function, and the effective management of garnishee orders.

Monitoring the payroll function

Payroll fraud is real and represents a threat to all organisations. At the Gauteng Department of Health an internal audit in early 2014 resulted in 143 "ghost" employees being removed from the payroll, saving the province more than R1.2 million (Dlamini, 2014). The general extent of remuneration-related fraud is revealed in the Association of Certified Fraud Examiners' (ACFE) *2012 Report to the Nations on Occupational Fraud and Abuse*. The report is based on 1 388 cases of occupational fraud in nearly 100 countries on six continents that were reported by the Certified Fraud Examiners who investigated them. The findings reveal that:

1   Payroll fraud happens in 27% of all businesses.

2   Small businesses with fewer than 100 employees are more vulnerable to payroll fraud. It was found to occur nearly twice as often (14.2%) in small organisations with fewer than 100 employees than in large ones (7.6%).

3   The average instance of payroll fraud lasts about 36 months (ACFE, 2012).

To avoid these problems, the payroll system should be audited regularly as part of the internal audit program and/or by external auditors. This should include that the payroll is reconciled at least quarterly by someone other than the person who runs the payroll. The focus should be on identifying and eliminating remuneration-related fraud such as the falsification or abuse of overtime, or creating "ghost" employees on the payroll.

Managing garnishee orders

A further area of remuneration where HR professionals or the payroll department can make an ethical difference concerns the effective management of garnishee orders. Garnishee orders or emolument attachment orders are issued by magistrate's courts and compel employers to deduct money owed from workers' salaries.

The results of a study undertaken by the University of Pretoria Law Clinic, entitled *The Incidence of and Undesirable Practices relating to Garnishee Orders – a Follow-up Report*, identify many areas of abuse, such as

1   Fraud by court officials who collaborated with law firms applying for orders

2   Orders being granted without the amounts owed being stipulated, resulting in debtors paying instalments with no prospect of ever settling their debts

3   The charging of excessive fees, incorrect calculations of interest and inadmissible charges being levied (University of Pretoria Law Clinic, 2013).

Verifying all garnishee orders, checking for the accuracy of the amount owing and the fees and interest being charged, and managing the duration of the deductions should be recognised tasks within the scope of payroll officers. HR can also fulfil a valuable role by communicating with its employees about the pitfalls of garnishee orders and by ensuring that employees who are affected by these deductions are kept fully informed about the validity and progress of the orders.

To all these issues can be added remuneration tensions among ordinary employees battling to manage financially. It may not be possible to resolve these issues – for example, to reduce the wage gaps – to the satisfaction of all parties. However, given these problems and accompanying dissatisfactions, organisations should strive to ensure that their management of all aspects of remuneration is completely ethical.

3.10 A CODE OF ETHICS: GETTING THE BASICS RIGHT

Codes of ethics and codes of conduct have long been accepted within organisations as a fundamental part of their ethics and compliance programme. This applies not only to private sector companies, but organisations of all kinds. By way of example, at a briefing in February 2014, the Institute for Justice and Reconciliation proposed that South Africa needs a code of ethics to ensure the long-term prosperity of the country (eNCA, 2014).

While these codes can, and should, serve a valuable role within the organisation, all too often employees know little of either the intent or the contents of their company's codes. There are five factors that provide useful guidelines for drafting or revising a code of ethics and would significantly improve the usability and value of a company's codes.

Is a code of ethics or a code of conduct needed?

Ideally, organisations should have a code of ethics that comprises two parts: a code of values that defines the organisation's values, vision and mission, and a code of conduct that outlines the standards of behaviour required within the organisation. This combination is based on the recognition that ethics (encompassing ethical conduct and an ethical culture) is shaped both by building an increased commitment to the company's values and by improving compliance with the organisation's rules and policies.

Distinguishing between the code of values and the code of conduct is also warranted to realise the benefits of their differences. Values and value-based initiatives are a more effective approach to improve ethics and ethical conduct, while rules, regulations and policies (as contained in the code of conduct) are generally a more effective mechanism to curb or reduce unethical conduct.

What is the purpose of the codes?

The purpose of the code of ethics, as a conglomerate term for the code of values and conduct, needs to be clear to all employees and to anyone else to whom it may apply (such as business partners).

The code of ethics should take account of business best practice as well as current, applicable legislation. It should form an integral part of the company's initiatives aimed at managing ethics in the workplace. These initiatives taken together should be aimed at creating an ethical culture in terms of which ethical conduct is the norm within the company and relative to all stakeholders.

The code of values should clarify the organisation's values so as to align workplace behaviour effectively with an organisation's values. The code of values should therefore serve as the foundation of the code of ethics as well as underpin the code of conduct. As such, the company's values should be clearly linked to the expected conduct, for example, as the value of honesty would relate to a fraud and corruption policy.

The purpose of the code of conduct is to clarify the standards of behaviour that are expected of employees and to provide guidance to employees with regard to what this entails, with the aim of preventing or reducing unethical behaviour. Unacceptable behaviour is generally addressed in the code of conduct in the form of separate policies. These are usually intended for employees, although certain policies can also be directed to external stakeholders to define standards of behaviour when dealing with the company.

Factors that promote the effectiveness of the codes

There are three especially pertinent factors that promote the effectiveness of an organisation's codes.

The code of ethics (especially the company's values) needs to reflect reality and avoid creating ethical gaps between what is stated and what is lived. If the code says the company is committed to "the highest ethical standards" but this is in fact a huge overstatement, it will erode the effectiveness of the code and risk undermining the individual employee's commitment to ethics.

Fairness is crucial to ensure that the codes (especially the code of conduct and its supporting policies) are seen as legitimate mechanisms. There cannot be different or selective applications of the codes and policies. Instead, equity dictates that the company's policies are consistently applied to all people.

The company should have a plan in place to maintain ongoing awareness and knowledge of its codes. This can be done by its inclusion in employee inductions, via a well-developed communications plan and as part of the company's ethics training programmes. As regards the type of training, refreshing employees' knowledge annually can be done effectively via customised e-learning modules, allowing face -to-face training in order to focus on the more challenging aspects of workplace ethics.

Reviewing codes and updating policies

A code of ethics, and particularly a code of conduct, should be reviewed annually to ensure that it complies with current legislation and promotes best business practice. Employees can also be involved in this process, for example, by providing feedback on the practical application of policies.

A review that simply checks for the absence or presence of policies does not qualify as an adequate review. Each policy needs to be appraised, for instance, to ensure it addresses all that it is meant to as clearly as possible and to eliminate any contradictory content relative to other policies or company documentation.

Since many policies "belong" to certain departments – typically when that department is expected to champion and enforce the policy – the department can be resistant to change, especially if the review is being done by an external consultant. To minimise this resistance, the review should be a shared process. Also, rather than simply writing new policies, where possible, current policies should be used and updated.

Factors that create a user-friendly code of ethics

There are five factors that should be taken into account to create a user-friendly code of ethics:

1   In pursuit of transparency, the codes need to be written in clear, plain language so that they are understandable to all stakeholders. This may warrant translating the codes to accommodate the dominant language/s amongst employees.

2   In order to create a user-friendly code of ethics, it should be as succinct as possible. This applies in particular to the policies contained in the code of conduct where the need to be comprehensive should be continually balanced against the need for brevity. For policies that warrant more detail, it is preferable to include only a summary in the code of conduct and to reference the location of the full version of the policy, for example, via a hyperlink.

3   The code of ethics should endeavour to encompass all the issues and policies that are pertinent to ethics in the organisation so that it serves as a "one-stop" location for the company's ethics documentation and ethics-related policies. Since a number of policies may be referenced to the department responsible for that issue (for example, the code of conduct could reference many issues addressed in the HR employee handbook), the company needs to ensure that this does not undermine the status of the code of ethics as the primary repository.

4   A list of definitions (in alphabetical order) should be included to provide readers with a concise summary of the meaning of the issues, topics, terms and concepts used in the code of ethics. However, the code should specify that these definitions are intended as a guide, and that the identification of misconduct, as well as actions against misconduct, will not be limited by these definitions.

5   To promote ease of use, the code of ethics should include a table of contents and the code of conduct should include an alphabetical index of issues and topics that are addressed, as well as the name of the policy in which those topics are addressed. Where necessary, more than one topic can be listed for a policy. For example, the bribery, corruption and fraud policy would be referenced alphabetically under all three words (bribery, corruption and fraud).

Ensuring that a company's code of ethics is a well-designed element of its management of ethics and compliance is a valuable start. Making the code a visible aspect of the company's ethics management and ensuring its fair and consistent application are important subsequent steps towards building and maintaining an ethical culture.

3.11 PRACTICAL GUIDELINE: ISSUES TO BE ADDRESSED IN A CODE OF CONDUCT

A code of conduct and supporting policies can include a variety of topics and issues. Many of these do not, strictly speaking, relate to behaviour in the workplace or provide a guide for behaviour from an ethical perspective. Rather, they reflect employment conditions or business practices – such as medical aid, study leave or maternity benefits.

Issues such as broad-based black economic empowerment, employment equity, HIV/AIDS, and corporate citizenship (including the pursuit of a triple bottom line) are specifically relevant in South Africa. However, these are likely to be addressed in a code of values rather than a code of conduct.

Apart from policies focused on values, employment conditions and business practices, the following list includes examples of issues that should be addressed in a code of conduct or a supporting policy. This list is not exhaustive, as different operating conditions may warrant other inclusions:

1   Bribery, corruption and fraud
2   Compliance
3   Confidentiality and intellectual property rights
4   Conflicts of interest
5   Disciplinary code and procedure
6   Dishonest conduct
7   Disorderly conduct
8   Electronic communications
9   Employee ethics reporting / ethics hotline
10 Entertainment
11 Ethics assessment and reporting
12 Expenses
13 External work
14 Gifts
15 Grievance processes
16 Health and safety
17 Insider trading
18 Relationships between business partners
19 Sexual harassment
20 Smoking
21 Substance abuse and dependency
22 Theft

23   Travel expenses
24   Use of company property and facilities
25   Workplace violence.

The code of conduct can also encompass the many activities in an organisation that need ethical underpinning and that ought to be guided by ethics. They include coaching and mentoring, performance management, promotions, selection and recruitment and reward and remuneration.

3.12 PRACTICAL GUIDELINE: CODE OF CONDUCT GIFT POLICY

The giving or receiving of a gift should display a positive sign of appreciation or thanks. However, the potential for unethical behaviour has prompted some organisations to adopt a no-gift policy. Such policies stipulate that its employees may not accept gifts, hospitality, reward or other benefit, either directly or indirectly, from vendors, suppliers, customers, potential employees, potential vendors or suppliers or any other individual or organisation under any circumstances.

But many companies still accept that the giving and receiving of occasional gifts between people with whom the company does business is not unusual, but is rather part of normal social exchange. However, the potential for abuse warrants that the organisation has a very clear policy.

The crucial principles and issue that should be addressed (which can be customised for specific companies or business circumstances) are as follows.

Scope

The policy should define to whom and to what it applies, for example, relative to all the company's employees in relation to the giving, accepting and/or soliciting of gifts at any time, on or off work premises.

Objective

The purpose of the policy needs to be clearly stated to encompass both what the policy addresses and what it aims to achieve.

Thus the purpose could be to clarify guidelines and criteria regarding the giving and receiving of gifts and to clearly distinguish between behaviour that considered normal and acceptable in relation to gifts and what is regarded as unethical, criminal or contrary to good corporate governance and best business practice.

The intended outcome of a gift policy could be phrased as aiming to prevent unethical or illegal practices related to the giving or receiving of gifts and to promote equal treatment and unbiased professionalism in relation to all the company's internal and external stakeholders, potential employees, customers or suppliers.

Definitions

To ensure the highest level of clarity, it is preferable to include definitions for key terms and concepts. In most instances, sound definitions are contained in the Prevention and Combating of Corrupt Activities Act 12 of 2004. The following terms should be defined:

Acceptor or recipient

The acceptor is defined in the Act as "any person who directly or indirectly accepts or agrees or offers to accept any gratification from any other person, whether for the benefit of himself or herself or for the benefit of another person" (South Africa, 2004:10).

Corruption

Corruption is broadly defined in the Act. A person is guilty of corruption where the giving, accepting and/or solicitation of a gift or gratification amount to "unauthorised or improper inducement to do or not to do anything" (South Africa, 2004:10).

Donor, giver or briber

The donor or giver is any person who gives or offers the gift, which can include suppliers, service providers, customers, employees, potential suppliers, customers and/or employees, or other stakeholders, individuals or organisations. The giver is defined in the Act as "any person who directly or indirectly gives or agrees or offers to give to any other person any gratification, whether for the benefit of that other person or for the benefit of another person" (South Africa, 2004:10).

Gift

The Act defines gifts very comprehensively under various terms: gratification, property and valuable security. A gift can be considered any tangible article, benefit, favour, gratification, product discount not in the normal cause of business, commission, occasion, entertainment or function (such as sporting event tickets) that is given to the employee to keep, use or attend at no cost. A gift can include anything of value given or received as a result of a business relationship for which the recipient does not pay fair market value.

The policy should apply to both direct and indirect gifts. Therefore, a gift given to or received by an employee's spouse or family member should be considered a business gift if motivated by, or related to, a business relationship. Such gifts should be subject to the gift policy in the same manner as other gifts.

Give

In terms of the Act, to give or agree to give or offer to give is interpreted to also include to "promise, lend, grant, confer or procure; agree to lend, grant, confer or procure or offer to lend, grant, confer or procure" (South Africa, 2004:9-10).

Gratification

The Act's definition of gratification encompasses money, donations, gifts, loans, property, and avoidance of a loss or other disadvantage, discounts, commission, bonuses, deductions, contract of employment or any status, honour, right and/or privilege (South Africa, 2004:5).

Induce and improper inducement

The underlying principle in the Act is that anything that is given or received with the intention to improperly induce is illegal. Both the person who gives and the person who receives are guilty. Induce is considered to include "persuade, encourage, coerce, intimidate or threaten or cause a person" to do or not to do something (South Africa, 2004:6).

Guiding principles

The key principles that should underpin a gift policy are transparency and disclosure, which should be built into the policy's procedures.

Unacceptable gifts

This should clearly set out what is not acceptable and what employees may not accept. The most common mechanism is to specify a monetary value above which gifts may not be accepted. In the event that the recipient is uncertain about the value of the gift, the policy should direct the recipient to consult a superior, such as his/her line manager or the Ethics Officer, who should be empowered to make a final decision.

Typically, this section of the policy would specify the circumstances under which it is not permissible to accept a gift, such as the following:

1   Employees may never solicit gifts from any third party under any circumstances.

2   Gifts in the form of cash, including cash vouchers, gift vouchers, shares, and/or leisure gifts such as flight tickets and accommodation, are not permissible under any circumstances.

3   A gift may not be accepted at all under the following circumstances:

 a   When it is given to obtain a business favour

 b   When it is accompanied by any direct or indirect suggestion, hint, "understanding" or implication that some expected or desirable outcome is required in return

 c   When it is intended to act as an improper incentive or to exert an improper influence on the recipient, for example, to influence the decision to do business with the giver

 d   When it has the appearance of improperly influencing the recipient.

The company should be aware when formulating these provisions that the essentials of a bribe are the receipt of the bribe and that it was given and received as an inducement. In terms of the law, it is not necessary to prove that the person bribed did what he/she was bribed to do (Claassen, 2013:SI,16).

It is preferable that there are no exceptions to these criteria. Relative to executives, for example, it could be argued that the nature and value of the gift should take into account if it would have any influence on the recipient, having regard to his/her income and/or status. While, in theory, this could be justified, in practice it is likely to be viewed as unfairness by more junior staff and it risks eroding the positive role model effect of the company's leaders.

Acceptable gifts

This should define what the company considers acceptable gifts. Normally this would include conventional hospitality, infrequent and modest tokens of appreciation and small, unsolicited gifts of a promotional nature that bear a company logo or advertising. For added clarity, the value of these gifts should be defined as below the threshold for unacceptable gifts.

Approval and declaration

Even though the policy defines what may and may not be accepted, it is still best practice to have a clear approval and declaration procedure to give effect to the principles of transparency and disclosure.

Ideally all gifts should need to be approved, for example, by the line manager of the employee who received the gift. Similarly, the company should have a gift register and all gifts should be declared and recorded – which process should specify details such as how promptly the gift must be declared. This can be limited to gifts above a nominal value, for example, to exclude having to declare items as small as a calendar or a bunch of flowers. The declaration of gifts should extend to gifts that are refused and not accepted.

Procedure for gifts that cannot be kept

The policy should detail what employees should do when gifts cannot be accepted, such as returning the gift to the donor within a particular time frame. This would also warrant a declaration and the company should record all such instances. The policy should also make provision for the possibility that it not possible or inappropriate to return the gift to the donor, and outline what procedure should be followed in that case. The gift could, for instance, be handed to the Ethics Officer, who will make a decision as to donating the gift to a worthy recipient, such as a charity.

Offering and giving gifts

This section should include the same criteria that are applied to the acceptance of gifts. Thus, ideally, gifts to clients or other stakeholders should be uniform and branded. It is also useful to issue all client gifts at a specific time of year (such as at year-end) so that there is no inference of either favouring specific clients or attempting to influence corporate relations. However, regular and ongoing entertainment of the same customers or suppliers should be discouraged on the grounds that it may create a suspicion of impropriety.

The policy should acknowledge what behaviour is unethical, against the law and contrary to good corporate governance. This would generally include that no director, officer, employee or representative of the company may offer or provide gifts and/or entertainment with a view to improperly influencing or inducing that person in order to obtain some benefit or result.

Business gifts that are given should also be reported (for instance, to the employee's line manager) and recorded in the company's gift register.

Reporting policy infringements

As for many policies in a code of conduct, the gift policy should include details of how employees (or others) could report infringements of the policy. This would normally include an anonymous ethics hotline.

3.13 PRACTICAL GUIDELINE: CODE OF CONDUCT CONFLICT OF INTEREST POLICY

A conflict of interest between, typically, the company and an employee can lead to a number of risks. The employee's choice, judgement, decision or action relative to one interest may be unduly influenced by another interest. It is also possible that the competing interests may undermine the employee's impartiality, compromise the performance of his/her workplace duties or limit the employee's ability to meet the responsibilities of his/her organisational role. These potentially negative consequences warrant that all organisations adopt a conflict of interest policy.

Scope

The policy should define to whom it applies, for example, any conflicts or any potential conflicts of interest between the company and its employees. This can be expanded, if pertinent, to encompass conflicts of interest between the company, inclusive of its agents, representatives and employees, relative to its employees, agents, representatives, clients or stakeholders.

Objective

The objective of the policy would be to avoid any conflicts or any potential conflicts of interest between the company and its employees.

The employer's stance would normally make it clear that employee behaviour that constitutes or gives rise a conflict with the company's interests will not be tolerated and will be addressed decisively.

Definition

The policy should include a definition to ensure clarity about the term. For example, a conflict of interest refers to a situation in the workplace when an employee has competing interests, allegiances or loyalties that are or could be in conflict with each other. The conflict can apply to employees in organisations of all kinds – the public sector, private sector or not-for-profit sector – and would typically be between the employee's self-interest and what is in the best interests of the organisation.

For organisations with multiple subsidiary companies or widespread ownership interests in other companies, it is recommended that these are specified in the policy. This disclosure ensures that it is clear that these entities fall within the ambit of the organisation's area of interest and it makes employees aware that they must avoid conflicts with these other entities too.

Policy requirements and prohibitions

The policy would generally list the behaviours or actions that employees are required to do, such as:

1   To disclose any involvement in any trade or dealings between the organisation and any other party, either when the organisation has a direct or indirect interest, irrespective of whether the employee stands to gain in any way from such dealings or not.

2   To disclose the involvement of any close family member in any trade or dealings between the organisation and any other party, either when the organisation has a direct or indirect interest in that party.

3   To disclose annually gifts and hospitality received.

The policy would also generally list the behaviours or actions that its employees are not permitted to engage in, such as:

1   To perform or undertake to perform work for remuneration outside the organisation.

2   To do any work on the organisation's premises that is not related to the employee's duties either for him/herself or others.

3   To use the organisation's resources or equipment for private purposes.

4   To engage its employees for private purposes or permit such employment by others, even if there is no payment for the services or work.

5   To accept any commission, fee, reward or ownership interests, monetary or otherwise, from sources outside the organisation in respect of the performance of his/her duties within the organisation.

6   To be involved directly or indirectly in any trade or dealings between the organisation and any other party, either when the organisation has a direct or indirect interest in that party or when the employee stands to gain in any way from such dealings.

7   To misuse his/her position to promote personal interests at the expense of the organisation.

8   To do business in competition with the organisation.

The conflict of interest policy should also outline the potential sources of conflicts of interest that are most common in its industry or that are particular to its business and how these can be identified. The policy should include guidelines about how to manage and avoid conflicts of interests and detail the procedure for compliance with the policy. The procedure is likely to entail immediate and full disclosure of any conflict or potential conflict and, when relevant, the employee's withdrawal from any involvement or action relative to the conflicted deal, interaction or process.

The consequences of non-compliance also need to be clearly set out in the policy, for example, that transgressions will be dealt with in terms of the disciplinary code and that employees found guilty of a conflict of interest may face dismissal.

Exceptions

A general exception would be for work such as community-related work or charity work. If the organisation chooses to include other exceptions, these should be subject to written approval by an executive.

Reporting policy infringements

The policy should include details of how employees (or others) can report infringements, for example, via a particular executive or department and via an ethics hotline for anonymous reports.

Conflict of interest in the public sector

Corruption Watch, a civil society organisation that gathers, analyses and shares information on corruption in South Africa and investigates complaints sent to it by citizens, provides very comprehensive details of conflict of interest in the public sector.

Their website lists the various pieces of South African legislation that are pertinent to a conflict of interest in the public sector, details the laws regarding conflict of interest in procurement at national, provincial and local government level and outlines examples of conflicts of interest in the public sector (Corruption Watch, nd). Examples include public officials influencing government tender processes so that their family members and friends are awarded state contracts and using their public position to benefit their private interests.

Corruption Watch also summarises what this means for public servants in terms of what they must and must not do. For example, senior public officials must disclose their financial interests and public officials must withdraw from supply chain management processes if they have an interest in the contract being awarded.

3.14 CAN YOU TEACH ETHICS?[iii]

Since creating an ethical workplace is increasingly being recognised as an important corporate goal, it is necessary to pay attention to the factors that could accomplish this goal. Improving ethics can be done to varying degrees via a combination of numerous elements and influences, such as leadership, values, ethical codes, policies, systems and training. In particular, training as an approach to addressing workplace ethics has flourished to the extent that it has become a growing industry, with business schools, ethics organisations and consultants all offering support for organisations' ethics training programmes. Its value is especially relevant given the outcomes which effective training can realise.

Effective ethics training serves to increase the level of ethical awareness in an organisation, which is a significant contributing factor to building and maintaining an ethical culture. For ethical employees, training should strengthen their ethical commitment, while for those who are "ethically challenged", it should provide clear guidelines of what will not be tolerated in the workplace. Ethics training interventions also present the opportunity to address those circumstances and influences that could impair ethical behaviour, to discuss and resolve ethical dilemmas within the organisation and to clarify the application of the company's values and rules relative to its decisions, strategy and changes. This ongoing engagement has the effect of keeping ethics alive and of making it a real part of the organisation's focus.

The importance of ethics training and education is recognised in many professions. Admitted attorney and legal academic at Rhodes University, Helen Kruuse, spoke on legal ethics education at the Legal Ethics Summit in Durban in February 2014, convened by the Law Society of South Africa and the National Association of Democratic Lawyers. She said that there needed to be a compulsory course on ethics in the Bachelor of Laws (LLB) degree curriculum at all universities, adding that most universities did not have it. She noted that law students needed to be encouraged to appreciate the significance of ethical dimensions of legal practices (Manyathi-Jele, 2014).

Writing about teaching ethics in the field of investment management, Robert Dannhauser, head of capital markets policy at the CFA Institute, noted that "ethics education, in conjunction with adoption of a code of ethics, is critical to investment firms seeking to establish a strong ethical foundation and to provide an environment in which employees routinely engage in ethical conduct" (Dannhauser, 2012).

In terms of the extent of ethics training, this was assessed in the *National Business Ethics Survey of the US Workforce*, which is conducted annually by the Ethics Resource Center, the United States of America's oldest non-profit organisation devoted to independent research and the advancement of high ethical standards and practices in public and private institutions. The 2013 survey revealed that the percentage of companies providing ethics training rose from 74% to 81% between 2011 and 2013 (Ethics Resource Centre, 2013:16).

However, ethics training programmes often do not appear to have sufficient impact. There are seven factors that influence the effectiveness of ethics training and that should be taken into account in the selection of a training provider and/or the design of a training programme.

Do not teach participants what they already know

Attending a training course is generally an effective way to improve learning, for example, to develop one's ability in finance or labour practices by building knowledge and understanding of those topics. But this does not apply to the same extent to ethics, the reason being that employees almost always already know what is right and wrong in the workplace. They therefore do not need to be taught these basics as if it was unknown or new knowledge.

It follows that ethics programmes should not focus on what the participants already know, such as the details of policies on fraud, bribery and corruption.

It is appropriate that this is addressed at ethics induction training or a refresher course on ethics to provide employees with the gist of company's policy, procedure and where it can be sourced. But for ongoing ethics training, this detail should not be a primary focus. The message can be captured in one sentence to reinforce the company's stance on such behaviour: "The company does not tolerate fraud, bribery or corruption under any circumstances."

Training time is better spent addressing ethical challenges that occur in the workplace, such as the difficult decision where there is not easy "right" answer. Training should also aim to build clarity about how the company's values translate into behaviours and what this implies for the individual participants within the scope of their roles and responsibilities.

Take into account the "knowing–doing" gap

Related to the fact that employees already know what is right and wrong is the "knowing–doing gap". This factor recognises that misconduct – "doing" – is rarely the result of a lack of "knowing". Rather, conduct stems from the individual's choice between good and bad and right and wrong, which, in the case of misconduct, reflects a gap, the "knowing–doing" gap.

This should be taken into account in designing a training course. Therefore, instead of the course being aimed at just trying to add knowledge, the overarching goal becomes influencing the ethical choices people make and encouraging a change of attitude that will achieve more ethical behaviour.

Confine teaching to workplace ethics

An issue that can seriously derail workplace ethics training is the focus on religion and on personal ethical behaviour (that is, outside the workplace).[6]

While the employee's values and personal ethics influence their behaviour in the workplace, the training material should avoid personal, non-work related examples, questions and scenarios for two reasons: firstly because they infringe on the employee's right to exercise their values as they choose in their private capacity and secondly because that intrusion is likely to create a barrier to the employee's further learning or engagement with the training material. Activating a response such as "what I do in my private life is my business" – whether said or just thought – is likely to deflect attention away from the intended outcome of the training and even create resistance to the intervention. This approach echoes the principle advocated in Chapter 1 as regards the company's values: that while employees may hold their own values, they are expected to adhere to the company's values in the context of the workplace and the employer–

---

6   Paying undue attention to personal values and ethics is discussed in the article "Personal values versus company values" in Chapter 1.

employee relationship. Teaching ethics should reflect this same context.

Religion can have the same negative effect. Since almost all the world's religions are premised on sound values and ethical principles, it should, in theory, provide a perfect platform for teaching ethics. However, in practice, there are many divisions and differences between religions, some of them still very emotive and underpinned by extremely strong views. While the inclusion of religion may engage the few who support that religion even better in the company's pursuit of ethical conduct, it runs the far greater risk of alienating others who are part of other religions or who do not hold religious beliefs.

Ethics training or ethics awareness training?

The fact that employees have their own personal values and ethics and that they already know what is right and wrong lends itself to another potential obstacle, namely that employees could regard the training as implying that they are not ethical (and therefore need further training and teaching), or that they do not know what ethics is.

A simple solution to preventing both these challenges is to label the training as "ethics awareness training". This is arguably a more accurate term, as ethics training serves to strengthen the employee's awareness of the company's commitment to ethics and reinforce the key ethical principles that are pertinent to its operation. High levels of ethics awareness also act to enhance people's good intentions and to deter possible misconduct by reminding those who may be tempted to stray of the ongoing attention the topic enjoys.

Teach ethics based on the company's ethical reality, not on abstract theory

In addition to training being directed to ethics in the workplace, the training should also be based on the organisation's current ethical reality. Using the results of an ethics assessment (such as the Ethics Monitor web-based ethics survey) allow the course content to be customised to address the organisation's actual ethical strengths, vulnerabilities and weaknesses, which significantly enhances its relevance for the company and the participants.

This also aims to ensure that ethics is not treated or regarded as a separate issue from the ongoing operation of the business. Instead, it should be promoted as an integral part of the business, as part of its DNA.

Use relevant content

The content of an ethics training programme needs to be customised as much as possible for the organisation. For example, the content should be centred on the specific intended outcome of the intervention as well as the ethical issues most pertinent to the company and its industry. It would, for instance, be a big mistake to ignore safety in an ethics programme in the mining industry.

The content should also take into account the level of the participants. While ethics and what constitutes ethical conduct in the workplace do not differ between board members and blue collar workers, it is still ideal to design the programme with the audience in mind as they are likely to face different ethical challenges in their roles.

A general ethics programme should consider including content that addresses the following:

1   What is ethics: understanding ethics in your workplace

2   Does ethics matter: does it make good business senses?

3   Ethics management system: how do you manage ethics?

4   Ethical leadership.

5   Ethical decision making and ethical dilemmas.

Use appropriate teaching methods

Face-to-face training sessions or workshops provide the opportunity for the most effective engagement with participants. This is particularly suited to addressing the practical application and the potential implications of the company's ethics in the workplace and to providing the opportunity for in-depth discussions on ethical challenges and dilemmas. These sessions should be done at least twice a year for all employees, with particular emphasis on the organisation's leaders and top talent based on their influence as role models.

The design of these sessions should take into account what achieves optimal learning. One-way lecturing is clearly at the lower, less effective end. An interactive approach is ideal to increase participation and hence meaningful interaction with the course material. Case studies are especially effective. The goal is not to try to teach the participants how to react in each unique situation, but rather to use "real life" situations to enhance the participants' understanding of the underpinning ethical principles and issues in the case and to promote the critical thinking and analysis necessary to understand different situation and how best to respond.

Ethics induction training or on-boarding for new employees, and annual training to reinforce and refresh employees' knowledge and understanding of the organisation's ethics policy, code of conduct and supporting policies, need not be done face to face. A web-based course or e-learning modules are well suited to this, with the added advantage that it is a much quicker intervention. The design and presentation of this type of training need to be focused on retaining the participant's engagement. While it would typically be structured around multiple-choice questions, the design can also include, for example, an audio track, graphics, animation, and short video clips to add content.

As regards e-learning content, the questions and answers should be clear and informative. While the participants may know the answers to many of the questions, the exercise nonetheless serves a valuable role to increase ethical awareness. However, the questions should not be so simplistic that the exercise is not taken seriously. Another trap to be avoided is the inclusion of lengthy scenarios that are not sufficiently relevant to the organisation's business or which add too little learning or insight relative to the amount of time they take.

While no amount of ethics training or education could deter those who are committed to being unethical, for the majority of employees, ethics awareness training can make a difference. These design features, supported by relevant content, help ethics to be taught much more effectively. But realising its full value is not automatic. It relies also on leadership's commitment to ethics and on a comprehensive, integrated approach to managing, improving and inculcating ethical behaviour in the organisation.

RECOMMENDED CASE STUDY AND COMMENTARY

Finder, J. 2007. The CEO's Private Investigation. *Harvard Business Review*, October. HBR Reprint R0710A.

"If there was ever a time when a chief executive should commission some quiet snooping on her colleagues, this might be it."

FURTHER READING

Schoeman, C. 2014. The Ethics of HR in Maphoshe, P. (editor) 2014. *Strategic HR Management: An African Perspective*. Johannesburg: Knowledge Resources. (To be published later in 2014)

Endnotes

i.   Acknowledgement: Original, abridged version of this article first published in HR Future magazine.

ii. Acknowledgement: Original, abridged version of this article first published in HR Future magazine.

iii. Acknowledgement: Original, abridged version of this article first published in HR Future magazine.

CHAPTER 4

MANAGING WORKPLACE ETHICS

INTRODUCTION

The central task of managing ethics is the focus of this chapter.

This is addressed in Part I at a bigger picture level that crucially includes a comprehensive ethics management system as a framework for managing ethics effectively. Related topics that are discussed are the challenge of tackling misconduct and how best to recover from ethical failure. The question of avoiding ethical divides explores gaps such as between a limited focus on misconduct and compliance versus a more inclusive focus on ethics. The extension of ethics to achieve a situation of borderless ethics is addressed in the article "Ethics without borders".

Part II provides insight at a more detailed level into a selection of issues that are pertinent to the management of ethics. The topics explored are care, social media, collusion, cybercrime, counterfeiting and supply chain ethics. Other topics that are addressed elsewhere in the book include bribery, ethics training, conflict of interest and gifts.

The chapter also includes a workplace discussion topic, four recommended *Harvard Business Review* case studies and commentaries, and suggested further reading.

PART I: ETHICS MANAGEMENT:
THE BIG ISSUES

4.1 ETHICS MANAGEMENT SYSTEM

It is crucial to understand what ethics is, why ethics matters, and the extent to which it makes good business sense. But those areas of knowledge and insight are essentially a prelude to the central task of managing ethics.

Management within the workplace is taken for granted relative to probably every area of the organisation. It would apply to operations, people, diversity, resources, organisational goals and more, and its primary intent would be, in general, to optimise the effectiveness and efficiency of the organisation. Similarly, ethics needs to be managed. Ethics may be present or some employees may display ethical conduct in the absence of any guidance or intervention. But that creates a serious risk of misconduct arising from the increased opportunity which the lack of management allows. Therefore, organisations need to ensure that they have a sound ethics management system in place.

Many organisations tend to focus their attention or their ethics programme only on unethical conduct. This should be avoided. Instead, the aim of an ethics management system should be to create an ethical culture via a dual focus on both increasing and promoting ethical conduct **and** reducing and discouraging unethical conduct.

The author's ethics management system encompasses all these features.

Ethics management: structure

The ethics management system is made up of a supporting structure and select focus areas and processes.

The way the organisation is structured and the associated lines of reporting are likely to vary for different organisations. However, it is important that ethics is clearly and formally assigned within the company's structure and that people's roles and responsibilities relative to ethics are clearly defined. This does not mean that these groups or individuals assume the sole responsibility for ethics and that therefore no one else has to concern themselves with it. Quite the contrary: it remains a core feature for leaders, HR professionals, line managers and anyone who has subordinates, namely that they consciously and actively strive to achieve sound ethical behaviour among their employees. What is necessary is that the roles and responsibilities of those formally tasked with managing ethics define what is done by whom to ensure that ethics is managed effectively.

The social and ethics committee, as a board appointed committee, might be the most relevant senior structure, unless the organisation has a more senior ethics officer. (The roles and responsibilities of the social and ethics committee are detailed in Part II of Chapter 3.) The social and ethics committee or the group ethics officer could also be supported by other structures or individuals, such as an ethics forum or ethics officers. The company's leadership and its HR department also have a distinct role to play as regards ethics (as outlined in Chapter 3). Other organisational functions may also have links to the primary ethics structure, such as the compliance, internal audit and risk function.

Ethics management system

The process for managing ethics has been labelled the ethics management system, and it comprises six pillars. It is given effect via the ethics management structure (discussed above).

Integrated ethics

While all six pillars of the ethics management system together form a robust, effective system, the management approach adopted by many businesses is often inadequate to achieve this outcome. A primary cause of this lies in a lack of integration.

In pursuit of improving the management of ethics, organisations tend to identify and action a cluster of initiatives. While many of them may be relevant to the field of workplace ethics, the disjointed nature of the initiatives reflects a lack of integration that undermines achieving an optimal outcome. For example, the initiatives do not necessarily enhance, leverage or even relate to each other. The result is that the employees whom the company is trying to influence do not recognise it as an integrated, co-ordinated ethics programme. Instead, the strength of an ethics management system lies in the integration and interaction between the component parts, as in the ethics management system advocated below.

Foundational and actions elements

The ethics management system is made up of three foundational pillars or elements and three action elements, as illustrated in Figure 4.1. The foundational elements are ethics goals and strategy, ethical standards and leadership. While they exist as separate factors, they also support and add to each other. Ethical goals therefore set the direction and define the desired outcome, while ethical standards clarify the boundaries of behaviour in terms of which this can be achieved. These factors are so named because managing ethics rests primarily on these factors, and the absence of any of them would minimise the effectiveness of the ethics management system. This applies in particular to leadership.

The three action pillars are ethical awareness, assessment and reporting, and operational ethics. While organisations can give effect to these factors without addressing the three foundational factors, it is not ideal or optimal: it runs the risk of a lack of integration, clarity and direction. For example, the communication and training that is central to ethical awareness is compromised if there are no clear ethical standards against which it is designed. Crucially, without the support of leadership, all the action initiatives are eroded.

These foundational and action elements together provide a sound, comprehensive system for realising the goal of an ethical culture.

Figure 4.1: Model of the ethics management system

The model illustrates the three foundational pillars or elements of the ethics management system at the centre, with dotted lines to indicate that they relate to and depend on each other. The outer three action elements of the ethics management system should flow from and be based on the foundational elements. They too are not rigidly separate, but interact to boost and support each other. The combination of these six pillars creates a framework for achieving the optimal goal of an ethical culture, hence its placement at the centre of the model.

Ethics goals and strategy

Defining the organisation's ethics goals and strategy is an important starting point and a primary pillar of the ethics management system. Without this clarity, the initiatives that follow risk not being focused or aligned. Paraphrasing what the Cheshire Cat said to Alice when she asked for directions in Wonderland without a destination in mind: "If you don't know where you're going, any road will do". While different organisations may identify different ethics goals, creating an ethical culture is an ideal, optimal objective for most organisations.

Ethical culture as an optimal goal

The concept of organisational culture surfaced in the late 1970s and is as relevant in the workplace today as it was then. Among the wealth of theories and thought leadership on the topic, the definition of culture as "the way things are done around here" is well recognised. Getting to "the way things are done" derives from, among other factors, the leadership, values and rules of the organisation. Organisation culture is also influenced by the nature of the business and the industry.

Irrespective of the nature or type of workplace culture, the crucial point that is widely accepted is that culture acts to shape behaviour in organisations, for good or for bad. Clearly an ethical culture is very desirable, not least because the optimal outcome of an ethical culture is trust, which delivers great value and multiple benefits to the organisation and its people. Given this, the quest for more ethical workplace conduct makes culture especially pertinent and, in particular, it makes culture an appropriate ethics goal for the organisation.

As acknowledged in Chapter 1, in addition to being a driver of behaviour, culture also acts as a reflection of behaviour by mirroring the norms and standards of the actions and conduct by employees and relative to external stakeholders. Therefore, culture serves as a communication channel to "show" employees what is considered acceptable and unacceptable in the workplace and, since it is ongoing, to reinforce those behaviours. As this often takes the form of non-verbal communication, its impact is strengthened, because actions have a far greater effect than words. This role as an effective self-reinforcing mechanism not only makes the attainment of an ethical culture a high-priority goal, but also adds to the validity of culture being the optimal ethics goal.

The value of an ethical culture consolidates its role as an ideal ethics goal and leaders who aim to achieve this goal therefore need to ensure that the value of an ethical culture is fully appreciated. Over and above creating a high-trust environment, it also produces higher levels of individual accountability and avoids the need for excessive regulation. An ethical culture serves to improve employee commitment, investor and market confidence and customer loyalty, which collectively enhance the company's reputation and brand equity. A sound ethical culture also has a positive impact on risk management, reducing the likelihood of high costs and other negative consequences associated with ethical breaches.

It is clearly important also to understand how ethical or unethical the organisation is, as this is directly manifest in its culture. The assessment of the organisation's ethical status forms a separate part of the ethics management system (addressed below).

How to create an ethical culture rests on a number of factors: leadership commitment, sound ethical standards, high levels of ethical awareness, and the extent to which ethics is put into practice. These issues are all addressed below as separate facets of the ethics management system.

Strategy to realise the goal of an ethical culture

The success of realising the goal of an ethical culture will also rest on the quality of the strategy that is put in place. Sound intentions without clear actions, plans and resources are not adequate.

Most frequently, an ethics strategy is almost exclusively focused on reducing unethical conduct. While this is crucial, it is not sufficient, because minimising misconduct does not necessarily ensure proactive ethical conduct. Therefore, the ethics strategy needs to include a distinct additional emphasis on improving ethical conduct, which should encompass two goals.[1]

Firstly, there needs to be a focus on increasing ethical maturity, which at higher levels implies that ethical behaviour is driven more by a commitment to values, rather than simple compliance with laws and rules at lower levels of ethical maturity. Secondly, attention must be given to expanding the organisation's ethical boundary to ensure that its values and ethics apply to all its stakeholders and embrace a triple bottom line.

There are two principles that should underpin an ethics strategy. It should follow a proactive approach, rather than a reactive one; and all ethics initiatives should be integrated to maximise the impact, as opposed to diminishing it via a fragmented set of initiatives.

Leadership commitment

In addition to defining the organisation's ethics goals and strategy, the other equally important element of the ethics management system is the commitment of the organisation's leaders to ethics and an ethical culture. Leadership in this regard encompasses the formal structures that are responsible for ethics as well as those who occupy executive or senior positions. As discussed in greater length in Part I of Chapter 3, leadership exerts the greatest impact on organisational ethics. Should this commitment be lacking or be intermittent, it will negatively affect the realisation and maintenance of an ethical culture.

The challenge for leaders is that the seniority of their position brings with it a great degree of scrutiny of their behaviour. Much like an actor on stage, the visibility of leaders and their behaviour effectively amounts to their also being "on stage" all the time. Added to that, as role models, leaders are mostly expected to abide by a higher standard of conduct than others. This expectation will almost certainly extend to conduct both inside and outside the workplace – the reason being that their behaviour would generally be directly linked to the company and any inappropriate behaviour in their private capacity would risk negatively

---

1   This is addressed in Part I of this chapter in the article "Beware the ethical divide".

impacting the company and its reputation. While this can be viewed as eroding their right to privacy and their freedom to do as they choose in their private lives, in reality, it is simply the cost of occupying a high profile position in an organisation. An extreme version of this is what celebrities experience. The public's interest is never confined to the source of their fame, whether it be their role as an actor or a sports star, but extends to every facet of their lives. Therefore, leaders need to strive to conduct themselves ethically at all times.

Ethical standards

Setting the ethical standards of the organisation constitutes another pillar of the ethics management system.

Code of ethics

The primary mechanism for an organisation's ethical standards is via a code of ethics. This code needs to be clear and well communicated and should comprise the organisation's values, its code of conduct, and other supporting policies for ethics-related matters. The code should be signed off by the board and endorsed by the all board members. The article entitled "A code of ethics: getting the basics right" outlines what drafting a sound, effective code necessitates and has not been repeated here.[2]

The effectiveness of these core ethical standards rests on unwavering equality in enforcement and the steadfast commitment of leaders at all levels in the organisation. They need to be seen to be "walking the talk".

Goals and measurements

Ethical standards should also be incorporated in other operational goals and measurements. In its best form, this allows sensitive issues to be monitored in pursuit of reducing unethical behaviour. For instance, the mining industry has very visible safety targets and comprehensive measures of safety incidents. However, operational goals and measures need to be carefully considered in terms of their unintended or potential consequences, as they can have the effect of encouraging unethical behaviour.

The example of time-based billing has already been mentioned. Unrealistic or unattainable "stretch" targets can also encourage unethical or undesirable conduct. By way of example, a survey by the Association of Teachers and Lecturers in the United Kingdom found that, because of pressure to realise unrealistic exam targets, 80% of teachers surveyed admitted that they "teach to the test" instead of teaching a broad and balanced curriculum. The effect of focusing their teaching primarily on just the content that the pupils need to pass the test is, of course, negatively impacting on children's education (Paton, 2014).

---

2   This is addressed in Part III of Chapter 2.

The Ford Pinto provides a much more extreme example of the consequences of decisions that were based on the metrics of a cost-benefit analysis. In the 1970s Ford President Lee Iacocca's goal of a compact car that weighed less than 2 000 pounds and was priced at less than $2 000 resulted in the production of the Ford Pinto. During the period of only 22 months from concept to production, Ford had been aware of the design defects. However, under competitive pressure from other small car manufacturers, the company was not open to any delay in production and therefore did not change the design, deciding instead that it would be cheaper to pay off possible lawsuits. The defect? In a rear-end accident the car could leak fuel and burst into flames. Figures vary as regards the number of deaths, but it is conservatively estimated at 27 (Bazerman & Tenbrunsel, 2011:59–60).

When formulating goals and measures, leaders cannot afford to be naïve or innocent with regard to the potential unintended consequences. This issue is expressed well in Graham Greene's book *The Quiet American*. Thomas Fowler is a world-weary British journalist in Indo-China and Alden Pyle is the idealistic and apparently innocent "quiet American" who seeks to promote democracy in a volatile political situation. Fowler's initial instinct to protect Pyle, however, gives way to the opposite impulse, and he comes to recognise the peril that innocence poses: "Innocence always calls mutely for protection when we would be so much wiser to guard ourselves against it; innocence is like a dumb leper who has lost his bell, wandering the world, meaning no harm" (Greene, 2002:37).

Performance management

Ethical standards should also be built into the organisation's recognition programmes and its performance management system.

Understanding the extent of employee support for and commitment to the organisation's values and ethical goals and their advancement provides useful insight into an important facet of the organisation's ethics. This can be assessed via a performance management system that includes the organisation's values and ethics as key performance criteria, which effectively makes ethics both a performance goal and measure for individual employees. Such an approach recognises that an employee's contribution to the organisation derives from the output of his or her functional position as well as from behaviour relative to the company values and ethics.

A performance management system also promotes ethical behaviour by balancing work outputs against values, thereby providing a guideline that avoids pursuing business results – such as signing a deal, making a sale or achieving turnover targets – at any cost. Elevating ethics to the extent that it is recognised and rewarded also helps to make sure that employees continue to focus on ethics.

In terms of recognition programmes, ethics should be built into initiatives such as employee of the month nominations. When these criteria are based on specific ethical behaviours or the company's values, it serves the further purpose of creating visible examples of the practice of ethics and of making those issues "real" and recognisable.

The combination of standards in the company's code of ethics, its goals and measures, and its performance management system should provide a strong, integrated system of ethical guidelines. Of course, when leaders tells others to "do whatever it takes" to get the desired results, it risks action being outside these standards and courts ethical disaster.

Ethical awareness

Ethical awareness is generally an under-used and under-valued ethics tool. But achieving a high level of ethical awareness makes a valuable contribution to both increasing ethical conduct and, especially, to reducing misconduct. As such, this constitutes another of the primary elements of the ethics management system.

The positive results derive from the regular, constant focus on ethics, creating a level of consciousness that permeates the actions and behaviour in the company, thereby continually reinforcing ethical conduct.

Reducing unethical conduct derives from a "big brother is watching" effect. In the workplace, this translates into the company being perceived to exercise a high level of vigilance relative to misconduct. This, in turn, increases the potential culprit's awareness that the undesirable consequences of misconduct will be enforced. Together, this amounts to an effective deterrent. It will not prevent all unethical behaviour, but it can make a meaningful difference. The example of visible policing has been used in this book to illustrate that the awareness created by, for example, the neighbourhood security patrol effectively acts as a deterrent to crime in that area.

Tom McLeod, author of *McLeod Governance: The Weekly Wrap*, relates an interesting example of the effect of ethical awareness with a simple solution. Following some disturbances in front of the McDonald's restaurant near their offices in Melbourne, a sign was erected in the car park reading "reserved for police vehicles". McLeod notes that although he has never once observed a police vehicle in the designated spot, there has never been any further trouble at the McDonald's restaurant. The awareness which the sign created acted as an effective discouragement to any further disturbances (McLeod, 2014).

Ethics awareness is achieved in numerous ways among which communication and training are key. Ethics needs to be communicated regularly and consistently – not just now and again. This can easily be done via newsletter articles, posters or pop-up messages on employees' computers. And ethics needs to be talked about, which means, for example, that it should be mentioned at staff meetings and, crucially, that it should be included on the agenda at strategy sessions, executive committee meetings and management meetings. If it is not on the agenda it is very unlikely that it will be discussed.

Ethics training also boosts ethical awareness significantly.[3] In this regard, organisations need to source effective training that adds value: two days spent on the minutiae of a code of conduct are likely to be boring and considered a waste of time – and therefore would be ineffective. Training needs to be done via appropriate delivery methods, ranging from face-to-face interactive discussions to e-learning. Most importantly, training needs to move beyond only telling employees what they already know (yes, they do know that bribery and corruption are wrong). Workplace misconduct rarely happens because employees did not know right from wrong. Instead, it is more likely to arise because of unethical choices. Training therefore needs to focus also on the question of ethical choices and ethical decision making. After all, better choices and better decisions make for better conduct.

In addition to training as a source of guidance for ethical issues, the company can also consider setting up an ethics helpline to deal with queries and concerns.

Ethics assessment and reporting

Assessing and reporting on the organisation's ethics and its ethics performance is an essential facet of the ethics management system. Its importance is reflected in the fact that it is the focus for the whole of Chapter 5. Consequently, the content included below is a brief summary of this topic.

Assessing ethics

Managing ethics and building an ethical culture both warrant an understanding of the organisation's ethical status. It provides the starting point from which to move forward and against which to track the company's ethical progress or regression over time. The assessment and monitoring that this necessitates is recognised by both the Companies Act 71 of 2008 and *King III*.

The Companies Act mandates that the social and ethics committee monitors ethics, while *King III* advocates the assessment and monitoring of ethics via an internal and external assessment as best corporate governance practice. *King III* recognises that the ultimate objective of the assessment (and reporting and disclosure) is to improve the company's ethical culture by enhancing its ethical

---

3   Ethics training is discussed in greater depth in Part III of Chapter 3.

performance (IoDSA, 2009:27). At a straightforward level, the measurement of ethics and ethics performance also contributes to the management of ethics inasmuch as it is much easier to manage that which you can measure. As such, the assessment or measurement needs, in the words of Jack Welch, renowned head of General Electric (GE) for 20 years from 1981 to 2001, "to face reality as it is, not as it was or you wish it to be" (Tichy & Sherman, 1994:15). Tichy and Sherman stress this by pointing out that "facing reality, in good times and bad, is an ethical obligation for managers – indeed, for anyone whose actions affect other people" (1994:125).To realise this and meet the outcomes of the Companies Act and *King III*, the choice of the assessment tool or process is important. This choice should rest on three criteria,

Firstly, the assessment should provide accurate, quantitative measures. This supports better risk management and allows management to identify where to act to improve ethics.

Secondly, to ensure the credibility of the results, all employees should be given the opportunity to share their experiences and perceptions of ethics in the workplace. When the assessment includes only a small sample of employees, the validity of the results runs the risk of being queried – by management if the results are unexpectedly poor, or by employees if the results are unexpectedly good. Similarly, the opinion of just the board does not constitute a representative view of the whole organisation and all its employees.

Thirdly, the assessment tool used must ensure the anonymity and confidentiality of the employees and their responses, which is vital to access their honest responses.

An instrument such as the Ethics Monitor meets all these criteria. It offers employees total confidentiality to share their experiences and perceptions and thereby serves as a very useful "listening" exercise to identify ethical and unethical issues in the workplace, to quantify ethical risks, and to identify what actions need to be taken, and where, to improve ethics.

Ethics reporting

Ethics reporting supports the maintenance of an ethical culture and the management of ethics via the focus and attention that is achieved by sharing the organisation's ethics performance results and ethical strengths and weaknesses with others.

Ethics reporting is also stipulated in the Companies Act and *King III*. *King III* recommends the reporting and disclosure of ethics to the board, management and external stakeholders. As for assessment, *King III* recognises that this serves the ultimate objective of improving the company's ethical culture by enhancing its ethical performance (IoDSA, 2009:27).

But ethics reporting is mostly still in its infancy.[4] An ethics report **may** include the board's view of the company's ethics, unethical incidents and how they were resolved (such as a high profile incident that could not be ignored), and some details of the organisation's ethics programme. The report seldom stems from an accurate, representative assessment of ethics within the company and thus rarely includes quantitative measures of the organisation's ethical status, strengths, risks and performance or information about remedial action taken for ethical risks and the outcome thereof. But it should include all of this if the intention is to provide meaningful insight into the company's ethical status.

A facet of reporting that also promotes ethical awareness and an ethical culture and that is rarely acknowledged is reporting to the organisation's employees. For organisations using the Ethics Monitor survey to assess their ethics, the ethics report of their results would be presented both to the executive team and to their staff. For employees this report-back is, in effect, sharing their own views with them, but the response is always extremely positive. Even for companies with less than ideal ethics results, the transparency that underpins the disclosure creates a platform for the company to be able to address the feedback. When the company responds to remedy poor results, it creates a strong, positive spiral, building confidence among employees that their tough feedback has been heard **and** acted on.

Another reporting system that can support ethics management is an employee ethics reporting system or ethics hotline. The latter can and should add value, but is generally used very little. As an executive said at a recent meeting, "the only calls we get are wrong numbers". It is the focus of the section in Chapter 5 entitled "Ethics hotline reporting: who will tell?"

Operational ethics: ethics in practice

The final pillar of the ethics management system is to include and merge ethics into the operation of the organisation. It cannot be a mere "add-on", conveniently included when necessary to create the right impression.

Echoing this, the Ethisphere Institute, an American-based independent centre of research, best practices and thought leadership in corporate ethics, annually chooses the World's Most Ethical (WME) Companies. This accolade is awarded to companies that truly go beyond making statements about doing business "ethically" and translate those words into action. WME winners not only promote ethical business standards and practices internally, but exceed legal compliance minimums and shape future industry standards by introducing best practices (Ethisphere® Institute, 2014).

---

4   This is discussed in the Chapter 5 article "Business ethics reporting: what should you tell?"

Putting ethics into practice entails giving effect to the pillars of the ethics management system as these impact on systems and procedures (as discussed above). Therefore, it involves the following:[5]

1   Leaders need to commit to being ethical and promoting ethics at all times.

2   The social and ethics committee needs to avoid a "tick-box" approach and strive to add real value by advancing ethics in the organisation.

3   HR, compliance, risk, internal audit and other functions need to pursue the application and enforcement of ethics in their roles, from recruitment to internal auditing.

4   An ethics goal needs to be articulated and widely shared among employees.

5   A supporting strategy needs to be formulated and implemented.

6   Standards need to be well defined in a code of ethics (including a code of conduct) and uniformly and consistently enforced, for example, via the company's disciplinary code.

7   Ethical goals and measures need to be carefully chosen. They should be visible in potentially sensitive areas and should form part of the company's performance management system.

8   Awareness needs to be constantly driven via communication and training and by putting ethics on the agenda.

9   Ethics needs to be regularly assessed and reported on.

Using these six integrated building blocks will provide an organisation with an ethics management system that is equipped to manage ethics and meet the goal of creating an ethical culture.

4.2   PRACTICAL EXERCISE: HOW ETHICAL IS YOUR COMPANY'S CULTURE?

The following paper-based exercise is useful as a quick and easy "dipstick"-type tool to surface the views of executive and employees regarding the ethical status of the company's culture. This is particularly suited to small and medium sized companies that can administer it themselves.

The value of the exercise lies in comparing the results to assess how aligned or different the views are among management and employees and how divergent this is from the culture that the company espouses or aspires to.

---

5   Building on these actions to operationalise ethics, the sections that follow focus more detailed attention on specific facets of ethics management, namely tackling misconduct, avoiding ethical "gaps", managing ethics "without borders", and recovering from ethical failure.

Since ethics can be viewed as sensitive information, the risk exists that employees will score the culture in terms of what they think the company would want to hear, rather than what the actual situation is. It is, therefore, preferable to allow this be completed anonymously.

The exercise entails the following:

1   The company can either select all the paired criteria from the list below or only those that are considered pertinent. These should be included in the participant scoring sheet (Table 4.1).

2   The participants score the paired criteria on the participant scoring sheet.

3   The score, ranging from 1 to 10, should be given based on the extent to which that behaviour or action is practiced or present in the organisation, using 1 as the lowest/worst score to indicate it is not practiced or prevalent at all and 10 as the best score to indicate that the behaviour is very widely practiced throughout the company.

4   The scores for each pair of factors, such as respect and disrespect, should then be transferred to the graph (figure 4.2) and, using the ethical conduct score on the vertical axis with the unethical conduct factors on the horizontal axis, the intersection of the scores should be plotted on the graph.

5   To identify each pair of factors the letter for that factor should be written at the point of the final score. For example, if an employee scored honesty as 8 and dishonesty as 2, he/she would write the letter A at the point of intersection, which would be in the upper left/lighter zone (as illustrated on the graph in Figure 4.2).

The result of each completed graph would be a very clear visual representation of the ethics of the culture because more strongly ethical scores would fall within the lighter left hand side of the graph, while more unethical conduct would be within the darker right-hand-side triangle.

Table 4.1: Participant scoring sheet to assess the ethics of the company's culture

Code to identify Factors	Factors that indicate ethical conduct		Factors that indicate unethical conduct	
	Score on the vertical axis	Score 1–10	Score on the horizontal axis	Score 1–10
A	Honesty		Dishonesty/fraud/ corruption	
B	Respect		Disrespect	
C	Fairness		Unfairness/ discrimination	
D	Ethical leadership		Unethical leadership	
E	High accountability		Low accountability	
F	Behaviour shaped by values		Behaviour shaped by rules	
G	Transparency		No transparency/non-disclosure	
H	High ethical awareness		Low ethical awareness	
I	High social responsibility		Low/no social responsibility	
J	Responsibilities		Rights	
K	Empowerment		Control	
L	Triple bottom line focus		Single bottom line focus	
M	Interests of stakeholders taken into account		Interests of shareholders not taken into account	

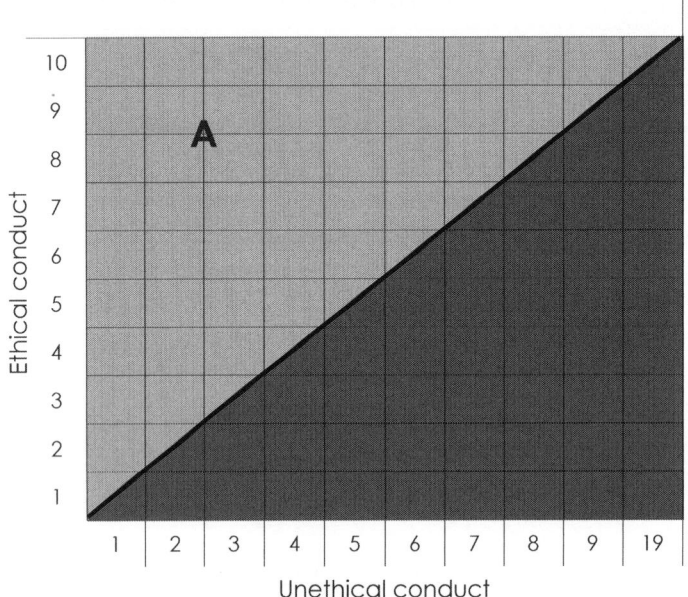

Figure 4.2: Graph of the company's ethical status

The scores for each pair of factors from the participant score sheet (Table 4.1) are captured on the graph, where the ethical conduct score on the vertical axis and the unethical conduct factors on the horizontal axis create a single point of intersection on the graph. The example of honesty scored at 8 and dishonesty scored at 2 is illustrated by the score marked A. The placement of the majority of the factors in either the ethical lighter area or the less ethical darker zone provides a clear picture of the overall ethical status of the company's culture, which provides the basis for a discussion as to which factors should be improved and why.

4.3   TACKLING MISCONDUCT

Managing misconduct is often described as "a fight", whether against corruption, bribery, fraud or a range of other unethical and illegal behaviours. This captures the fact that seeking to eliminate or even to reduce misconduct is not an easy task: it can feel like an ongoing battle. But it is an important area of ethics management that warrants serious attention and a clear framework.

In fact, the extent and magnitude of misconduct and the plethora of examples that encompass such a wide range of misdemeanours make it impossible to ignore. Just a few examples that were exposed in early 2014 illustrate the scale and scope.

1   Computing multinational Hewlett-Packard is to pay American regulators $108 million to settle a corruption scandal involving employees at subsidiaries in Poland, Russia and Mexico, who were charged with bribing government officials to win and retain IT contracts (Garside, 2014).

2   The Bank of America has agreed to refund as many as 2.9 million customers $727 million and pay $45 million in fines for illegal credit card practices that both deceived consumers and unfairly billed them for services not performed (Puzzanghera, 2014).

3   Foreign donors have suspended $150 million of aid to Malawi until a scandal involving the alleged looting of more than $100 million from government coffers by civil servants, MPs and businesspeople is cleared up (*Mail & Guardian*, 2014).

The reasons why organisations need to actively manage misconduct should be self-evident. As these few examples reveal, the costs and consequences are high.[6] It can include fines, losses, damaged corporate reputations, terminated careers, reduced share prices and eroded customer and investor confidence, among many other negative outcomes. Often the negative costs of breaches of ethics are not only borne by the perpetrators alone (assuming they are caught). It can also impact victims who can also sometimes suffer losses or damage. However, this section does not focus on the many costs but rather concentrates on providing content that can assist organisations to fight misconduct more effectively.

Who commits misconduct?

Understanding who is most likely to commit misconduct is a good start and provides valuable insights – provided it is used appropriately and does not lend itself to supporting prejudices or the like.

The Ethics Resource Center conducts a regular business ethics survey. Their *National Business Ethics Survey 2013* found that a relatively high percentage of misconduct is committed by managers and that 60% of misconduct involved someone with managerial authority from the supervisory level up to top management (Ethics Resource Center, 2013).

Further insight is offered by the PwC *Global Economic Crime Survey* released in 2014. The survey was conducted among 5 128 senior representatives from over 93 countries during the fourth quarter of 2013. In South Africa, 134 organisations across 17 industries took part in the survey. The survey revealed that the typical internal fraudster is male, aged between 31 and 40 and has acquired a first university degree or higher. Globally, almost half of all frauds are committed by employees with 6 or more years of experience and almost a third (29%) are committed by employees with 3 to 5 years of experience. The findings also

---

6   The cost of corruption is the topic of a section in Chapter 2.

showed "an alarming shift in the perpetrator profile in South Africa since 2009, with senior management now regarded as the main perpetrator of economic crime committed by insiders". Senior management fraud now amounts to 41% of all internal fraud (PwC, 2014).

While this might appear alarming – given that senior managers are the very people who are supposed to set a good example of ethical conduct and make sure that employees behave ethically – it makes sense when one considers the factors that create the opportunity for fraud. Deon Rossouw, in his book *Business Ethics in Africa*, identifies three such factors.

> The person must be in a position of trust or must have access to people in positions of trust within an organisation.
>
> A person must have knowledge of the control systems of the organisation. Knowledge gives one the ability to beat them.
>
> A person should have access to the assets of the company (2002:160).

He notes that when these factors combine it creates the opportunity for committing fraud and that this is most likely for those in more senior positions – hence fraud is often viewed as a white collar crime (Rossouw, 2002).

How can you fight misconduct?

The number of frameworks, methodologies and approaches to the management of misconduct is such that it could confuse more than assist. The ethics management system outlined in the previous chapter provides a good basis for tackling misconduct: that is, by integrating the seven pillars, namely ethics goals and strategy, leadership commitment to ethics, ethical standards, ethical awareness initiatives, ethics assessment and reporting and operational ethics in systems and practices.

At the level of the individual employee, Mary Gentile, author of *Giving Voice to Values* and Senior Research Scholar at Babson College, provides a clear set of guidelines about how to challenge unethical behaviour at work. She offers the following set of questions as a way to formulate a plan of action:

- What is the conflict at hand, and what is your position on it?

- What's at stake for the key parties, including those who disagree with you?

- What arguments are you trying to counter? That is, what reasons and rationalisations do you need to address?

- What responses to those reasons and rationalisations would be most powerful and persuasive? Do you have all the information you need to craft a sound argument?

- To whom should the argument be made?

- At what time has your audience had a change of heart before? What can you learn from those examples?

- What timing is optimal? Should your efforts be sequenced in some way?

- Which allies, if any, will help you make your case?

- What forum is right for the conversation – off-line or in public?

- What communication style do you prefer? What style best suits this situation?

- What sources of support do you have inside and outside the organisation? Are they adequate? (Gentile, 2010:117).

To provide a broader perspective of this field, two different frameworks have been described and a few common approaches and pitfalls have been addressed. These inputs have been combined with the seven pillars of the ethics management system to create a more focused framework for tackling misconduct.

Punishment, incentives, deterrence and pitfalls

A popular approach to managing misconduct is to attempt to deter it via punishment or the threat of punishment. The effectiveness of this rests on the punishment being consistently enforced. If, for instance, it is only imposed sporadically, it will significantly erode the effectiveness of punishment as a deterrent. Thus low prosecution rates would erode the efficacy of this mechanism by allowing wrongdoers to assume that, even if they are caught, they will not be successfully prosecuted. An example is the low rate of convictions that the Independent Police Investigative Directorate (IPID) is achieving relative to its investigations into South African Police Service members (Eliseev & Whittles, 2013). In the workplace the same applies when punishment is intermittent or, worse, selective (applied to some but not to others): it fails to deter potential offenders.

If the sanction is too lenient relative to the transgression, it will also having little or no effect. The cost can, in fact, be accepted as an unwelcome cost of doing business. The fines imposed on the construction industry in South Africa for collusive practices in work done in the lead-up to the 2010 Soccer World Cup were seen by many to be far too lenient. In June 2013 15 South African construction companies agreed to pay fines totalling R1.46 billion.

The issue of punishment can also be viewed as incentives that aim to encourage good conduct and discourage bad. Fines or penalties are therefore imposed for bad or unacceptable behaviour and rewards or bonuses are offered for desirable or good behaviour. Steven Levitt and Stephen Dubner, in their bestselling book *Freakonomics*, recognise three types of incentives: economic, social and moral. For organisations that use incentives, the distinction is important, as the example they quote reveals. A study undertaken by Uri Gneezy and Aldo Rusti at a daycare centre explored the issue of parents collecting their children late. In an effort to curb this, a fine was imposed for late collections. However, the fine backfired completely because, in effect, it replaced a moral incentive with an economic one. Thus, instead of the parents' behaviour being guided by a sense of consideration for the daycare centre staff and the guilt of being late, it was replaced with a fine, allowing parents to "buy off their guilt" (Levitt & Dubner, 2005:16–19).

Although these examples reflect situations where the threat or risk of punishment is not effective, it can be very effective in many situations. An extremely powerful message (warning) is sent when, for example, a senior executive is fired for misconduct.

Another factor that can undermine the management of misconduct is a delay in acting against culprits or in seeking their prosecution. While the legal process can take a long time, organisations should strive to act – and be seen to act – quickly. An undue delay would easily be translated as a lack of commitment to ethics. Similarly, it is counter-productive to dismiss an employee rather than pursuing an internal disciplinary process or laying legal charges. It not only allows the employee to perpetrate the same misconduct at another organisation, but communicates the lack of consequences for misconduct to other employees.

The clear lesson is, therefore, that organisations need to enforce punishment and penalties in accordance with the law and the company's policies (typically a disciplinary code or policy) that are severe enough to be effective as promptly as possible every time there is a breach of ethics.

Features of effective fraud, bribery and corruption management

A useful framework is contained in Ernst & Young's (EY) 2013 Europe, Middle East, India and Africa Fraud Survey, entitled *Navigating Today's Complex Business Risks*. The report identifies the features that are common to those businesses that manage the risk of fraud, bribery and corruption most effectively (EY, 2013).

- They own the problem. Boards and senior management acknowledge that the risk is real for them and their business.

- They deal with the issues. Teams across businesses, functions, geographies and grades understand that the risks are relevant to them and their work.

- They communicate the risks and the benefits. The costs of fraud, bribery and corruption are understood at an individual level. Behaviour is not only limited by controls, but is driven by a common culture.

- They focus effort. Squeezing inefficiencies out of shrinking resources is a necessity in today's environment. Identifying specific risks and focusing resources on these is, therefore, increasingly important.

- They ask questions and demand answers. Management is not afraid to ask difficult question or turn over stones, knowing that what is hidden cannot be ignored (EY, 2013:3).

The message from the survey is that businesses face significant threats and must be aware and take action to navigate these risks.

Governance from the CEO down

A comprehensive approach used by Ben Heineman Jr, who was the Chief Legal Officer at GE for nearly 20 years, sought to merge the high performance demands at GE with equally high integrity (Heineman Jr, 2007).

Heineman notes that the primary governance focus within corporations is on the relationship between shareholders and the company and between the board and the CEO. However, at GE, they recognised the vital "third dimension" of governance, that being from the CEO down. In pursuit of such "governance on the front lines" he shares the set of seven inter-dependent principles and practices that they viewed as essential to avoid "integrity land mines" and to create and support such a high performance-high integrity culture (2007).

1   *Demonstrating consistent and committed leadership.* Heineman stresses that "in no area of corporate life is leadership commitment more important than in creating an integrity culture" (2007:102).

2   *Going beyond formal financial and legal rules.* For multinational companies global standards that are higher than the financial and legal requirements in a particular jurisdiction should be considered relative to issues that are most important for key stakeholders.

3   *Staying ahead of the sheriff.* This translated into GE systematically gathering information on financial, legal and ethical developments to ensure they remained up to date and could respond timeously, for example, to adopt new standards or practices.

4   *Building standards into business processes,* which GE supported by giving business leaders the primary responsibility in their divisions for performing with integrity.

5   *Encouraging finance, legal and HR to be both partner and guardian.* This needs to be accompanied by the most senior leadership's understanding of the tensions between these two roles and their encouragement to occupy both roles.

6   *Giving employees a voice.* GE found that a particular challenge to their goal of a high performance-high integrity culture was educating and training employees across multiple countries. Enabling employees to share on-the-ground concerns was seen as key to creating a culture of openness and accountability. Employees have four major channels through which to report issues: the ombuds system that included anonymous reporting, via each business unit's annual assessment, to the internal corporate audit staff and to business units' financial, legal and HR staff.

7   *Holding business leaders accountable with integrity metrics*, specifically to evaluate how leaders carry out their integrity responsibilities (Heineman Jr, 2007:102–108).

While some of these principles or practices have particular applicability for multinational organisations, many can be used in organisations of all sizes.

Misconduct management framework

There is clearly no one method for tackling misconduct in all organisations. However, the seven pillars from the ethics management systems woven together with GE's approach and the common features identified by Ernst & Young create the following valuable framework, a misconduct management framework, which should be able to be used in almost all organisations:

1   *Leadership:* Consistent, committed leadership who live ethics and acknowledge the risk of misconduct

2   *Goal and strategy*: Formulating a clear corporate ethics goal and implementing a supporting strategy that focuses effort and resources

3   *Standards:* Defining standards and building them into business processes and systems that go beyond minimalist compliance

4   *Awareness:* Using ongoing ethical awareness initiatives that focus on staying informed of financial, legal and ethical developments and communicating the risks and the benefits to all employees

5   *Partners and guardians:* Encouraging wide-spread support within the organisation for promoting ethics and reducing misconduct, specifically that finance, legal, compliance and HR act as both partners and guardians

6   *Assessment:* Assessing the organisation's ethics, holding leaders and managers accountable with performance-related integrity metrics, asking questions and demanding answers

7   *Reporting:* Reporting on ethics to external and internal stakeholders and creating safe, effective channels for employee reporting.

4.4   BEWARE THE ETHICAL DIVIDE

Since ethics in the workplace is becoming an increasingly important focus area, it warrants paying attention to those factors or circumstances that could undermine ethics or even limit its effectiveness. This particularly applies to divides or gaps between ethical issues, choices or situations.

Some of these gaps have already been addressed as separate topics, such as managing gaps between employees' personal values and the company's values.[7] Creating maximum alignment is crucial to creating an ethical culture.

---

7   This topic is addressed in Chapter 1.

Organisations also need to consciously manage the gaps that can occur between what is ethical and illegal and unethical but legal. The assumption that what is ethical is legal and what is unethical is always illegal ignores many ethical divides.[8]

An issue that is discussed later in this chapter is supply chain ethics, which is likely to become an increasingly high profile ethical divide. The requirement to conduct business ethically is gradually extending to an expectation that the organisation also strive to influence how their suppliers conduct their businesses. This is a very noteworthy extension of the company's ethical responsibilities, which lends itself to an ethical divide between the company and its suppliers, especially as regards suppliers' labour practices.[9]

There are other ethical gaps that need to be recognised as they bring with them various risks.

Improving ethics or reducing misconduct

One of the most fundamental gaps or imbalances that can occur is when organisations focus virtually all their attention in the field of workplace ethics on curbing misconduct. While this focus is vital, it is not sufficient. Minimising or even eliminating misconduct does not necessarily promote or ensure proactive ethical conduct, nor is it a sufficiently effective factor to create an ethical culture on its own. While in language being ethical is the opposite of unethical, in practice diminishing or eradicating misconduct does not imply that it will result in all that being ethical entails, such as the positive actions associated with sound values. Therefore, the ethics strategy that guides the organisation's ethics management system needs to include a distinct emphasis on reducing misconduct **and** promoting and improving ethical conduct.

The effect of the divide between ethical conduct and misconduct is illustrated and supported by well-known research done by American psychologist Frederick Herzberg. His motivation-hygiene theory – also known as two-factor theory or dual-factor theory was based on research into employee satisfaction and dissatisfaction. It showed that they were shaped by separate factors and that the absence of dissatisfaction did not lead to satisfaction (Herzberg, 1968:13). Similarly, as discussed in Chapter 1, the absence of misconduct does not lead to the deliberate, positive actions that constitute ethical conduct. Interestingly though, the presence of ethics and an ethical culture will positively impact compliance and thereby help to reduce misconduct.

8   This is included in Chapter 1.

9   This subject is discussed in detail in Part II of this chapter.

Doing the right thing versus minimalist compliance

The tendency to focus largely on tackling misconduct is sometimes coupled to an internal focus on compliance instead of a comprehensive focus on ethics. Recognising this distinction, *King III* recommends that business leaders should "do business ethically rather than merely being satisfied with legal or regulation compliance … or limiting themselves to current social expectations" (IoDSA, 2009:20).

However, the increasing demand to be compliant with a multitude of laws and regulations is making compliance an onerous task in many countries. Compliance officers are battling to balance the many duties of the function, including establishing standards for business conduct, ensuring compliance with anti-bribery and corruption requirements, tracking and analysing regulatory developments, board reporting, amending policies and procedures and liaising with internal stakeholders and control functions. Two 2013 surveys provide interesting insights into the consequent pressures.

Thomson Reuters Governance, Risk and Compliance (GRC) surveyed more than 800 compliance practitioners from financial services firms in 62 countries covering Africa, the Americas, Asia, Australasia, Europe and the Middle East between November 2012 and January 2013, to canvass their views on the costs of compliance and the greatest challenges they expected to face during the year ahead. The survey, the *Cost of Compliance Survey 2013*, confirmed that compliance requirements have increased, as has scrutiny from regulators and consumers. As regards ongoing increases, 43% of the respondents said that they expect the amount of regulatory information published by regulators to be significantly more over the next 12 months than today. (Thomson Reuters GRC, 2013:4). The survey report specifically noted that, given the continuing lack of interaction between internal audit and compliance, the alignment between these two functions needs to be improved (2013:12).

Regulation in the financial services sector may be more demanding than in other industries. However, the Deloitte and Compliance Week *Compliance Trends Survey 2013*, which was conducted among American compliance executive across many industries, confirms this pressure. The survey found that the majority of companies still run compliance with relatively tight budgets and staffing (Deloitte & Compliance Week, 2013:8). The survey also identified that the biggest operational issue around managing compliance risks was monitoring employee compliance with policies (2013:11).

Adding to this picture is the fact that many regulators are striving to be more proactive, rather than reactive. At an operational level a solution to the demands of this role lies in working with and leveraging resources in other functions, such as legal, IT, HR and internal audit to achieve compliance goals. However, compliance is still likely to remain a very challenging role.

This could be used to justify a "tick box" approach to compliance, which is clearly not ideal, not least from a risk perspective. However, the far greater problem that can arise is that compliance comes to be seen as the totality of the organisation's ethical focus and ethics initiatives – that companies decide that no more time, funds or resources can be allocated to anything else beyond compliance. This risk is enhanced by the reality that compliance is almost always obligatory (for example relative to legislation) while much of ethics can be considered voluntary. This echoes how Lord John Moulton, an English jurist writing in the early 1900s, described the law and ethics as drivers of human action – as amounting to "obedience to the enforceable" and as "obedience to the unenforceable" respectively (in Kidder, 1995:66–67).

The distinction between compliance and board-based ethics is reflected in the legal recognition of the letter and spirit of the law. Obeying just the letter of the law limits behaviour to the literal interpretation of the legislation, often in a minimalist manner. However, this ignores the intent, the spirit, of the law. A purposive interpretation of the law, on the other hand, entails acting to give effect to the intention of the law, which is viewed as acting in a more comprehensive and ethical manner. So too for ethics: only complying with the rules does not necessarily extend to the intended bigger-picture outcome of an ethical workplace.

The unsatisfactory consequence of a choice in favour of compliance instead of broad-based ethics would be to limit the company's ethics to only one facet of ethics, the rule-based side of ethics. However, to be an ethical organisation and create an ethical culture require an equal focus on fostering value-based behaviours, which, as discussed above, are much more sustainable and contribute significantly to an ethical culture. Rules and compliance are not sufficient to achieve an ethical culture. Therefore, the question of whether an organisation needs values and rules or only one and not the other should not be a choice. Both are necessary. And organisations need values **more** because ethical behaviour can be achieved with sound values and very few rules, but not *vice versa*. Thus, ironically, more focus on fostering value-based behaviour, increasing ethical maturity and creating an ethical culture directly support the compliance function since the commitment it entrains includes compliance.

The gap between saying and doing

The most common example of an ethical divide is the gap between what is said and what is done. This often takes the form of a gap between the company's values, code of conduct or policies relative to their culture and practices. Examples of this are as endless as they are damaging to the organisations and its leadership. It occurs, for example, when the value statement includes respect but employees are demeaned in front of colleagues or clients, when the code of conduct is explicit about expensive gifts from clients or suppliers but ignores this at year end and when the recruitment policy is not applied when a family member of the boss applies for a job. The most junior employee is easily able to recognise the lack of alignment – if not outright contradiction.

Similarly, an approach of "do as I say, not as I do" will rarely achieve the desired behavioural outcome – as most parents have long since worked out. When leaders are the guilty parties, the added consequence is that their actions erode the leadership credibility in the organisation and the leader's position as a positive role model.

Another classic facet of this divide centres on making promises or commitments and not delivering on them. Vanessa Hall, the author of *The Truth about Trust in Business*, recognises expectations, needs and promises as the three key elements of trust. When promises, whether implicit and explicit, are not met, trust is eroded or broken. Confirming this, research she conducted in Australia found that 65% of the respondents said that keeping promises was the most important way for businesses to build trust (Hall, 2009:49). Given how obvious this is, one wonders why so many people will make promises to colleagues or clients that they are not able to or do not intend to keep when they know the cost of not meeting those commitments.

These types of saying–doing ethical divides are made all the more harmful because actions serve as a very effective communication medium. The ethical status of a leader or an organisation is judged not on intentions, but rather on demonstrable behaviour.

Gaps between senior management and employees

An ethical divide is also created when leaders and senior management are seen to be "above the law" or when their actions flout the values and rules of their organisations. The privileges of leadership do not and should not include exemption from compliance when commitment is what is expected.

Similarly, if organisations discriminate between senior management and employees in how they handle incidents of misconduct, this, too, creates a problematic divide. Choosing to handle serious leadership misconduct internally and in secret, rather than openly or by referring it to the appropriate authorities, is often defended on the grounds that publicising such unethical behaviour can have a detrimental effect on the organisation. It can negatively affect its reputation, its customer relationships, and even the share price for publicly traded companies.

However, the risks are far greater if the misconduct is kept quiet and then exposed by another party, such as the press. In this event, the organisation will have to deal not only with the inherent discrimination, but also with its earlier secretive handling of the matter, which is likely to exacerbate the consequences.

The many potential ethical divides in the workplace all pose risks and bring with them negative consequences. If organisations are aware of these pitfalls, they can mostly be avoided quite easily. However, this will probably not earn them any noteworthy recognition: while misconduct is punished, good behaviour is mostly taken for granted. But it will ensure that their path to an increasingly better ethical status, with all the associated rewards, continues to progress without unnecessary setbacks.

4.5   ETHICS WITHOUT BORDERS[i]

For organisations that strive to be ethical, there are two important criteria for earning and maintaining an ethical status: the continual, consistent application of their values to all their stakeholders, and their ongoing adherence to all applicable laws and regulations. If a company's commitment to their values or their compliance with regulations is irregular or applied selectively, it erodes their ethical standing. The constancy and widespread scope of ethical behaviour reflects the practice of "ethics without borders" or "borderless ethics".

Borderless ethics

Borderless ethics necessitates that the organisation has a very inclusive ethical boundary, whereby ethics is exercised beyond self-interest and includes all stakeholders affected by the company's operations. By contrast, an exclusive ethical boundary which implies that ethics is exercised only for the organisation's own benefit and relative to a select few stakeholders (typically shareholders) contradicts an approach of ethics without borders. While the exclusion of other stakeholders does not necessarily mean that the company is behaving unethically, it does highlight the fact that the company prioritises their own goals and needs above those of others, or that they do not give equal priority to their various stakeholders, such as communities which are impacted by the company's operations. Added to that, organisations are rarely obliged – for example, by law – to include all stakeholder groups formally within their ethical boundary. So, although technically such companies may not be behaving unethically or illegally, their limited application of ethics means that they would rarely be regarded as ethical organisations.

There is a further challenge to following an approach of ethics without borders. This emanates from the recurring discourse in workplace ethics that ethics differs for different people, cultures, countries and situations.[10] This view needs to be addressed not only because it appears to invalidate the possibility for ethics without borders, but also because it undermines the pursuit of common and shared organisational ethics. The globalised nature of the world of work particularly makes for a multitude of differences in the workplace. Yet, ironically, globalisation makes the practice of ethics without borders all the more valuable, not least for the clarity it offers all affected parties and the fairness it embodies by operating in terms of the same ethics globally.

---

10 This issue is addressed slightly differently in Chapter 1, focusing on personal versus company values.

What is actually different in the workplace?

To realise a situation of borderless ethics, organisations need to surface and focus on the apparent ethical differences in their workplace. This is best done by considering the two primary clusters of factors that shape ethics and by recognising that these are applicable at a personal and a work level. This includes the relevant laws, rules and regulations and the values, norms or culture and the leadership of the group, such as those of an organisation or community.

Laws, rules and regulations

In a given context, national laws and organisational rules and regulations would probably be common to the organisation and its employees. Therefore, this does not constitute a difference. There are also increasing similarities in legislation between countries, such as laws addressing bribery and corruption. For example, in South Africa, there is the Prevention and Combating of Corrupt Activities Act 12 of 2004 and the Companies Act 71 of 2008; the United Kingdom has the UK Bribery Act, and the United States of American has the Foreign Corrupt Practice Act and the Sarbanes-Oxley Act.

However, there are many countries that do not have adequate legislation or satisfactory legal enforcement. This manifests itself, for example, in the area of counterfeiting where outsourced manufacturers in foreign countries cannot easily be held to account for producing and selling fake goods. The best solution for the problem of globally inconsistent or inadequate legislation is a combination of an understanding of the relevant country's legal system and a commitment to abide by the law in the organisation's country of origin or primary operation.

Values and norms

The pursuit of a situation of ethics without border is, however, subject to the differences as regards values. Personal values and norms can differ significantly from those of the organisation as the individual's values are affected by a variety of factors including upbringing, culture and the behaviour of their leaders and role models. This can represent a serious ethical divide for an organisation that threatens to destroy the ideal of aligned personal and organisational values and norms.

However, as discussed in Chapter 1, though different individual values and norms may be held, it is essential that in the workplace the organisation espouses a set of values that reflects what constitutes acceptable ethical conduct in that environment. The crucial point is that values in the workplace are not a means for accommodating the full spectrum of values – from impeccable to appalling – among employees and stakeholders. They serve, instead, to define the criteria and standards by which an organisation strives to operate and to act as a guide for ethical behaviour.

Therefore, within the workplace context adherence to the company's values is what is expected of employees and deviations from these values would largely be unacceptable.

Do values mean different things in different organisations?

A further challenge to the concept of borderless ethics is that ethics, and specifically moral values, means different things in different organisations or, phrased differently, that values can differ.

This argument has very little substance. Core moral values such as honesty, integrity or fairness do not lend themselves to a range of different behaviours **when they are exercised in an ethical manner**, which means they are applied equally to all stakeholders and without variation. When the values are not exercised in an ethical manner, they can differ – but the crucial issue then is that such action is not ethical. As an added precaution against this view, companies that operate across different geographies and employ a culturally diverse workforce should ensure that appropriate definitions are included in their code of ethics to promote a common understanding of their values and desired behaviours across all their operations.

A difference that can occur is the way in which the values manifest themselves in practice. A good example is respect. Although it is a widely held value, it can **look** very different in different cultures. The different displays of respect do not mean that it is not respect that is being exercised. It simply requires an understanding and acceptance of the varying expressions of the value.

What about cultural norms?

Cultural norms can also give rise to differences that threaten the goal of ethics without borders.

The business practice of giving gifts is one example. Whereas in many Eastern countries, such as China, gifts are common incentives to doing business and are routinely given, in many Western countries gifts and personal perks would easily be classified as bribes and are often subject to a zero tolerance approach.[11]

While there is no single easy solution for this clash, a combination of transparency, discussion and respect can be effective. This includes, for example, focusing on customers that have similar values and being aware at the outset of business dealings of this potential area of difference. For those companies where bribes have become common practice, it is best to actively avoid doing business with them: the cost of complicity in misconduct is unlikely to warrant the potential benefits of the business (Shuibo, 2011:132).

---

11   The recommended case study included at the end of Chapter 1 addresses this issue.

Bribery is another example of a practice that is regarded as a "cultural norm" in many countries.[12] The crucial point is that organisations should avoid treating a bribe as acceptable because it is commonly practised in a particular country or industry. The extent to which it is practised neither makes it right, nor does it invalidate applicable legislation. This view is also projected by the OECD Anti-Bribery Convention, which holds that "an offence is committed irrespective of, amongst other things, the value of the advantage, perception of local custom [or] the tolerance of such payment by local authorities" (OECD/AfDB, 2012:11).

In countries where the prevalence of bribery is such that an organisation could not easily operate without succumbing to being part of the problem, the choice should be reviewed as to whether to enter that market or whether to continue operating there. This is especially pertinent when corruption extends beyond cultural norms to a political norm. In a country such as Russia, for example, the repercussions for displeasing the state can be severe. The case of Russian lawyer and anti-corruption activist, Alexey Navalny, illustrates this. In 2010 he founded RosPil, a web-based initiative to expose corruption in Russia (Healy & Ramanna, 2013). However, his success has come at a personal cost: he has been arrested numerous times by Russian authorities, and in February 2014 he was placed under house arrest and prohibited from communicating with anyone other than his family or from using the Internet (Agence France-Press, 2014).

Therefore, much as bribery may be accepted in a specific context and may "facilitate" access to lucrative markets, this gain needs to be weighed up against the potential longer-term cost. Even when the organisation may not risk prosecution in the "bribe-friendly" jurisdiction, it does not imply it will not be held accountable elsewhere, such as in its home country. Organisations are also being held to the higher standards of conduct by their external stakeholders. And public and investor opinion is not to be ignored.

As to what can be done to maintain ethics without borders: large multinational organisations are increasingly showing that they can use their power to combat bribery and corruption, which is to be encouraged. Companies must also train their staff in how to handle demands for bribes and, crucially, back them up when they refuse to pay (Healy & Ramanna, 2013).

Clearly, therefore, ethics without borders is not without its challenges. The benefits, however, exceed the challenges. A policy of borderless ethics can build and maintain excellent levels of trust with stakeholders – including shareholders, employees, customers, suppliers and investors – which, in turn, can enhance a company's reputation and facilitate other advantages such as easier access to capital or a lower cost of capital.

---

12 This topic is also addressed in Chapter 1 in terms of the conflict between ethical and illegal and unethical and legal.

The sound ethical status it accords a company delivers a further very valuable benefit. It can serves as a unique source of competitive advantage that eclipses the limited scope of competitive opportunity offered by many other sources. The unique nature of ethics as a source of competitive advantage rests on the fact that it cannot easily be copied; nor can it be bought, sold, owned, delegated or loaned. It can be realised only by practising it.

Leaders therefore need to equip themselves with an understanding of the flaws in arguments against borderless ethics in order to deflect them effectively. And, for those leaders who make the choice to follow an approach of ethics without borders, they need to recognise that the responsibility for living by that approach will be demanding and will warrant their ongoing support and commitment – and that it will be a rewarding route to follow.

4.6   RECOVERING FROM ETHICAL FAILURE

There is hardly an issue of a newspaper or business magazine which does not include at least one story about a new or brewing ethical scandal. Sometimes, but regrettably not always, the perpetrators have to face the costs and consequences of their misconduct – whether these may be the loss of their position, fines, or jail sentences.

However, once that price has been paid, those individuals or organisations face the challenge of how to recover from ethical failure. In most instances the damage cannot be corrected by simply cutting costs before the next set of results.

The misconduct may be so serious that recovery appears impossible, whether because of the severity of the ethical breach or because it is a repeated offence. For Wendy Machanik, founder of the South African estate agency group in her name, being found guilty of accessing the company's trust account over 90 times to the extent of over R217 million was that serious that it ended her company and her career in the real estate industry – and the damage was not lessened by her admission in a press opinion piece (Machanik, 2012). However, mostly, one incident will not render the person or company unethical for the rest of time.

Martha Stewart is still a good example of a successful recovery. Having built her business, Martha Stewart Living Omnimedia, to become America's first self-made female billionaire, she was convicted of lying to investigators about a stock sale and served five months in prison in 2004. While the company suffered some losses in 2004, it returned to profitability the following year and continues to go from strength to strength – and still under her name. Her response to how she recovered was a well-designed PR plan, a new board, and a strong measure of resilience. To that needs to be added a tough attitude, captured on the cover of the November 2005 issue of *Fortune*: "I cannot be destroyed" (Sellers, 2005:47–56).

In South Africa this attitude of being indestructible is also evident, often coupled to an apparent lack of any sense of embarrassment or shame at having been caught out. This exceeds the typical ostrich approach of merely pretending nothing has happened, by trying also to convince others of that. Attacking the media for inaccurate reporting or passing the buck are other familiar tactics.

However, what these approaches neglect to do is to re-establish a measure of confidence in that person or organisation. This is a critical step to getting back to a situation of some trust, which is an essential ingredient for a successful – or even for a functional – relationship with all stakeholders, whether employees, customers, unions, followers, voters or citizens.

Alice Tybout and Michelle Roehm advocate a four-step approach to manage a crisis response. First assess the incident, making sure that this concentrates on the client's perspective. Second, acknowledge the problem promptly. They advocate avoiding premature statements related to the cause, focusing instead on the process of investigation and the prevention of further harm. Third, formulate a strategic response based on a cost–benefits analysis related to customers' relationships over the long-term. Fourth, implement the response strategy, using the services of marketing and communication specialists (Tybout & Roehm, 2009:85).

An alternate approach that is specifically focused on building confidence and re-establishing trust is the author's A^5 approach. This entails five steps, namely, admit, apologise, take accountability, make amends and do not do it again.

Admitting as a first step is crucial. This may well cause damage, but when the facts are exposed by someone else, such as the press, it is almost certain to cause more damage. If a business leader admits to the problem as soon as it comes to his/her attention, the admission can even be positioned as being transparent.

A good example of this, which is still used as a best practice case study, is the 1982 Johnson & Johnson Tylenol case, when Tylenol capsules laced with cyanide led to seven deaths in the Chicago area of the United States of America. Johnson & Johnson's admission extended to the action of recalling 31 million bottles of Tylenol capsules and offering free replacements in the safer tablet form. After reintroducing their tamper-proof product, in just a year they had regained a 30% market share from a prior 37% share of the market. The role their credo (values or code of ethics) played was pivotal. It shaped, informed and kept aligned the myriad decisions which needed to be made and the priorities which underpinned them (Rehak, 2002).

Admitting can also take the form of keeping relevant parties informed when there is a reasonable suspicion or a formal allegation of misconduct. A South Africa example where this was really badly handled involved Pinnacle Holdings, a prominent provider of information and communication technology products and services. An executive director of the company, Takalani Tshivhase, was arrested on 5 March 2014 (and released the same day on bail) after allegedly offering a R5 million bribe to a member of the South African Police Service to secure a multimillion IT contract. He appeared in court on 24 March 2014 – and the company waited until then before informing the market. The result? A massive 40% fall in the company's share price. The fall was not based on shareholders' pre-emptively judging the executive to be guilty. Instead, it was caused by the failure to communicate. Under the circumstances – the seriousness of the charge and the company's claim that the director is innocent and that it was a "misunderstanding" – shareholders would have expected the company to be transparent and forthcoming. Instead, the information was withheld for almost three weeks – as was shareholders' confidence thereafter (Dolan, 2014 & Wynn, 2014).

Apologising is a critical step, ideally done in conjunction with admitting. It will not right the wrong, but it can create a platform for moving forward. An apology can also have a moral value as well as an economic or business value if, for example, it reduces the damage of an ethical failure.

Mark Sanford, the former South Carolina governor and congressman whose political career appeared to have been ended by a scandal involving an extramarital affair, has had a triumphant return to politics with his victory in April 2013 in a Republican primary for his former South Carolina House. According to Scott Sobel, a crisis management specialist in Washington, a "heartfelt" apology is key in the quest for redemption. For voters, it appears that Sanford's admission and apology were enough to move him from scandal to rehabilitation to recovery (Walshe, 2013).

However, this is one of the things Rupert Murdoch got wrong in his handling of the *News of the World* cellphone hacking scandal in 2011. His apology to the family of Milly Dowler, the murdered British teenager whose phone was hacked, was followed the next day with two full-page public apologies in many of Britain's national newspapers. This should have helped. But its delay, coming more than 10 days after the accusations first appeared and a week after the *News of the World* was closed, eroded the benefit (O'Carroll, 2011).

Taking accountability is an important step that recognises the principle that one should be answerable for what one does. This should build on the guilty party's apology by acknowledging the wrongdoing. The lack of individual accountability – when, for example, subordinates are blamed – often exacerbates unethical incidents and increases public outrage. Taking accountability is also often avoided under the guise of avoiding potential legal liability and costs.

Politicians are often seen as among the people most guilty of avoiding accountability. While the best way of creating accountable governance is to hold guilty officials to account and to impose the prescribed punishment, this is undermined by those who are politically and financially powerful, who enjoy apparent impunity. The result, of course, is to erode citizens' confidence in those politicians or sometimes even in the entire political party.

A recent example where this did not occur concerned the forced adoption of 250 000 babies taken from their mothers in Australia – most of them young and unmarried – between the 1950s and 1970s. In March 2013 former Australian Prime Minister, Julia Gillard, offered a national apology to those affected by forced adoptions. Her apology took accountability for the action and was coupled to the Australian government providing A$5 million to improve access to specialist support, records tracing and mental health care for those affected by forced adoption (ABC News, 2013).

A rare example is when a leader or senior executive escalates the principle of accountability by taking responsibility for the action of a subordinate. This happened when Oswald Grübel resigned as CEO of UBS, a Swiss global financial services company, after the bank revealed that one of its traders had made unauthorised trades that resulted in a $2.3 billion loss for the company. Grübel acknowledged that ultimate responsibility rested with the chief executive (Simonian, 2011).

Making amends is a crucial next step. Clearly this should not be a token gesture, but should recompense those negatively affected appropriately.

This has not yet worked out for Italian pasta maker Barilla following a global storm caused by Guido Barilla, its chairman, who stated during a radio interview in September 2013 that he would never use a gay family in his advertising. Calls by gay rights groups to boycott their products led to the company attempting to make amends by saying it planned to make the company more diverse and to run a more inclusive TV ad campaign. The success will, however, rest on whether they can convincingly show that this is not just "window dressing" (Reuters, 2013).

Another factor to take into account is timing. When the remedy or compensation that is due to the victim is not forthcoming in a timely fashion, it risks invoking the saying "justice delayed is justice denied". In legal terms it means that that if the legal redress that is available to the person who has suffered loss or damage is delayed, it is effectively the same as having no redress at all.

Ensuring that the ethical failure does not happen again is the final step. However, this is easier said than done. It entails not only ensuring that the specific incident does not occur again, but also avoiding another ethical failure. For example, the company found guilty of collusion will suffer as much damage if found guilty thereafter of fraud as it would for a repeat charge of collusion.

The sincere apology that got Mark Sanford back into politics after his breach of ethics did not work for his compatriot, Anthony Weiner. He was a rising Democratic star until his political career imploded in May 2011 when he resigned from the American Congress after a texting scandal involving sexually charged messages and photos. Press reports in April 2013 revealed that he appeared to be orchestrating his comeback, announcing that he was considering running for Mayor of New York City. This included press "confessionals" designed to unlock the power of public contrition and defuse the "sexting" issue (Katz & Lemire, 2013). However, his plan did not proceed after it was revealed that he had sexted yet again (Chumley, 2014).

Ensuring that misconduct does not occur again necessitates taking on the task of improving the ethics in the whole organisation. This entails a sound ethics management system, which includes that ethics is managed proactively, rather than reactively, and that it is managed regularly, rather than on an *ad hoc* basis.

Together, these five steps can contribute significantly to re-building confidence and re-establishing trust among stakeholders.

PART II: ETHICS MANAGEMENT: A DETAILED FOCUS

4.7   FOCUS ON CARE: THE NEGLECTED VALUE

The importance of care as a value within organisations is not often recognised. Recapping a few of the facts about organisational values is a good starting point to explore the relevance of care.

Recapping organisational values

Organisations of all kinds identify themselves with values, whether in a value statement, code of ethics or credo. As discussed in Chapter 1, values are an integral facet of ethics. The organisation's values should represent its fundamental beliefs and are intended to serve as guiding principles that define how employees are expected to behave. Values are also a key determinant of the ethical choices between what is considered good/right and bad/wrong.

As regards the commonality of values, Rushworth Kidder, founder of the American-based Institute for Global Ethics and author of *How Good People Make Tough Choices: Resolving the Dilemmas of Ethical Living*, compiled data from the participants at their many Ethical Seminars held in several countries, including South Africa. He identified a common set of five values, namely, truth or honesty, respect, responsibility, fairness, and love or care or compassion (Kidder, 1995:90–91). An informal review of values across different companies and industries would support this finding that the first four values are widely held: honesty or truth or integrity, respect, responsibility and/or accountability and fairness. But the moral value that is often not appreciated or adopted in the workplace is care.

Care in non-profit organisations

The impact of care is often well illustrated within volunteer, not-for-profit and NGOs to the extent that, in some cases, care is their *raison d'être*. An organisation such as Doctors without Borders is a volunteer organisation that provides assistance to populations in distress, to victims of natural or man-made disasters and to victims of armed conflict irrespective of race, religion, creed or political convictions. Similarly, Oxfam International defines its purpose as helping to create lasting solutions to the injustice of poverty. Care is not included in either of their mission statements or purpose, but their commitment to making a difference clearly reflects deep care for the plight of others.

Care in government

But what about care in governments? This is especially pertinent since their influence extends to a whole country and all its citizens, many more people than are impacted by, for example, a company or even a group of companies.

Care is likely to be reflected in a focus on the citizens' well-being and development. But, according to retired Constitutional Court Judge, Zak Yacoob, the South African government's provision of socio-economic rights, such as housing and proper health services, lacks both care and sensitivity (SAPA, 2014).

The central point of his speech at the University of KwaZulu-Natal in March 2014 was about taking corrupt politicians to task for public sector corruption. This arguably represents the greatest threat to the exercise or perception of care. One reason is that corruption deflects money from its intended purpose to benefit the country's people. Thus, for example, instead of all the funds being put towards building community amenities or delivering public services, only a portion is productively used. This, in turn, risks cost-cutting that can translate into lower quality building materials or reduced services.

However, the more impactful erosion of care occurs when the focus of the power and influence that comes with senior governmental roles and positions is not directed at the well-being of others or serving the public as public servants are appointed to do. When that focus is instead directed at personal gain or self-enrichment, when officials serve only themselves and when those in power amass personal wealth without benefiting their people, it sends a very clear message of lack of care.

There are, of course, pockets of excellence in government that can be credited with great integrity, such as the office of the Public Protector. But the overall statistics for corruption in South Africa and Africa are not encouraging.[13]

Care in business

In the corporate world, care for others often manifests itself as corporate social responsibility or corporate social investment. While this may sometimes be driven by compliance requirements (such as for a BEE rating), it can and should serve as a valuable facet of the company, for example, to build sound relationships with the local community or to improve employee engagement via employee volunteer programmes.

Care is also an important facet of leadership in the workplace. A simple test using two questions but focusing only on the answer to the second question illustrates this point: Who was the best boss you ever had? Why was that person your best boss? While many reasons may be shared, most of them tend to fall into two categories: care, and growth or development (Schuitema, 1998:24–25). The best boss was understanding, caring or supportive in a particular time of need. Or the best boss was committed to helping you grow and develop. These roles – care and growth – represent two crucial aspects of leadership from a motivational and a productivity point of view and are arguably as close as one can get to the "magic formula", the approach that is most likely to get the best out of followers.

But can care really be implemented in the organisation? Would a policy of care be of value or deliver value?

An ostensible area of conflict stems from the fact that the event or circumstance that warrants care, compassion or understanding is often not work related: a sick child, a partner with AIDS, or going through a divorce. If the company subscribes to a "work is work and home is home" view, these issues would fall

---

13 Transparency International's Corruption Perceptions Index produces reliable annual statistics of perceived levels of public sector corruption. The Index reveals that in 2013, sub-Saharan Africa was the most corrupt region. On a scale from 0 as "highly corrupt" to 100 as "very clean", 90% of the sub-Saharan countries scored below 50, compared to an average of two-thirds of countries worldwide (Transparency International, 2013). South Africa's scores over a four-year period were all in the lower, increasingly corrupt half of the scale. In 2010 on a 0 (highly corrupt) to 10 (very clean) scale South Africa scored 4.5, which declined even further in 2011 to 4.1. In 2012 South Africa scored 43 on a slightly changed scale of 0 to 100, which declined to 42 in 2013. (Transparency International. 2010, 2011, 2012 & 2013, http://www.transparency.org/cpi2010/results [Accessed 26 March 2014], http://www.transparency.org/cpi2011/results [Accessed 26 March 2014], http://www.transparency.org/cpi2012/results [Accessed 26 March 2014] and http://www.transparency.org/cpi2013/results [Accessed 26 March 2014].

outside its boundaries – although the impact would still affect the employee at work. But if the company recognises that the impact of work and home co-exist in employees, helping them – as a supportive leader or by providing access to suitable counselling – becomes mutually beneficial.

Another apparent obstacle to the inclusion of care in the workplace centres on the pursuit of productivity and results. It would easily be assumed that accommodating employees' personal problems would erode productivity and have a negative impact on results. But care does not and should not imply that the employees' responsibilities and deadlines disappear. Nor should it negate necessary discipline. Incorporating care into the company's values (as for other values) requires that employees understand what it does and does not entail and what it means in terms of their behaviour and their work. Care should be a two-way exercise that addresses both parties' needs.

An instance when care matters and when it would be of greater value is when the company faces retrenchments or downsizing. This is a tough experience for all affected employees. **How** the process is managed and employees are treated is crucial. Displaying care would involve, for example, that:

1   All the termination meetings are attended by a senior executive such as the HR Director. Avoiding the difficulty and stress of being part of the process by delegating it to a more junior HR employee sends a very uncaring message.

2   Employees' feelings are acknowledged and support in the form of counselling is made available.

3   Assistance is provided to increase the employees' employability, for example, by including training opportunities or skills upliftment in the termination package.

All of these care-based actions can help employees to cope better and could even reduce the likelihood of legal challenges or CCMA (the Commission for Conciliation, Mediation and Arbitration) action for the company. It also sends a positive message to those employees remaining in the company's employ about the extent of the company's care.

Therefore, instead of viewing care as a "soft" approach that allows employees to take advantage of the organisation, it should rather be seen as an "investment" approach, stemming from the recognition that the company's employees represent its intellectual investors.

This approach is supported by the changing role of business in society. Under the banner of good corporate citizenship and a triple bottom line, organisations are increasingly facing two related expectations: to move towards a more inclusive stakeholder approach (as opposed to only shareholders) and to add social and environmental responsibilities as the two extra "bottom lines". Both these factors encompass taking the interests of those affected by the organisation and its operations into account – in other words, caring for their interests. Interestingly, this mirrors one of the key defining features of being ethical, namely, that moral values should apply not only to oneself, but to others as well.

Care and safety

In the context of the expanded responsibility of business beyond just producing profit to include greater emphasis on care for others, safety has become even more of an issue in many industries around the world, such as in manufacturing, construction, transport and mining. When an event reflects the absence of care, it exacerbates the consequences and the public outrage.

The February 2014 vehicle recall by General Motors (GM) for an ignition-switch flaw that was found to be behind 13 deaths is such an example. GM started investigating the problem in 2004. By 2007 it had received more reports, including at least one involving a fatal accident (Associated Press, 2014). At a meeting on 15 May 2009 it was confirmed that the data in the black boxes of Chevrolet Cobalts revealed that a potentially fatal defect existed in hundreds of thousands of cars. But in the months and years that followed, GM claimed that it did not have enough evidence of any defect in their cars. The company acted only in February 2014, recalling 1.6 million Cobalts and other small cars and finally admitting that if the ignition switch was bumped or weighed down it could shut off the engine's power and disable air bags (Stout, Vlasic, Ivory & Ruiz, 2014). The company's subterfuge and delay cost 13 people their lives – and it speaks volumes about their lack of care for the drivers of those vehicles.

Care and ethical decision making

Care can also fulfil another role in both private and public sector organisations and this is as a guide for ethical decision making.

Despite ethics being "the right thing to do", practising it is not always easy. This is particularly so where ethical dilemmas entail two desirable but mutually incompatible "rights".[14] In the workplace this can mean a conflict between two ways of resolving a problem where each option represents a right thing to – when, for example, justice is incompatible with mercy or loyalty with honesty. An ethical dilemma can also arise between social and environmental priorities when business development damages the environment but also creates employment and training opportunities for local communities.

Such ethical dilemmas are different from right versus wrong choices. The official who accepts a bribe and the employee who defrauds the company have not grappled with an ethical dilemma: rather, they have succumbed to what can better be described as "moral temptation" (Kidder, 1995:17). While the ethics of right versus right choices is often ignored in the face of more frequent right versus

---

14 This is a particular focus in Chapter 6.

wrong issues, it warrants particular attention because right versus right issues are likely to be the toughest of ethical decisions to make.

The standard inspirational answer to resolving ethical dilemmas to "do the right thing" often offers little help. There are various approaches that strive to help resolve ethical dilemmas. Rushworth Kidder includes "care-based thinking" as one of three approaches to do so (Kidder, 1995:25). Care-based thinking reflects the golden rule to "do unto others as you would like them to do to you". It has the advantage of being a well-recognised approach and a principle at the centre of most religions. It echoes a philosophy of reversibility, which entails testing actions by imagining oneself in the other person's position and assessing the situation from that perspective. It also requires giving the same weight to the interests of others as to one's own (Singer, 1993:11).

There is therefore a sound argument to be made for embracing the value of care within the workplace. It remains to be questioned why it is still such a neglected value.

4.8 FOCUS ON COLLUSION: HOW ENTRENCHED IS IT IN SOUTH AFRICA?

The fines against construction companies for collusion continue to be in the news and, rightly, raise the question of how entrenched this kind of behaviour is in business in South Africa.

The construction industry is a high-profile example of how extensive anti-competitive behaviour is – or has been. The South Africa Competition Commission identified 300 collusion cases in projects worth R47 billion between 2000 and 2010, which included the 2010 Soccer World Cup stadiums, road works, dams and private-sector projects. However, it limited its investigations into collusion in the construction industry to 160 projects between early 2006 to late 2009, fining 15 construction and engineering firms a total of R1.46 billion for collusion (Allix, 2014).

Advocate Oliver Josie, acting deputy commissioner of the Competition Commission who led the construction industry investigation, said at a University of the Witwatersrand School of Law seminar in March 2014 that senior members of construction and engineering groups were part of numerous cartels in Gauteng, the Western Cape and KwaZulu-Natal (Allix, 2014). The Commission's findings show that this was very entrenched behaviour. Instead of there being competitive bidding processes, the various companies – including senior executives – met regularly and agreed among themselves on issues such as who got which bid, compensation payments for the companies that would not get the bid and inflating margins. According to Josie, normal margins in large infrastructure projects are between 5% and 6%. Margins in the building of the 2010 Soccer World Cup stadiums were found to be up to 16.5%. "One can see immediately that the competitive bidding process was sidelined. Municipalities started to see that costs were much higher than initially anticipated," Josie said (Allix, 2014).

But the construction companies are not the only ones guilty of collusion. It extends to other industries as well. In 2010 Pioneer Foods was made to pay just over a R1 billion settlement for bread price-fixing. In 2012 oil companies Engen and Shell were fined almost R29 million and R26 million respectively for bitumen (a crude oil by-product) price collusion.

This suggests that this kind of conduct has been widespread. But, countering this view, construction company Murray & Roberts claim that of 2 500 tenders submitted by them in the 10-year period to 2010, only 21 transgressions were found, of which 17 were settled with the Commission (Clark, 2013).

But how extensive collusion was is perhaps not the best question. Instead the more pertinent question would be, does it look less likely going forward?

In this regard, the effectiveness of the Competition Commission is definitely discouraging such behaviour, if not eliminating it. In particular, their use of a Fast Track Settlement process was very successful for the construction industry investigations, whereby the guilty companies were offered leniency for admitting liability and for honest disclosure. While this process has been criticised, it undoubtedly allowed the matter to be resolved much more quickly. All too often legal processes take so long that it appears the offenders will never actually be held accountable. In this case, the timeous outcome is to be welcomed. The Fast Track process also succeeded in disbanding the existing construction industry cartels.

The fines imposed by the Commission may not be a serious deterrent, but they do ensure that the guilty companies are identified and held accountable, and that their boards are made to answer to their shareholders. The high level of publicity given to these cases is also likely to act as a disincentive going forward, given the potential to harm the reputation and share price of the companies involved. Pressure is also mounting for the prosecution of the company directors allegedly involved. If this occurs, it will add a whole new dimension to deter future collusive practices

While these consequences may not be a perfect remedy, it is to be hoped that they will serve as a meaningful warning to such conduct.

4.9   FOCUS ON COUNTERFEITING

Counterfeiting is not new. Goods of all kinds have been copied for ages in numerous ways.

Recommendations on responsible business conduct for multinational enterprises by the OECD contain the central message that production can be outsourced, but the corporation's responsibility cannot be outsourced (OECD, 2002). While this is used in relation to supply chains and supply chain ethics, it has an interesting relevance for the counterfeiting problem of so-called "third shift" products.

Counterfeit goods are defined as products bearing a trademark that its maker had no authority to use, while a knock-off is a broad term encompassing counterfeits as well as "look-alike" items that do not use forged trademarks. A "third shift" product, on the other hand, represents an unauthorised product made by an authorised contractor and arises when companies outsource the manufacture of their goods (Parloff, 2006).

The first two shifts produce goods for the company in terms of their outsourcing contract, but the third shift produces additional goods that are distributed and sold for the benefit of the manufacturer. The problem is compounded by outsourcing manufacture often being conducted in foreign countries that do not always have adequate legislation. Detection is hampered by the fact that the third shift goods are identical to the legitimate products in every way, having the same fabric, design, workmanship and trademark labels. The only differences are likely to be the price and the sales outlets (Parloff, 2006). The effects are significant, including not only losses for the original company but, more importantly, damage to brands arising from cheap substitutes, fakes or "third shift" products.

Counterfeiting is, of course, not limited to handbags and clothing. Trade in illicit cigarettes is a problem as regards both counterfeit cigarettes and tax evasion. In South Africa, as elsewhere, steep "sin" taxes comprise the major part of the cost of a pack of cigarettes. Avoiding paying those duties would, of course, increase profits. Therefore, a low-risk environment in terms of being caught and fines that are not too big create the opportunity for an active illicit trade. As evidence of this, the loss in tax revenue from counterfeit cigarettes in South Africa is estimated as being in excess of R2.5 billion annually (*De Rebus*, 2014:5). The author was interviewed by Alec Hogg on the TV programme CNBC Africa Power Lunch in December 2013 about the extent of these activities. What started as a South Africa Revenue Service (SARS) investigation into a local tobacco manufacturer grew into an investigation by SARS and the Hawks, the Police's Directorate for Priority Crime, into South Africa's top three cellphone companies, MTN, Vodacom and Cell C. They were accused of providing the tobacco manufacturer with cellphone records, which were apparently used to spy on SARS investigators in an attempt to deflect their tobacco manufacturer probe (CNBC Africa Power Lunch, 2013).

Counterfeit medicine is one of many more areas of concern. The risks associated with fake medication include that it can be contaminated, contain the wrong ingredients or no active ingredient, be the incorrect dose, or be falsely labelled. The scale of this problem adds to its risks. In October 2013, Interpol announced that more than 100 tons of illicit and counterfeit medication – antibiotics, birth control pills and anti-malarial and analgesic medication – were seized in Angola, Malawi, Swaziland, Tanzania and Zambia. In a statement, Interpol said that "the seized illicit and counterfeit medicines, both branded and generic, are estimated to be worth approximately ... R35 million" (SAPA, 2013a).

In South Africa and elsewhere there are many examples of counterfeiting official documents, such as identity documents, passports, drivers licences, residents permits and work permits. These "legal forgeries" would, of course, be sold. For example, in Umlazi, KwaZulu-Natal, four arrests were made following the sale of a learner's and a driver's licence for R5 500 each (SAPA, 2013b).

The potential consequences are noteworthy: fake driver's licences compromise road safety, false IDs create an opportunity for identity theft, and false passports provide safe passage for criminals or terrorists. An example of the latter was the issuing of a fraudulent South African passport to Samantha Lewthwaite, one of the world's most wanted terrorism suspects and a suspect in the September 2013 attack on Westgate shopping centre in Nairobi that killed 67 people. Even prior to this incident, in February 2009, the lack of security of South Africa passports saw Britain for the first time impose a visa requirement on all South Africans entering the United Kingdom. In her announcement of this in the National Assembly, the then Home Affairs Minister, Nosiviwe Mapisa-Nqakula, disclosed that the decision by the British government was "based on its concerns regarding the ease with which non-South Africans can acquire genuine SA travel documents" and use them to travel to the United Kingdom (SAPA, 2009).

Adding to these negative consequences, the cost of counterfeiting is considerable. Cape Town attorney Vanessa Ferguson, head of anti-counterfeiting at law firm DM Kisch Inc. and the convener of the International Trademark Association (INTA) Middle East, Africa and South East Asia anti-counterfeiting subcommittee, spoke on 13 February 2014 at a round table on the fight against counterfeiting. She said that because South Africa has the largest economy in Africa (now second largest after Nigeria), it is the top destination for counterfeit goods. In addition to significant losses in taxes, she stated that in 2010 counterfeiting was responsible for 14 400 job losses in the textile and clothing industries alone (*De Rebus*, 2014:5). The threat of counterfeiting makes the need to improve anti-counterfeiting measures imperative. In South Africa, the applicable legislation is the Counterfeit Goods Act 37 of 1997, which is jointly enforced by the Companies and Intellectual Property Commission, SARS and the South African Police Service. Organisations working to address this problem include the INTA, a global association of trademark owners and professionals dedicated to supporting trademarks and related intellectual property that is operational in South Africa. Their anti-counterfeiting committees actively work towards improving enforcement and education about counterfeiting.

However, the task of tackling this is enormous. It is an area where consumers can and should join forces with the authorities and the organisations working to eliminate – or at least curb – this scourge. The crucial contribution the public can make is simply not to buy any counterfeit goods at any price irrespective of the quality. As in all market situations, if the demand were to reduce, so too would the supply.

4.10 FOCUS ON CYBERCRIME: WHAT IS THE COST OF SECURITY?

Cybercrime or computer crime in its simplest definition amounts to criminal activities carried out by means of computers or the Internet. Typical instances of cybercrime are the distribution of viruses, illegal downloads of media, phishing and pharming, and theft of personal information such as bank account details or financial data.

Cybercrime is increasingly extremely sophisticated, the depth of which is not addressed here. It is generally enabled by so-called malware (short for malicious software), which extends to software that enables hackers to penetrate computer systems. According to Venkatramana Subrahmanian, a University of Maryland expert on hacker black markets, this type of software, described as "absolute power", can be purchased on "more than two dozen illicit online forums and through at least a dozen clandestine brokers" (*The Economist*, 2013:57).

This form of crime has been massively enabled by the powerful technology and hyper-connectivity that is now a normal part of virtually every organisation and by the ever increasing number of connected people and devices. As noted relative to social media, connectivity and access also have a dark side in that it affords users enormous power and reach. In the wrong hands, cybercrime is the result.

The extent of the problem

There are a lot of statistics and a vast amount of information on incidents of cybercrime that quantify the extent of this problem.

In South Africa one in five small and medium businesses have been targeted by cybercrime (Mungadze, 2014). A March 2014 *Financial Mail* report states that the United States of America's Federal Bureau of Investigation has flagged South Africa as the sixth most active country involved in cybercrime and that a 2013 report by multinational security software company Norton found that South Africa had the third-highest number of cybercrime victims, after Russia and China (Mungadze, 2014).

Cybercrime was one of the focus areas of PwC's *2014 Global Economic Crime Survey*, which canvassed the views of over 5 000 respondents from around the world. The findings reveal that nearly half of the respondents (48%) believe the risk of cybercrime has increased, a 23% increase from 2011, making it the fourth-most reported type of crime in the 2014 survey (PwC, 2014:6). The percentage of all respondents who experienced cybercrime over the survey period was 24% and 11% of these suffered financial losses of more than US$1 million (2014:29).

Quantifying the cost of cybercrime, Microsoft South Africa COO, Zoaib Hoosen, put the business cost at almost US$500 billion: $127 billion to improve security and $364 billion to fix data breaches (Mungadze, 2014).

Looking at the impact and cost of just one incident of cybercrime would suggest that these numbers may be conservative. At the end of November 2013, the biggest retail hacker attack in American history (thus far) occurred at Target, the second-largest retailer in the United States of America. In the days prior to Thanksgiving in 2013, malware designed to steal the details of all credit cards used at the company's 1 797 American stores was installed in Target's security and payments system. In theory, the company was prepared for this scenario. It had begun installing a $1.6 million malware detection tool and had a team of security specialists in Bangalore to monitor its computers around the clock. But when the Bangalore office notified the security team at the retailer's headquarters in Minneapolis at the outset of the attack, they failed to act. The results: 40 million credit card numbers and 70 million addresses, phone numbers and other pieces of personal information were stolen (Riley, Elgin, Lawrence & Matlack, 2014).

The repercussions have been similarly big and continue to grow. Customers and banks have filed more than 90 lawsuits against Target for negligence and compensatory damages. Among many other costs, the company spent $61 million responding to the breach and is covering the cost of fraudulent credit card charges (Riley et al, 2014).

The enormity of the problem was reflected in the World Economic Forum's 2014 *Global Risks* study, in which "digital disintegration" was among the three risks explored in depth. While it is recognised that "so far, cyberspace has proved resilient to attacks", this is viewed against the especially pertinent fact that the online world has always been much easier to attack than defend. The report acknowledges that should the ability to secure online interaction be significantly eroded, it would mean that "the Internet would cease to be a trusted medium for communication or commerce" (WEF, 2014:10). It labels the worst-case scenario "Cybergeddon" (2014:40).

Addressing the problem

Against this backdrop, drafting a company policy seems like a futile response. Although it could be said of virtually all policies that they are essential but not sufficient, it seems more pertinent against such an amorphous risk as cybercrime. However, it is nonetheless one of the basics that should be put in place, especially to ensure that the company's employees understand what is and is not allowed as regards the usage of the company's computers, its network and the Internet and, crucially, that they understand – and do not underestimate – the risks that cybercrime poses.

Drafting an electronic communication policy or an information and communication technology (ICT) policy would typically aim to address and achieve the following:

1 Protect the company and its employees from potential liabilities that may result from the inappropriate and unprofessional use of the network facilities, the Internet and email.

2 Protect and safeguard confidential and proprietary information belonging to the company and its clients from loss or unauthorised access.

3 Protect the company's networks and systems from being disabled, damaged or destroyed by, among other things, the introduction of computer viruses or access by unauthorised persons.

4 Regulate the manner and instances in which employees are entitled to utilise the company's network facilities, the Internet and email facilities.

5 Ensure that the professional reputation and integrity of the company is not harmed or otherwise infringed by the inappropriate and unprofessional use of the network facilities, the Internet and email.

South Africa's response as regard cybercrime and cyber security is generally regarded as poor: it is seen to be lagging behind most countries. Professor Basie von Solms, director of the University of Johannesburg's Centre for Cyber Security, says cybercrime is largely unregulated by government agencies. The Cabinet passed the National Cyber Security Policy Framework in March 2012, which is intended to co-ordinate government actions on cyber security and ensure co-operation between the government, the private sector and civil society on tackling cyber threats. However, as of early 2014, the policy is not yet publicly available. And from March 2012 the Department of Communications took 18 months to appoint the National Cyber Security Advisory Council in October 2013. The Electronic Communications and Transactions Act 25 of 2002, which provides for inspectors to enforce cyber security in South Africa, has not been fully implemented and is now being rewritten (Jones, 2014).

Professor von Solms acknowledges that a lack of urgency in implementing measures to tackle cybercrime is a major obstacle to addressing the threat effectively, as is a shortage of skills (Jones, 2014). Given this, it is not surprising that South Africa ranks poorly relative to other countries.

Around the world there are a range of responses to address cyber security. Among them, counter-intelligence tactics are becoming more common. *The Economist* reported in April 2014 that a midsized American bank has set up a project, known internally as "Honey Banker", to expose fraudulent payments. This involves creating a group of non-existent bankers, with fake email addresses and biographies, whose details appear on bogus web pages not linked to the rest of the bank's website. If a transfer request comes in to one of these aliases, it is likely to be from a fraudster and the bank is able to block the sender's Internet address, pending further investigation (*The Economist*, 2014).

However, a factor that complicates addressing cybercrime is the issue of transparency. PwC's 2014 *Global Economic Crime Survey* reports that:

> ... even when it is detected, cybercrime often goes unreported. Outside of privacy breaches in regulated areas such as identity theft, there are few regulatory conventions requiring disclosure. And often – such as in the case of theft of key intellectual property – there may be compelling competitive reasons for organisations to keep such losses confidential (PwC, 2014:29).

The overarching importance of a trusted, secure cyberspace is behind the World Economic Forum's Global Risks 2014 report strongly advocating that "fresh thinking at all levels on how to preserve, protect and govern the common good of a trusted cyberspace must be developed" (WEF, 2014:10). To this can be added that organisations of all kinds need to take this threat seriously, which requires them to keep themselves informed of the nature and form this can take and source expert assistance to ensure that they have taken the best precautions they can to protect and secure the organisation's critical electronic communications and infrastructure against unauthorised electronic access and related threats.

4.11 FOCUS ON SOCIAL MEDIA: A NEW ETHICAL TERRAIN

The impact of social media is so extensive that it appears to belie the fact that Facebook and Twitter were founded as recently as February 2004 and March 2006 respectively. Clay Shirky, an American writer and teacher on the social and economic effects of Internet technologies and author of *Cognitive Surplus*, explains the profound change this represents: "We have gone from a world with two different models of media – public broadcasts by professionals and private conversations between pairs of people – to a world where public and private media blur, and where voluntary public participation has moved from non-existent to fundamental" (Shirky, 2010:211).

Complements of powerful technology and hyper-connectivity, the participative elements of social media have been accompanied by unprecedented scope, reach and amazing levels of immediacy and permanence of the content. All these features – and potential benefits – have been amplified by increasing scales of usability. As a result, social media has quickly moved from predominantly personal, individual use to use by organisations as well.

The dark side of connectivity

The primary challenge for organisations is not, as some assume, whether or not to allow employees access to social media during working hours or on workplace resources – not least because access via their cellphones makes the use of company resources largely irrelevant. Instead, the workplace challenge that warrants attention is achieving the appropriate and ethical use of social media by employees and avoiding the many risks emanating from unethical online conduct.

The primary ethical issue that this raises stems from the enormous power this communication medium confers on its users. Whereas in the past communication that realised equivalent degrees of influence and reach was limited to governments, large organisations or extremely powerful individuals, today that power lies in the hands of ordinary individuals. And when those individuals lack ethics, the potential for far-reaching ethical breaches is huge. This was recognised in 2012 as a global risk, aptly entitled The Dark Side of Connectivity, by the World Economic Forum: "While significant material and human resources were required in the past to exercise political or economic influence on a global scale, borders have become permeable as power shifts from the physical to the virtual world" (WEF, 2012:11).

This risk is characterised by two pertinent issues. Firstly, social media within an organisation can serve the dual purpose of an employee benefit and a business tool. The latter can deliver significant business value, for example, by providing a targeted audience for legal direct marketing and by enabling the company to better understand its customers and build its brand and brand loyalty. However, this can backfire, as JPMorgan Chase & Co. (JPM) found out. A Twitter debate in November 2013 on the #AskJPM hashtag hosted by a senior JPM investment banker was intended in part to give college students an opportunity to communicate directly with a senior executive. But it had to be cancelled when genuine questions were overtaken by insults and criticisms (Kopecki, 2013).

Secondly, it is often not the company that has established a social media account, but rather employees of those businesses who tweet or post on behalf of the business. This juxtaposition of the individual and the organisation raises a number of ethical issues pertinent to social media.

One such risk relates to who owns these social media accounts and the goodwill they encompass. Spoor & Fischer's *Point* publication mentions the example of Laura Kuenssberg, a BBC political correspondent who tweeted on behalf of the BBC via her Twitter handle, @BBCLauraK. However, when she left the BBC to join ITV, her account was renamed @ITVLauraK and she took her 60 000 followers with her to the competitor news station (Spoor & Fischer, 2013). Had this been a traditional client list, it would have been considered theft – but social media often lacks this clarity. Therefore, for organisations that utilise social media for business purposes, the question of ownership needs to be clearly addressed – whether in employment contracts or otherwise.

Another factor that affects social media is the reality that, because values are often different for different people, organisations are likely to encounter a spectrum of employee values that can differ significantly from the organisation's espoused values. While it is the leader's role to align employees' values behind the values of the organisation, this is generally focused on the application of values in the workplace or the scope of business. However, under the guise of different values, employees' private use of social media – especially senior employees' use – can give rise to many circumstances that can cause damage to the company. This can include, for example, sharing confidential information, defaming a client, or being unduly critical of the company. Added areas of company risk deriving from employee conduct include copyright and trade mark infringements and possible vicarious liability for discrimination and harassment.

New acronyms are a keen reflection of big issues within society. It is therefore noteworthy that "NSFW" – not safe/suitable for work – is now in fairly common use, even with its own Wikipedia entry. An incident in April 2014 illustrated how serious this can be. US Airways, in a Twitter response to a customer complaint about a delayed flight, sent out a very NSFW tweet to its more than 420 000 followers. Included in the message was a link to an explicit pornographic image. Unfortunately, it took nearly an hour before the company recognised the problem and deleted the tweet, enough time for the offensive image to go on to become one of the day's top trending topics on Twitter, ahead of announcements of the Pulitzer Prize winners. Major news outlets – from the BBC to CNN – also ran stories on the incident (Holmes, 2014). While it has been largely viewed as a mistake, Ryan Holmes, CEO of HootSuite, who posted an account of the incident on LinkedIn, says it should be "a wake-up call" for large companies (2014).

The merged individual and company use of social media also creates the potential for ethical dilemmas – most notably, it can place the individual's right to privacy and freedom of expression in opposition to the company's right to appropriately protect its interests. As such, where a company has IT systems in place to monitor possible breaches, the organisation must be conscious that this does not amount to an invasion of privacy. (As the furore around the United States of America's "monitoring" activities have revealed, spying under the banner of safety and security is still spying.)

Social media risks from external sources

Organisations also need to manage the social media risks that can arise from external sources. An incident that illustrates this is the claim made by an artist on social media in October 2013 that Woolworths had plagiarised her work (a design in home furnishings) (Radcliffe, 2013). Although Woolworths' explanation of their processes refuted her claim, this was only after the issue had trended on Twitter and had made national radio news broadcasts.

While in this instance there was no serious damage done, what it nonetheless reveals is that companies need to monitor social media very closely to pick up these kinds of comments and proactively manage their responses before incidents spill over into the national arena. In particular, someone who is familiar with these communication channels should be assigned to this role so that the company is equipped to respond appropriately. The key factor is speed: it allows companies to manage the situation better and to minimise the possible damage.

False identities and hacked identities represent further ethical risks in the domain of social media. A White House official, Jofi Joseph, who was the director of nuclear non-proliferation helping negotiate nuclear issues with Iran, was fired In October 2013 after being uncovered as the author of an anonymous Twitter account which attracted much attention among Washington's power circles for its vitriolic and well-informed insults of public figures (Bruce, 2013).

Hacked identities arguably pose an even greater risk, such as a hacked LinkedIn message from a client claiming a personal problem and asking for money, or a message purportedly from the CEO's social media account to the company's clients berating the company or trying to extort money from them. Keeping the company's social media networks safe from such abuse is clearly imperative.

Managing social media

These issues warrant a social media policy that does more than provide guidelines on the dos and don'ts for the use of social media and clarifies who can and cannot act as a spokesperson for the company. The risk necessitates that the company's policy extends to the appropriate and ethical use of personal social media accounts where that has the potential to affect the company.

The law offers another mechanism to manage the ethical risks of social media. Although there is no legislation that explicitly deals with social media in South Africa, applicable legislation includes the Constitution, employment law, consumer protection law, and intellectual property law. The common law rules of defamation also apply equally to all social network sites and electronic communication media. Legislation has already been effectively applied in this regard, such as in the CCMA, where employees' dismissals have been confirmed as a result of derogatory Facebook updates.

In Australia, in the first Twitter defamation battle to proceed to a full trial (earlier decisions have considered defamatory comments on Facebook), an Australian court ruled that a former student, Andrew Farley, pay A\$105 000 compensatory and aggravated damages for making false allegations about music teacher Christine Mickle on Twitter and Facebook.

Commenting on the case, media law expert David Rolph, an associate professor at the University of Sydney Law School, said: "This case just reinforces that even private individuals are subject to defamation law on social media and should be careful about what they say" (Whitbourn, 2014).

However, a company's pure reliance on the law to manage their social media (or any aspect of ethics) is not ideal – primarily because recourse to legal mechanisms is an after-the-fact event and as such is reactive. An effective ethical management system should be inherently proactive and should incorporate a reactive arm only when necessary.

In this vein, organisations need to acknowledge the limitation of rules and rule-based mechanisms in the management of ethics, especially as a means of controlling the vast capability of social media. While legislation and company policies are essential, they are not sufficient to ensure ethical conduct. Broad-based leadership is needed to build and maintain high levels of ethical awareness and to continually strive to build commitment to common values such as integrity and respect. Together these represent a much more sustainable way to facilitate the benefits and minimise the risks of social media.

Illustrating this, the *Compliance Trends Survey 2013* conducted by Deloitte & Compliance Week found that while 78% of respondents said their businesses have a social media policy in place, more than half of that group admitted that they do not monitor employees' use of social media to see whether they follow the policy (Deloitte & Compliance Week, 2013:6). The reality is that monitoring all social media would be a very onerous task. While the necessary precautions should be taken, these should be coupled with a focus on building willing co-operation as well.

Clearly, the domain of social media is a vulnerable area for companies and it requires a great deal of vigilance. In pursuit of more effective management, Ryan Holmes recommends a number of practical steps:

1   Restrict access to social media accounts by using social media software that has variable permission levels, such as HootSuite.

2   Install "Are you sure?" checks for sensitive accounts.

3   Weed out offensive material with automatic filters.

4   Track changes in message volume with analytics software. Dramatic spikes in the number of retweets, for instance, would be a sure sign that something warranted attention – for good or bad.

5   Provide employees with social media basic training (Holmes, 2014).

What is encouraging in this debate is that achieving an ethical social media space does not rest with any one company. Online security is now considered a public good that necessitates a cooperative effort by all institutions. However, the importance of realising that should not be underestimated. As acknowledged by the World Economic Forum, "maintaining a healthy digital space is needed to ensure stability in the world economy and balance of power" (WEF, 2012:11).

4.12 FOCUS ON SUPPLY CHAIN ETHICS

As the scope of business ethics has developed from a shareholder-centric approach to a triple bottom line approach,[15] so too is the scope of ethics facing another extension. This centres on unethical practices among suppliers.

Supply chain management has long been a facet of normal business practice for many organisations, especially large multinationals. However, this is now being expanded to supply chain ethics, where corporations are increasingly expected to influence and improve ethical conditions among their suppliers. The rationale behind this shift in responsibility is that the large corporates have the power and influence to impact the behaviour of their suppliers.

This initiative is specifically supported by the OECD, and the *OECD Guidelines for Multinational Enterprises (MNEs)* are considered the most comprehensive set of government-backed recommendations on responsible business conduct. They address disclosure, human rights, employment and industrial relations, environment, combating bribery, bribe solicitation and extortion, consumer interests, science and technology, competition, and taxation. The governments of the 46 countries that adhere to the *Guidelines* aim to encourage and maximise the positive impact MNEs can have on sustainable development and enduring social progress (OECD, 2002). The central message being shared is that production can be outsourced, but the corporation's responsibility cannot be outsourced.

However, the title of an article written by Roel Nieuwenkamp, the Chair of the OECD Working Party on Responsible Business Conduct, is illustrative of the challenges inherent in this pursuit – *"Cut and Run, or Stay and Help*?" (Nieuwenkamp, 2014). The challenges that organisations confront to reform or improve issues among suppliers are evidenced, unfortunately, by the worst practices and disasters.

The garment industry is a particular case in point where gross violations in working conditions have cost many lives. One example was the collapse of the Rana Plaza in Savar in Bangladesh on 24 April 2013. The death toll of 1 129 made it one of the deadliest garment-factory accidents in history. Reflecting the abuse the garment workers faced, while other businesses in the building closed when major cracks were discovered, the garment workers were ordered to return to work.

Cocoa production is another area in the spotlight because of the widespread use of child labour. The children are subject to serious exploitation and, in some cases, are the victims of trafficking or slavery. The International Programme on the Elimination of Child Labour (IPEC), part of the International Labour Organisation (ILO), found evidence that suggested that nearly 12 000 of the 200 000 child labourers working in Côte d'Ivoire, the world's biggest producer of cocoa, had

---

15   For further details read the article "Workplace ethics in context" in Chapter 1.

been trafficked (IPEC, 2005:3). In 2012 CNN's David McKenzie travelled to Côte d'Ivoire to investigate children working in the cocoa fields. The investigation found that child labour, trafficking and slavery were still rife (McKenzie & Swails, 2012). This issue was given a major boost when it became a focus of CNN's Freedom Project, which is aimed at ending modern-day slavery.

While the major chocolate companies were slow to address the issue, they are now working together with NGOs to tackle the problem. For example, Nestlé, one of the major chocolate corporations, admits it drew up an action plan, the Nestlé Cocoa Plan, only in response to a report on Nestlé's cocoa supply chain in Côte d'Ivoire by the Fair Labor Association (FLA). On its website, the company has now made a commitment that it will "involve communities in Côte d'Ivoire in a new effort to prevent the use of child labour in cocoa-growing areas by raising awareness and training people to identify children at risk, and to intervene where there is a problem" (Nestlé, 2012).

Two other related factors that are driving a focus on supply chain ethics are corporate social responsibility (CSR) and sustainability.[16] CSR, which is equated with corporate citizenship, is considered to encompass the three dimensions of the triple bottom line, economic, social and environmental, and take into account the interests of affected stakeholders. These actions determine that CSR, in effect, supports a sustainable approach to business. Sustainability and sustainable development is widely accepted as "development that meets the needs of the present without compromising the ability of future generations to meet their own needs" (WECD, 1987:16) and therefore also embraces a social and environmental dimension. The ethical aspect that is being included in these concepts relative to suppliers is not merely to consider those relationships in terms of trading interests or sound business practices (for instance, that supplier payments are processed promptly), but also the suppliers' ethical conduct.

Thus supply chain ethics is also extending to industries where sustainability is the core issue. Palm oil is an example. This is an industry that has been characterised by deforestation, the destruction of peat lands, and human rights abuses. This also has ripple effect consequences: the deforestation in South East Asia is contributing to the endangerment of the orang-utan and the Sumatran tiger.

Numerous organisations – often not-for-profit organisations – are working for change, such as SumOfUs, a new world-wide movement for a better global economy, and Avaas, a global online activist network aimed at bringing people-powered politics to decision making everywhere. The positive outcome is to influence companies such as Kellogg's. In February 2014 Kellogg's committed to work with palm oil suppliers to source fully traceable palm oil that is produced in a manner that is environmentally responsible, socially beneficial and economically viable. The company announced that to do so, it would work through its supply

---

16 These topics are discussed and related to each other in the Chapter 1 article, "Workplace ethics in context".

chain – from suppliers to processors to growers – to ensure that the palm oil it uses is not associated with deforestation, climate change, or the violation of human rights (Kellogg's, 2014).

There are other organisations that are making significant efforts. Unilever, the international consumer products corporation, has been recognised for its supply chain accountability under the banner of sustainability, which is noteworthy given the scale of their supply chain: the company sources materials from over 150 000 suppliers. They manage this on a "prioritise and conquer" approach, setting goals for the top ten raw materials to move them to sustainable supply. For example, Unilever has set a target to exclusively use sustainable palm oil by 2015. The company admits that the return from this investment is variable but they believe that they will "see the return in years to come" (Beard & Hornick, 2011).

The scope of what supply chain ethics can involve and demand could prompt a "cut and run" approach, as recognised by Nieuwenkamp. Companies unwilling to take on this added responsibility may have been able to ignore the abuses happening in factories or plantations in areas remote from their corporate premises. There is even a recognised bias – the concept of indirect blindness – that blinds people to the unethical practice of outsourcing "dirty work" (Bazerman & Tenbrunsel, 2011:62). But for organisations that are reluctant to deal with the ethics of their suppliers, public pressure and, in some cases, the law can affect their inaction.

Public pressure has most frequently taken the form of product boycotts, such as the well-known boycott in the 1990s against Nike in Europe and the United States of America for unacceptable labour practices in their factories in Indonesia and Vietnam (Cushman Jr., 1998). This is especially effective relative to global corporations for which boycotts together with the consequent negative publicity have the potential to affect profits adversely – thereby linking supply chain ethics directly to the company's (economic) bottom line, which is mostly an effective motivator.

In the sphere of legislation, in California compliance with the landmark Transparency in Supply Chains Act of 2010 is now being required. The Act requires qualifying manufacturers and retailers to detail publicly – through a "conspicuous" link on their website – their efforts to eradicate human trafficking, slavery, child labour and forced labour from their worldwide supply chains. In 2013, the California Attorney General reportedly received a list of some 6 000 companies that, based on their tax filings, fall under the Transparency in Supply Chains Act of 2010 (Perkins Coie LLP, 2014). In the United Kingdom, the part of the Companies Act relevant to CSR came into operation in October 2007. The intention of the law reform was to ensure that organisations take their ethical, social and environmental responsibilities seriously and develop productive relationships with employees and those in their supply chain (IoDSA, 2009:11). In South Africa this is addressed in the Companies Act, which requires the social and ethics committee to monitor and report on the company's activities with regard to social and economic development, good corporate citizenship, the environment, health and public safety, consumer relationships, and labour and employment – which clearly includes suppliers.

The added responsibility which this entails should not be underestimated. Effectively managing supply chain ethics will require ongoing time, attention and resources and will therefore incur costs. But the consumer lobby for sustainable products and decent working conditions where their purchases are sourced or made is an ever increasing societal force. It is therefore likely that this will be an increasingly high profile ethical touchpoint that corporations will not be able to ignore.

 *WORKPLACE DISCUSSION*

How effective is your management of ethics?

Is ethics in your organisation viewed as a luxury you can't afford? Is it just an illusion (spoken about but not acted on), or is it recognised as a necessity? Is ethics valued to its full extent?

Consider the following:

- Do you have clear ethical goals that are well understood by your people?

- Do you have an ethics strategy or does it form part of the organisation's overall strategy?

- Do you follow an integrated approach to ethics or is its impact being eroded by a fragmented approach?

- Is ethics managed actively and proactively? Or is it managed reactively (after a problem has arisen) and on an ad-hoc basis?

- What is the level of ethical awareness among your employees? Is it high enough to be the effective management tool it could be?

- Do you consciously strive to avoid ethical gaps, for example, between what is said and done?

- What could be done to manage your organisation's ethics better or more effectively?

- Do you have a clear, comprehensive ethics management system and/or a misconduct management framework?

RECOMMENDED CASE STUDIES AND COMMENTARIES

Humphreys, J, Ahmed, ZH & Pryor, M. 2009. World-Class Bull. *Harvard Business Review*, May. HBR Reprint R0905B.

"Inspired sales ploy or ethical breach?"

Fryer, B. 2008. When Your Colleague is a Saboteur. *Harvard Business Review*, November. HBR Reprint R0811A.

"How can Mark regain his footing after being sabotaged?"

Nunes, PF & Mulani, NP. 2008. Can Knockoffs Knock Out Your Business? *Harvard Business Review*, October. HBR Reprint R0810A.

"Counterfeiting of Ruffin products is on the rise. The company's CEO is obsessed with putting a stop to it. How far should he go?"

Hasson, R. 2007. Why didn't we know? *Harvard Business Review*, April. HBR Reprint R0704A.

"A whistle-blower's lawsuit alerts Galvatrens to deep flaws in its system for uncovering misconduct. How should management and the board respond?"

FURTHER READING

Bazerman, MH & Tenbrunsel, AE. 2011. Ethical Breakdowns. *Harvard Business Review*, 58–65, April. HBR Reprint R1104C.

"Good people often let bad things happen. Why?"

Gentile, MC. 2010. Keeping Your Colleagues Honest. *Harvard Business Review*, March. HBR Reprint R1003K.

"How to challenge unethical behaviour at work – and prevail."

Hall, V. 2009. *The truth about trust in business*. Austin, TX: Emerald Book Company.

Healy, PM & Ramanna, K. 2013. When the Crowd Fights Corruption. *Harvard Business Review*, January-February. HBR Reprint R1301K.

"In Russia, citizens are cleaning up business and government."

Kramer, RM. 2009. Rethinking Trust. *Harvard Business Review*, June. HBR Reprint R0906H.

"Despite deceit, greed and incompetence on a previously unimaginable scale, people are still trusting too much."

O'Toole, J & Bennis, W. 2009. A Culture of Candour. *Harvard Business Review*, June. HBR Reprint R0906F.

"We won't be able to rebuild trust in institutions until leaders learn how to communicate honestly – and create organisations where that's the norm."

Tybout, AM & Roehm, M. 2009. Let the Response Fit the Scandal. *Harvard Business Review*, December. HBR Reprint R0912J.

"A step-by-step guide to tailoring your crisis response."

Endnote

i   Acknowledgement: Original, abridged article first published in *HR Future* magazine.

CHAPTER 5

MEASURING, MONITORING AND REPORTING ON ETHICAL PERFORMANCE

INTRODUCTION

Chapter 5 focuses on the core tasks of measuring, monitoring and reporting on ethics and ethical performance.

The chapter discusses the six reasons why businesses should actively manage, measure and report on their ethics. The Ethics Monitor is explained, including its design and key features and two practical exercises are included: to assess the organisation's level of ethics awareness and management and to conduct an ethics gap analysis. Building on the Ethics Monitor rating, the value of a AAA (triple A) ethics rating is examined. The issue of ethics reporting is addressed both from the perspective of employee reporting via an ethics hotline and corporate ethics reporting, and the chapter includes a sample ethics report.

The recommended discussion focuses on the question, do you know how ethical your organisation really is?

5.1 SIX REASONS TO MEASURE, MONITOR AND REPORT ON ETHICS

Within the workplace there are many reasons that demand, encourage or deter actions. Typically these would fall into two camps: doing something because you have to or doing something because you want to. The latter can be driven by the company's commitment to following a value-based ethical approach or by its desire to be seen to be doing the right thing. Irrespective of the underpinning motivation, the difference is significant because "wanting to" derives from intentional choice by the person or organisation and this internal locus of control makes it more sustainable. On the other hand, "doing something because you have to" is often dependent on an external party insisting on compliance, be that the law or your boss.

The following summary brings together the primary reasons – proactive, reactive, voluntary and obligatory – why organisations should measure, monitor and report on their ethics. These all support quantitative governance, which is considered far more valuable than a qualitative approach.

Reason 1: Companies Act 71 of 2008

Compliance with the law is always a good reason to do something. In this regard, the Companies Act mandated that all state owned companies, listed public companies and any other company that scores more than 500 public interest points in any two of the previous five years (which is based on the number of employees, annual turnover and third party liability) establish a social and ethics committee by 1 May 2012.

The roles and responsibilities of the committee are to monitor social and ethics issues, draw matters to the attention of the board as required, and to report to the shareholders at the company's annual general meeting.[1] The legislation does not specifically detail the intended purpose of the social and ethics committee but it can be interpreted as speaking directly the purpose of the Companies Act, in particular "to promote the development of the South African economy by … encouraging transparency and high standards of corporate governance" (South Africa, 2011:42, s 7(b)(iii)).

Should a qualifying organisation not set up a social and ethics committee the Companies Act Commission may intervene, for example, to engage with the company's shareholders to inform them of a general meeting and to convene a general meeting to appoint a social and ethics committee (South Africa, 2008:84(6); (7)). The financial implications of non-compliance are very low. The law therefore does not serve as a strong motivating factor. It is hoped that organisations will set up the committee for its own merits and the value it can to the effective management of ethics.

Reason 2: *King III*

The recommendations contained in *King III* offer another important reason to assess and report on ethics. Although *King III* is a voluntary code, based on the principle of "apply or explain", compliance with the *King Reports* is a requirement for companies listed on the JSE (IoDSA, 2009:7).

King III advocates the assessment, monitoring, reporting and disclosure of an organisation's ethical performance. Both an internal and an external assessment are recommended. An internal assessment is deemed necessary "to provide the board and management with relevant and reliable information about the achievement of ethics objectives, the outcome of ethics initiatives and the quality of the company's ethics performance", while an external assessment is needed "to provide internal and external stakeholders with relevant and reliable information about the quality of the company's ethics performance" (IoDSA, 2009:27). The external assessment is motivated on the grounds that "the independent assurance of the company's ethics performance, supported by an

---

1   This is discussed in greater detail in Part II of Chapter 3.

assurance statement (as part of the integrated report) enhances the credibility of the information provided to stakeholders" (IoDSA, 2009:27).[2]

King III recognises that the ultimate objective of the assessment, reporting and disclosure is to improve the company's ethical culture by enhancing its ethical performance (IoDSA, 2009:27).

Reason 3: Directors' liability and responsibility

Directors' liability in terms of the Companies Act and directors' responsibility in terms of *King III* warrant that they should **insist** on regular measurement and monitoring to enable accurate reporting of ethics.

Ideally they should support an independent assessment for the greater measure of impartiality it brings and they should stipulate that the views and experiences of all employees are evaluated (and, if relevant, key stakeholder groups) to ensure that they are provided with reliable, credible and accurate information on which to base their decisions. This applies particularly to non-executive directors who have limited opportunity to personally assess the business's ethical behaviour and risks.[3]

Reason 4: Improved management of ethics

The ethics management system in Chapter 4 outlines an optimal approach to managing ethics effectively in the workplace. An important facet of the ethics management system is the measurement, monitoring and reporting of ethics. Its inclusion rests on a number of sound business reasons.

Quantifying ethics makes it much easier to manage ethics. The ethics assessment tool used should clearly identify the areas where the organisation needs to act to improve ethics and how severe the issue is, thereby enabling the company to draw up a prioritised action plan to address problems or to retain ethical strengths.

Assessing the organisation's ethics is crucial to gain an understanding of the organisation's current reality as regards ethics. Its importance is illustrated by a shopping experience: the mall had a superb display portraying where all the stores were located. The problem for the new shopper was that it failed to include a "you are here" icon. Within the workplace, the importance of a "current reality" view of ethics rests on it defining the ethical status from which organisations need

---

2   The Ethics Monitor provides such an external assessment and consequent independent assurance and the ethics rating the survey produces should form a crucial part of the organisation's assurance statement.

3   Using a tool such as the Ethics Monitor will provide directors with reliable and accurate insight into the company's ethical status as perceived and experienced by all its key stakeholders, thereby allowing directors to make better-informed decisions with regard to the company's strategy or necessary remedial actions.

to build. As such, the assessment should canvass the views and experiences of all (or almost all) employees and key stakeholders to ensure a credible picture is obtained. Only once the current status is clear can the organisation decide how and where it should act to improve ethics. Understanding one's current reality also avoids organisations being able to pretend that everything is alright (think Enron) or to embark on an ethics management system on an assumed reality.

Having qualitative results for the organisations ethics also allows the value of ethics to be more fully appreciated. Ethics should be recognised as a key part of the organisation's intangible asset base, but its somewhat indefinite nature can lead to it still not being valued sufficiently. Quantitative assessment results that specify the extent of company's strength and weaknesses can overcome that problem.

Crucially, for the ethical organisation, measuring ethics also provides a clear measure of success. This leads on to the benefits of ethics reporting since a sound assessment rating or good assessment results can be viewed as legitimate "bragging rights" that warrant being shared with key stakeholders. The positive outcome of this is that it can enhance the company's reputation and bolster trust levels.

Reporting also serves a valuable role to keep stakeholders properly informed and this transparency effectively serves as a motivator to keep the organisation's focus on ethics and "encourage" them to maintain good ethics results.

There are therefore a number of reasons why the assessment and reporting of ethics supports the improved management of ethics and why it makes great business sense.

Reason 5: Risk management

Risk management is an important issue for most business. Ethical risks, in particular, need to be managed as the cost of ethical failure can be very damaging to the organisation, whether financially, in the forms of fines or legal settlements, in falling share price or in eroded market and customer confidence. The accurate, regular assessment of the organisation's ethics can provide the organisation with a sound ethics risk profile that highlights problem areas so that these can be remedied promptly, thereby reducing risks.

Monitoring ethics entails that ethics is assessed over time. This also directly supports risk management because it enables the company to track areas of improvements or deterioration.

Ethics reporting also supports risk management although mostly for the organisation's stakeholders. While current or past ethical performance is not a guarantee of future ethics, it is a noteworthy indicator. Thus, by providing stakeholders with relevant information about the organisation's ethics, it allows them to make better informed decisions relative to their relationship with the company, thereby reducing their risk.

Reason 6: Reputation management

Since the comprehensive assessment of an organisation's ethics and regular reporting both illustrate the organisation's ethical status, for ethical organisations this can provide an opportunity to increase the recognition they get for this asset from their stakeholders (such as shareholders and potential investors). This, in turn, can enhance the organisation's reputation, which is very advantageous.

A good ethical reputation, which can be equated with a high level of "ethical capital", brings with it many advantages. It increases brand equity, favours easier access to capital and a lower cost of capital, enhances employee commitment and customer loyalty, supports the recruitment and retention of top talent for employees and the board, and supports good stakeholder relationships.

Collectively there are, therefore, many sound reasons why organisations should measure, monitor and report on their ethics. The only decision should be how to go about it, not if.

5.2   THE ETHICS MONITOR

The Ethics Monitor is a web-based ethics survey that was designed and developed by the author in 2007 based on her development work and teaching in the field of workplace ethics. Its aim is to provide practical support to organisations to improve and more effectively manage their ethics and to build an ethical culture both within organisations and across industries.

The Ethics Monitor was designed to be easy to use and to produce meaningful results. The design features detailed below illustrate how they contribute to delivering high quality results. However, the ultimate value of the survey lies in the organisation acting on the results. The absence of any action is likely to erode the effectiveness of the survey, not least because it would diminish the employees' participation over time.

Company ethics surveys

Within the organisation the survey measures its ethical status based on the experiences and perceptions of its stakeholders, including executive management, employees and, if required, external stakeholders.

The Ethics Monitor survey differs from an ethics audit or an audit-type process, which would typically check for the presence or absence of policies and procedures and evaluate awareness based on a select sample of employees. Instead, the Ethics Monitor survey appraises ethics at a deeper level based on actual behaviour and performance and on the effectiveness of mechanisms that should increase ethics or reduce misconduct (such as policies). The Ethics

Monitor is therefore able to produce in-depth results that both quantify ethics and provide meaningful management information to address any areas of concern.

Industry ethics survey

An extended version of the Ethics Monitor has recently been developed to assess the ethical status of an industry. It is especially well suited to industry bodies that have the responsibility of managing their industry's reputation and governance. The industry survey would typically comprise multiple companies and consolidated results would be produced derived from the results of all participating member organisations. These would be shared with the industry body. (The industry survey can also be used for a holding company that has many subsidiary organisations.)

The principle of anonymity is also relevant for this type of survey. Therefore, all results from the participating companies would be anonymised, for example, by assigning numbers to each company instead of using the names.

The industry survey also accommodates giving each individual company its own results in the same manner as a company survey.

The industry survey serves as a useful tool to allow industry-type associations to play a meaningful role in the advancement of ethics in their industry and the proactive management of the industry's ethical perceptions. The survey would provide them with all the results for individual companies as well as enabling them to address any gaps or ethical risks that require industry-wide action, for instance, via custom designed training initiatives.

Survey concepts, questions and scale

The survey is based on a model comprising two key ethical concepts: behaviour and an ethical boundary.

Behaviour

Behaviour ranges from very ethical to extremely unethical. Unethical behaviour can vary from relatively minor misdemeanours to serious misconduct. The degree of ethical behaviour also ranges from low to high, directly mirroring the organisation's level of ethical maturity. Higher levels imply that ethical conduct derives primarily from commitment to shared values. This represents a sustainable foundation for ethics, because behaviour is driven by personal decisions. Lower levels of ethical behaviour reflect lower ethical maturity, indicating mainly rules-based behaviour where ethical action is largely a function of compliance with laws, rules, regulations and policies (often in the form of a code of conduct). Managing ethics by rules alone represents a "high maintenance" approach in the sense that it requires time and effort to supervise and police behaviour, and its effectiveness rests heavily on the successful enforcement of the rules.

Ethical boundary

An ethical boundary assesses the organisation's degree of inclusion or exclusion relative to stakeholders and the extent to which the organisation follows a triple bottom line approach (recognising an economic bottom line as well as social and environmental responsibilities). It is measured on a scale from inclusive to exclusive. High inclusivity reflects an ethical boundary that encompasses a wide range of stakeholders and affected groups as well as social and environmental concerns. High exclusivity, on the other hand, indicates a narrow ethical boundary that excludes all or most other stakeholders and the effects of the organisation's behaviour on parties other than itself. The ethical boundary therefore addresses one of the primary features of ethics, namely that ethics applies to others as well as to oneself.

Survey questions

Via these concepts, the survey questions explore and produce results for the primary ethical issues in the workplace, for example:

1   To assess employees' commitment to values.

2   To assess the extent to which leaders live the organisation's values.

3   To measure the effectiveness of the factors that promote ethical behaviour and to identify which factors best promote ethics.

4   To measure the effectiveness of the factors that reduce misconduct and to identify the factors that best reduce unethical behaviour.

5   To assess the extent of specific incidences of unethical conduct.

6   To evaluate the extent to which employees feel valued.

7   To measure the degree to which the organisation's values apply to its external stakeholders.

8   To assess how much the organisation does towards fulfilling its social and environmental responsibilities.

The survey includes 60 standard questions. The questions are written in clear language to ensure that respondents understand what they are being asked.

Survey scale

The scale for all survey questions ranges from "not at all" to "a lot", which is underpinned by a graphic (visual) progression of buttons. The scale does not include a numeric score. For example, a question would ask: "To what extent do your leaders live the value of respect?" The respondent would click on the button that represented his/her view between "not at all" and "a lot". As an added precaution to ensure that respondents score the questions accurately, the scale options "not at all" and "a lot" include smiley and sad faces as appropriate to the question.

Survey format

Although the Ethics Monitor is largely used in its web-based format, it is also available in hard-copy format where this is more convenient, for example, when employees do not have electronic access. The hard-copy survey can also be used for blue collar workers.

The survey is, however, not ideal for employees with low levels of literacy in English. This obstacle can be overcome in good measure by encouraging employees to engage the support of a trusted colleague to explain the questions to them as they complete it to ensure that they are expressing their views accurately.

Anonymity and confidentiality

The Ethics Monitor survey is designed to protect the anonymity of all respondents and the confidentiality of all responses. Therefore, the completion of the survey does not require the respondent's name and it does not use any passwords or other individualised log-in details that would create the perception that the response could be linked to the respondent. The survey is accessed via a single hyperlink that is common to all respondents. The survey also does not include any open-ended questions as these too could possibly be used to identify employees. An added security feature is that the survey is also located on the Ethics Monitor website, not on the company's.

In circumstances of low trust when employees think that even completing the survey on their own computer would allow response to be identified, it is recommended that the organisation sets up "Internet café" computer facilities in a private space in the office.

The value of the anonymity and confidentiality is immense because it improves the quality of employee responses by allowing them to respond honestly without fear of any come-back.

In many cases just the perception that responses are not confidential will distort the results. When, for instance, a telephonic survey is done, the employee at the other end of the telephone may still feel vulnerable to being exposed even if the survey is being conducted by a trustworthy external organisation. This perception has the potential to elicit the responses that the employee thinks would be acceptable, would not cause trouble, or would be what the company wants to hear.

The possible down-side of the anonymity in the Ethics Monitor survey is that employees could complete the survey more than once. This could sometimes be identified, for example, if more respondents completed the survey for a department or work level than the actual number. In such a circumstance, this could be taken into account in evaluating the results. However, it cannot be prevented. The likelihood of this would be far greater for dissatisfied employees, who may use the opportunity of the survey to repeat and emphasise their negative feedback. While this would skew the results, it is important that the organisation hears the negative messages too. It also serves as an indicator for action, for instance, to investigate what is behind such an exaggerated response. This potential problem is considered an acceptable risk in order to protect respondents' anonymity.

Survey timing

An obstacle to conducting the survey is often that employees are disinclined to do so, mostly because they feel it will take too long. The Ethics Monitor was designed with this inherent reluctance in mind. The survey takes about six minutes to complete, which lends itself to much higher percentages of employees being prepared to complete the survey.

Customisation

The Ethics Monitor is available as a standard or a customised survey. The customisation of the survey is done according the organisation's branches, departments or divisions, work levels, values, and the stakeholder groups that are pertinent to the organisation. An especially valuable facet of the customisation is that it allows the inclusion of additional questions to address company-specific issues or concerns. Therefore, for the mining industry, the added value would be safety; while for the government department, there may be extra questions around procurement abuses.

The customisation adds real value because it produces detailed results for all the organisation's branches, departments and work levels. The limitation is that all such criteria need to include at least ten employees to protect their anonymity. For example, if the HR department comprises only five employees, it will be combined with another department to provide the sense of "safety in numbers" for the respondents.

The customisation is restricted for organisations with less than 100 employees. In this case a standard survey is recommended to protect the anonymity of the respondents. Thus, for departments, the survey would read "all departments" and "all employees" for the work levels. This survey can be semi-customised with the inclusion of the organisation's values, stakeholder groups, and additional survey questions to address company-specific issues.

Credibility of the results

Because the survey provides the opportunity for all employees (and external stakeholders, if required) to express their views and experience of the organisation's ethics, it produces really credible results. This cannot be achieved via a select sample of employees.

As the Ethics Monitor is such a quick survey it also achieves good response rates. The average survey response rate within client organisations is about 70%.

Together these two factors – widespread opportunity and high response rates – avoid the results being challenged instead of being acted on. When results are not seen as reliable, the risk is that they will be called into question by management if the results are worse than they expected or challenged by employees when the outcome is better than they expected.

The credibility is also strengthened by the anonymity and confidentiality of the survey and the fact that the survey is not located on the organisation's website. With regard to the latter, this means the company does not have access to the raw data and the results can therefore not be manipulated.

Results

The design features and the quality of the questions translate into results that provide an in-depth understanding of the organisation's current ethical status. The results identify and prioritise actions to improve its ethics. Therefore, the results also serve as a comprehensive ethics risk analysis, with insight into the organisation's ethical strengths, vulnerabilities and weaknesses that should respectively be grown, monitored and addressed.

The results include an overall ethics rating for the organisation and scores for its performance by branch, department and work level relative to the two ethics concepts (ethical and unethical behaviour and ethical boundary) and supporting questions.

Ethics rating

Ethics ratings are ideally assessed on two key ethical concepts, behaviour and an ethical boundary, which is how they are derived for the Ethics Monitor. Based on the organisation's behaviour and ethical boundary results, it would be rated on a scale ranging from AAA to D, as indicated in Figure 5.1.

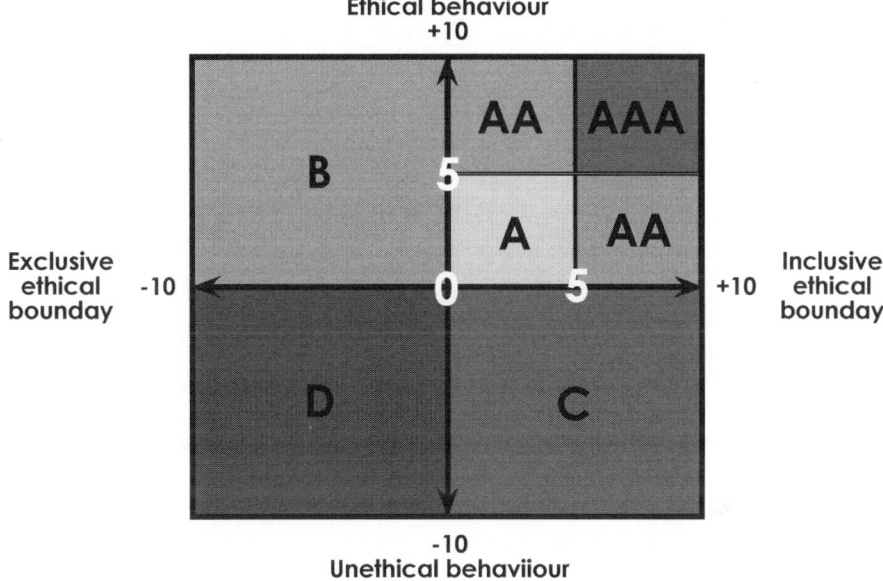

Figure 5.1: Ethics rating as per the Ethics Monitor survey model

A model of the two key concepts of the Ethics Monitor survey, behaviour and an ethical boundary, both on scales of +10 to –10. The model illustrates how the scores for these concepts translate into an ethics rating according to the quadrant in which the two scores intersect. AAA is the highest rating, which declines to D as the worst rating.

AAA, AA and A ethics rating

A AAA rating reflects the highest levels of ethical behaviour and ethical maturity and an ethical boundary that accommodates a very high degree of inclusivity relative to stakeholders and social and environmental issues.

The rating declines to AA when ethical maturity declines and ethical behaviour is more a function of compliance with rules and regulations (in the bottom right block of quadrant A/AAA in Figure 5.1), or when the degree of inclusiveness of the organisation's ethical boundary decreases relative to its stakeholders or the triple bottom line (in the top left block of quadrant A/AAA in Figure 5.1).

An A rating still reflects an ethical status, but illustrates a situation where both ethical behaviour is at its lower levels because it is largely compliance driven, and where the inclusiveness of the organisation's ethical boundary is not seen to encompass its stakeholders or its social and environmental responsibilities fully.

B ethics rating

While this indicates ethical behaviour, the ethical boundary falls within the exclusive zone, which shows that ethics is practised primarily with reference to the organisation's own interests (such as economic goals), excluding the interests of all or most other stakeholders or a triple bottom line. Although, strictly speaking, this represents an ethical status, prioritising profits and self-interest is increasingly being considered unacceptable in the face of the ongoing importance accorded to the interests of other affected parties and environmental concerns.

C ethics rating

This rating indicates unethical behaviour, but with an inclusive ethical boundary. This depicts an unusual situation that rarely occurs, in which the benefits of unethical conduct are not purely for self-gain, but are shared with others. A popular example of this is Robin Hood, who stole from the rich and gave to the poor.

D ethics rating

This is the worst ethical rating. It represents both unethical behaviour and an exclusive ethical boundary, where the misconduct is purely for self-gain, to the exclusion of the interests of others or the impact of such misconduct on other stakeholders, affected communities or the environment.

Ethical behaviour and ethical boundary results by branch, department and work level

Adding to the organisation's ethics rating, detailed results quantify the organisation's ethics and ethical performance by branch, department and work level relative to the two ethics concepts (ethical and unethical behaviour and ethical boundary) and relative to the various clusters of questions.

The results produced include the following:

1   An in-depth understanding of the organisation's current ethical status

2   Credible ethics results based on the experiences and perceptions of all employees

3   An accurate measurement of ethics for reporting purposes in line with *King III* and the Companies Act social and ethics committee

4   Actions to improve ethics identified and prioritised

5   A comprehensive ethics risk analysis, with insight into the organisation's ethical strengths and weaknesses

6   The ability to monitor ethical progress or regression over time throughout the organisation, and

7   An ethics rating to increase the organisation's reputation and ethical capital with external stakeholders.

The survey also produces specific results for each cluster of questions (as outlined above under the subheading "Survey questions").

The survey results and recommendations would typically be prepared in the form of a PowerPoint ethics report. This would be shared with the organisation's executive team to clarify the findings and to promote action to improve ethics. Results are also shared with the survey respondents if feasible. The latter is especially impactful: the transparency is viewed very positively and serves to build trust in the company's commitment to address any problem areas. The trust would, of course, be broken if the company did not fulfil its undertaking to act to remedy problems, but the rewards when it does are often very high – arguably disproportionally so, which the company should strive to achieve.

Ethics reporting

The Ethics Monitor survey produces accurate, reliable quantitative results of the organisation's ethical status and performance for reporting purposes in line with the Companies Act social and ethics committee requirements (if applicable) and *King III* recommendations. The ethics rating should form part of the assurance statement recommended by *King III*.

Ethics monitoring: survey frequency

The survey is intended to be used annually. This allows organisations to monitor their progress over time. It can, therefore, track any regressions, monitor the success of remedial actions to address sensitive areas and ensure the organisations' areas of strength are being maintained.

5.3   PRACTICAL EXERCISE: ETHICS CHECKLISTS

The importance of ethics assessment as a facet of a sound ethics management system has already been established. A comprehensive ethics assessment can be done with an instrument such as the Ethics Monitor. However, for smaller organisations, two in-company exercises are useful.

The Ethics Awareness Checklist

The Ethics Awareness Checklist serves as a quick and easy appraisal of the level of a company's ethics awareness, understanding and management. If the majority of the employees answer "no" or "don't know" to any of the nine questions, it indicates that further action should be taken to more effectively manage the organisation's ethics.

1	Do the directors, executives and employees share a common understanding of what constitutes ethics in your organisation?	Yes	No	Don't know

A clear, shared understanding is an essential foundation for ethical behaviour. It also serves to build greater levels of ethical awareness. Without a common understanding, differences can arise from divergent personal values, among other issues.

2	Do you understand why workplace ethics is important?	Yes	No

Insight into the benefits of sound ethics and the potential costs of unethical conduct strengthens employees' understanding of why workplace ethics matters in the workplace. Benefits include being able to attract and retain key staff and board members, strong customer loyalty, increased investor and market confidence, and easier access to capital. Costs can range from financial losses to fines, damaged reputations and, in extreme cases, jail sentences and the closure of the business.

3	Has your company appointed someone to manage ethics and to whom queries and problems can be referred?	Yes	No	Don't know

Smaller companies are generally not required to set up a social and ethics committee. However, all companies should appoint someone to manage ethics and to handle queries or problems. This could be an ethics officer or, if the company is too small to warrant a fulltime position, it could be a senior member of staff such as the CEO or the HR director.

4	Does your company have a clear ethics goal and a supporting ethics strategy?	Yes	No	Don't know

The company's ethics goal (such as building and maintaining an ethical culture) should be clearly articulated so that all employees understand what the company is aiming to achieve. Understanding or having some insight into the strategy means that more people are able to support and give effect to the strategy.

5	Does your company have an ethics management system?	Yes	No	Don't know

An ethics management system consolidates the ethics initiatives to create a greater impact on employees. In the absence of a sound, integrated ethics management system, the company risks its ethics initiatives being disjointed and not achieving the intended benefit.

The ethics management system needs to include six focus areas: ethics goals and strategy, leadership commitment, ethical standards, ethical awareness, ethics assessment and reporting and operational ethics

	Yes	No	Don't know
6 Does your company manage its ethics proactively and regularly?			

The benefits of ethical conduct and the costs associated with misconduct warrant that ethics is **not** managed reactively or on an ad hoc basis. Effective ethics management rests on proactive, regular attention.

	Yes	No
7 Does your company provide opportunities for its people to learn how to handle ethical dilemmas effectively?		

Effective ethics training can help build and reinforce an ethical culture. It also provides the opportunity to address ethical challenges in the workplace, makes employees more aware of ethical choices and decisions, and equips managers and supervisors with the necessary knowledge and understanding to manage ethics better among their people.

To ensure that ethics training programmes are impactful, the following design features should be taken into account: do not teach what the participants already know, take the "knowing–doing" gap into account, teach ethics based on your company's ethical reality, not on abstract theory, and combine appropriate theory and practice.

	Yes	No	Don't know
8 Does the company have an ethics policy, a code of conduct or other polices that provide clear guidelines about what behaviours are and are not acceptable?			

One of the key features of an effective ethics management system is defining the company's ethical standards in an ethics policy and/or a code of conduct with supporting policies.

	Yes	No	Don't know
9 Does the company report on its company's ethics?			

Ethics reporting is a recommendation of *King III* and a requirement of the Companies Act social and ethics committee. An ethics report should include the activities of the social and ethics committee, details of the company's ethics management system, and the annual measurement of the company's ethics, all of which should be presented in relation to the organisation's ethics goal/s and strategy.

Assessing ethical status: values gap analysis

A simple approach (also suited to smaller organisations) to get insight into the organisation's ethical status is to do a gap analysis of the actual values versus the desired values.

To do the exercise: List on Table 5.1 the company's stated values and any other values that are desirable. Score each of the company's values twice on a scale from 1 to 10, using 1 as the lowest score, and 10 as the highest. Firstly, score the value in terms of the extent to which it is actually practised and supported within the company; and secondly, the extent to which it would be desirable for it to be practised and supported. Use different colours or symbols to identify the different scores, for example, circle the score for the actual status and cross the score for the desired status.

The gap will reveal where action is required and to what extent. The exercise should include a discussion about why the gaps exist and/or what caused the differences, which should shape the action taken to bridge the gap.

A further distinction can be to consider the extent to which the company's internal views would be shared by other stakeholders, for example, suppliers or customers (Schoeman, 2012:41–43).

Table 5.1: Gap analysis of actual versus desired values

Value 1	Low	1	2	3	4	5	6	7	8	9	10	High
Value 2	Low	1	2	3	4	5	6	7	8	9	10	High
Value 3	Low	1	2	3	4	5	6	7	8	9	10	High
Value 4	Low	1	2	3	4	5	6	7	8	9	10	High
Value 5	Low	1	2	3	4	5	6	7	8	9	10	High
Value 6	Low	1	2	3	4	5	6	7	8	9	10	High
Value 7	Low	1	2	3	4	5	6	7	8	9	10	High
Value 8	Low	1	2	3	4	5	6	7	8	9	10	High

The actual extent to which values are practised in the company is scored in comparison with the score for the extent to which it would be desirable that the value should be practised. The scale ranges from 1 as the lowest, worst or least applicable score to 10 as the highest, best or most applicable score. The exercise generates two scores for each value (using different colours or symbols to identify them) which illustrate the gap between the actual and desired practice of values. Collectively the scores for all participants indicate the extent and severity of the gap, which provides an opportunity to act to correct the imbalance.

5.4 DOES YOUR COMPANY HAVE A AAA ETHICS RATING?

Ratings of all kinds are widely used to assess something in terms of quality and/ or quantity. For example, credit ratings are widely recognised as fulfilling an important role in evaluating the credit worthiness of businesses and governments. The rating is based on the rating agency's assessment of risk of the debtor's ability to pay back the debt and the likelihood of default. The value of a AAA investment grade rating is well accepted, as is the negative impact when a rating is downgraded.

Similarly, an ethics rating can add significant value to enable investors and other stakeholders to assess an organisation's ethical risks **and** for organisations to get recognition when they have been operating ethically. This extends to acting sustainably, since ethics is synonymous with a triple bottom line that is core to sustainability.

Despite its obvious value, organisations are rarely being recognised for being ethical. By way of an informal assessment I have asked audiences at various local conferences and workshops to identify just three companies operating in South Africa that have really distinguished themselves as being ethical. The very minimal number of companies identified is a telling sign – not that there are no ethical companies in South Africa, but rather than very few organisations have been widely recognised for being ethical or for their sound ethical culture. This represents a real waste of ethical capital. Seeing that organisations rarely waste other sources of capital, it is prudent that companies quantify their ethics to ensure they can leverage its inherent benefits. An ethics rating, specifically a AAA ethics rating, serves as a direct reflection of the organisation's ethical capital.

The value of an ethics rating is further increased by the correlation between ethics and risk. Transparency International's Corruption Perceptions Index offers reliable measures of public sector corruption in different countries. The top six least corrupt countries globally (that is, the most ethical countries) for the three year period 2011 to 2013 (the most current results) are listed in Table 5.2.

Table 5.2: Corruption Perceptions Index ranking for the top six least corrupt/most ethical countries globally

2011 (Transparency International, 2011)	2012 (Transparency International, 2012)	2013 (Transparency International, 2013)
1st New Zealand	1st New Zealand	1st New Zealand
2nd Denmark	1st Denmark	1st Denmark
2nd Finland	1st Finland	3rd Finland
4th Sweden	4th Sweden	3rd Sweden
5th Singapore	5th Singapore	5th Singapore
6th Norway	6th Switzerland	5th Norway

Comparing this cluster of countries with the findings of the latest (Q1 2014) Euromoney Country Risk (ECR) survey reveals a perfect overlap. Their tier 1 rating indicates the countries with the very lowest risk globally, and all the countries that feature as the most ethical according to the Corruption Perceptions Index, are classed as tier 1: New Zealand, Denmark, Finland, Sweden, Singapore, Norway and Switzerland, among a few others (ECR, 2014). This confirms what most people would intuitively assume: that sound ethics, as identified by an ethics rating, is associated with lower risk and, conversely, that a lack of ethics carries a higher risk.

An ethics rating, as the outcome of an ethics assessment, also serves as a crucial facet of an ethics management system. As such, it contributes towards the more effective management of ethics and, thereby, to reducing ethical risks and strengthening the organisation's ethical culture.

For these reasons, an ethics rating should be indispensable.

A web-based ethics survey such as the Ethics Monitor delivers just such an ethics rating, ranging from AAA, as the best rating, through AA, A, B and C to D as the lowest rating.[4] The confidentiality of the Ethics Monitor survey provides a mechanism to enable employees to report unethical behaviour honestly and more easily, without exposing themselves to reprisals. Adding to this, the assessment of ethics by means of the survey is based on the assumption that, when there is a breach of ethics, it is likely that someone within the organisation other than the perpetrator is aware of it. The survey results therefore provide a comprehensive ethics risk analysis (of ethical weaknesses and strengths) and identify and prioritise the necessary actions to improve ethics. Since the survey is

---

4   This is discussed in detail in the previous article in this chapter, "The Ethics Monitor".

based on the responses of all employees and executives, it also offers a credible, accurate measurement of ethics for reporting purposes.

Organisations should use their ethics rating to increase their reputation and to build their ethical capital with external stakeholders. For example, being able to increase the degree of trust between the company and its stakeholders would lead to many benefits, such as quicker, easier and more sustainable negotiations. And, in the same way that credit ratings are intended to be comparable across different sectors and regions, so, too, can the Ethics Monitor rating be used as a benchmark within industries, market sectors and regions.

Therefore, as governments and organisations aspire to the highest credit rating, so too should they aspire to a AAA ethics rating. To realise and retain this level of ethics rating necessitates ongoing commitment from leadership to a sound ethical culture. Ethics also need to be clearly identified as a high priority organisational goal and included as a core feature of the organisation's strategy. In the absence of this support, the pursuit of ethics risks being overtaken by operational targets. The concluding question is therefore whether governments and businesses have the political and leadership will to commit to this goal.

5.5 THE CASE FOR AN ETHICS DUE DILIGENCE

Due diligence is a term most commonly used for the process whereby a potential purchaser evaluates a target company for acquisition. It amounts to an investigation of a potential investment that includes reviewing all financial records plus anything else deemed material to the sale. Offers to purchase are usually dependent on the results of due diligence analysis.

The value of a due diligence is well recognised. The *2014 M&A Outlook Survey* conducted by KPMG LLP among over 1 000 merger and acquisition (M&A) professionals in American organisations found that an effective due diligence was considered to be the third most important factor for the success of the deal (KPMG, 2014).

But, as for many other business processes, the importance of a due diligence is well illustrated by its failures. One example was the due diligence conducted for Hewlett-Packard (HP) on Autonomy, the United Kingdom software company. HP subsequently claimed that Autonomy had inflated the value of the company prior to the takeover, which led to a write-off of more than $8.8 billion related to allegedly fraudulent accounting at Autonomy. This, in turn, led to HP facing $1 billion lawsuit from its shareholders. The class action suit named eight defendants who oversaw the botched deal and it accused them of conducting "cursory due diligence on a polluted and vastly overvalued asset". Among the defendants were HP's chief executive, Meg Whitman, her predecessor, Léo Apotheker, the company's former chairman, Ray Lane, and Autonomy founder, Mike Lynch (Garside, 2013).

While a breach of ethics is central to scandals such as this one, ethics has a further relevance for a due diligence.

A due diligence should serve to confirm all material facts, for example, in regard to a sale and it is intended as a means to prevent unnecessary harm to either party involved in the transaction. To realise this, a due diligence checklist would typically include a focus on issues such as assets, contracts, customers, employee agreements and benefits, facilities, plant and equipment, finances, the relevant legislation, suppliers and tax. The focus of a due diligence can also differ, from a financial due diligence to a legal due diligence or a commercial due diligence (Patel, 2013:4–5).

However, neither ethics nor an ethical due diligence is recognised in these facets of a due diligence. Nor was ethics identified among the top due diligence issues by respondents in KPMG's *2014 M&A Outlook Survey*. (The top three issues were assessment/volatility of future revenue streams at 34%; quality of earnings at 19%; and quality of assets at 11%) (KPMG, 2014).

But, in the absence of ethical conduct, the facts can be skewed by the company being sold, making the acquisition a future risk to the purchaser. This can range from liabilities and penalties associated with fraudulent practices to having to change the company's entire culture. And courts are unlikely to be sympathetic to a purchaser that neglects the due diligence process, either by failing to investigate adequately or by ignoring the information discovered.

Clearly the difference between an ethical and unethical company is noteworthy and consequently ethics – or, specifically, a lack of ethics – should be considered a material fact. As such, an ethics assessment should form a fundamental part of any due diligence to quantify the organisation's ethics (for example, in terms of an ethics rating) and provide meaningful information about any areas of concern. Taking into account *King III*'s recommendations, the assessment should be conducted by an external party because "the independent assurance of the company's ethics performance ... enhances the credibility of the information provided to stakeholders" (IoDSA, 2009:27).

Conducting an assessment of the organisation's ethics as part of a due diligence also adds considerably to the depth of insight into the target company. This warrants that the assessment extends beyond an audit-type exercise that would typically check for the presence or absence of policies and procedures and evaluate ethics awareness based on a random sample of employees. Instead, the assessment needs to evaluate ethics at the level of behaviours and practices among all relevant stakeholders and to assess the effectiveness of the mechanisms that should increase ethics or reduce misconduct (such as leadership and the company's values, policies, rules, and code of conduct). A comprehensive ethics assessment, in effect, should serve as an effective risk analysis because it illustrates ethical strengths and what needs to be done to remedy ethical weaknesses.

There are five additional issues that should be investigated to evaluate the status of a company's operational ethics:

1   If the company has a social and ethics committee, is this viewed as a compliance exercise, or is it expected to add value? The difference is a noteworthy reflection of the importance of ethics.

2   Does the company have an ethics strategy and clearly identified ethics goals? In the absence thereof, initiatives and actions to create an ethical workplace are likely to be disjointed and lose the benefits that an integrated approach can deliver.

3   Does the company report clearly on its ethics? It should, as ethics reporting is a specific recommendation of *King III* and a requirement for the Companies Act social and ethics committee.

4   How does the company manage its ethics? Dealing with ethics on an *ad hoc* basis and reactively after there is a failure of ethics as opposed to managing ethics regularly and proactively in terms of a sound ethics management system has major implications for the quality of the company's ethics management.

5   Does the company provide meaningful ethics training? Ethics training is an effective way to address ethical challenges and establish a high level of ethical awareness, both of which contribute to building and maintaining an ethical culture.

The optimal value of the inclusion of ethics in a due diligence should be to increase the level of assurance about the value of the seller's ethical capital. In fact, the seller with a sound ethical culture should **insist** on an ethics assessment to clarify that value. The inclusion of ethics is also important to minimise the risk of future problems. Although it may not be possible to prevent other scandals by means of better due diligence processes, ensuring that the due diligence is the best it can be should be a recognised goal.

5.6   ETHICS HOTLINE REPORTING: WHO WILL TELL?

The focus on reducing misconduct includes many different approaches and mechanisms. All of these are not equally effective, for example, as regards how well they act as deterrents.

A rule-based approach to reducing misconduct

A rule-based approach is common whereby laws, rules, regulations, a code of conduct and company policies are used to shape behaviour towards being ethical. However, a rule-based approach has the inherent challenge that good rules (and other regulatory measures) do not necessarily realise good compliance; nor do they automatically equal good enforcement. In some cases, good rules do not even mean consistent and fair implementation. In addition, when laws or regulations are used as a mechanism to correct ongoing or extreme unethical behaviour, they tend to overcompensate. The intended outcome of the law, regulation, rule or policy is almost certainly good, but the unintended consequences may erode that good.

In the United States of America it is a claim made against the Sarbanes-Oxley Act, which was enacted in 2002: the intended accounting reforms and protection for investors following the collapse of Enron and WorldCom are sound, but it has been criticised for making compliance too difficult and bringing with it huge compliance costs, factors especially onerous for smaller organisations.

A further factor influencing the effectiveness of strategies to diminish misconduct is the tendency to continually increase the number of laws and regulations. In society, many actions are now regulated that in the past were not legislated, such as smoking and fishing quotas. Organisations often copy this trend in pursuit of ethical outcomes, for example, writing lengthy policies when one sentence would suffice: "We do not tolerate theft under any circumstances". However, over-regulation does not increase compliance.

Rules and regulations are essential to ensure clarity about what is allowed versus what is not permitted. But while they are necessary, they are not sufficient to reduce or prevent unethical behaviour – and, least of all, to foster ethical behaviour.

Systems and procedures to reduce misconduct

Systems and procedures can also serve to shape behaviour towards being ethical. This can take the form of recruitment and reference checks, monitoring processes, such as internal audits, or reporting mechanisms, for instance, reporting the rate and frequency of disciplinary hearings.

The assessment of ethics, one of the key pillars of a sound ethics management system, can also support this outcome. The Ethics Monitor survey, for example, serves as an excellent "listening" exercise to allow employees and other stakeholders to share their views and experiences of the organisation's ethics. Since the survey is specifically designed to protect the anonymity and confidentially of respondents and their responses, it fulfils a valuable role as an ethics reporting mechanism.

Whistleblowing ethics hotline

Another system, beyond rules, regulations and assessment, that is increasingly being used in an attempt to minimise workplace misconduct is tapping into employees' knowledge as a way of exposing unethical behaviour. An ethics hotline or "whistleblowing" system is intended to provide an anonymous channel for employees (or others) to report knowledge of misconduct without threat of retribution. It rests on the assumption that although there are cases when knowledge of wrongdoing is limited to the perpetrator, in most cases there are other people who know, or at least suspect, that something is not right. It also reiterates the much-used law enforcement catchphrase, "If you see something, say something". But key to its effectiveness is the question: "Who will tell?"

Recognising the important role whistleblowing plays in combating crime, many countries have enacted or are considering enacting laws to protect whistleblowers from retribution. In South Africa legislation has already been passed: the Protected Disclosures Act 26 of 2000, the so-called "whistleblower" Act, specifically aims to protect employees from occupational disadvantage for reporting wrongdoing.

This legislative support should favourably influence the question of "who will tell what to whom", especially when two added factors are taken into account. Firstly, many larger companies have their own policy to protect employees and secondly, most hotline services are run by external providers further entrenching the security of reporting. (In the *Compliance Trends Survey 2013* conducted by Deloitte & Compliance Week, 62% of the (largely American) companies surveyed reported that they outsource ethics hotline operations (Deloitte & Compliance Week, 2013:5)).

While these factors should remove the obstacles to reporting, they do not necessarily do so. As evidence, Randy Cohen, who wrote a column on ethics, "The Ethicist", for *The New York Times Magazine* for 12 years, found that the most common ethical question he received from readers concerned the duty to report: that is, when they were aware of wrongdoing in others, they wanted to know when they had an obligation to come forward. The guideline Cohen offered was that when someone is acting in a way that presents an imminent, serious threat to other people, you have an absolute duty to come forward (NPR staff, 2012).

Report at your own peril

However, what about when that threat is to yourself? This is especially the case if the misconduct is happening at senior management level or if it is systemic in the organisation. Employees feel vulnerable to a range of adverse consequences, whether dismissal, demotion, compromised promotion opportunities or reduced prospects for salary increases or bonuses. The very real risk exists that reporting unethical behaviour can give rise to a situation where the institution "shoots the messenger" for bringing unwelcome news.

The reluctance to report is exacerbated by stories in the media about employees who have been victimised or disadvantaged in some way, illustrating that the assumption of reprisals is often factual. Supporting this, the *2013 National Ethics survey* of the American workforce conducted by the Ethics Resource Center, America's oldest non-profit organisation devoted to the advancement of high ethical standards and practices in public and private institutions, reported that retaliation against workers who reported wrongdoing continues to be a widespread problem. Among the employees who reported misconduct in the 2013 survey the percentage who experienced retaliation in return was 21%, virtually unchanged from the record high of 22% in 2011 (Ethics Resource Center, 2013:13).

More dramatic examples of whistleblowers are the revelations made by Edward Snowdon[5] and Bradley Manning (now officially Chelsea Elizabeth Manning).[6] In both cases, the United States of America has treated the disclosure of information as espionage and a breach of American law.

Even an apparently "successful" case that is seen as a victory for whistleblowers is likely to be a deterrent. One such situation is the case of Colonel Kobus Roos. Having uncovered and disclosed proof of widespread corruption in the Crime Intelligence unit of the South Africa Police, he was marginalised and placed in an unproductive position. The positive outcome in this case is that in April 2014 the Labour Court in Johannesburg ordered the Police Service to redeploy Roos to a similar position and to compensate him to the value of R156 250 for unfair labour practice (SAPA, 2014).

Interestingly, these disadvantages are not pertinent for a public reporting system. This is reflected in the success Crimeline has had in getting the South Africa public to report criminal activities. Launched in 2007 by Primedia, it offers an independent and anonymous service either via sms or email (which can be done via their website to ensure anonymity). Its success derives from a number of factors: the publicity that Primedia gives it via their various radios stations and newspapers maintains a good level of ongoing ethical awareness; it is endorsed by the South African Police Service who act on the information received; and, crucially, it has the advantage of some distance between the "reporter" and the "accused". This distance is, however, mostly not applicable in the workplace.

---

5   Snowden is an American computer professional and a former contractor for the American National Security Agency (NSA). In May 2013 he disclosed to several media outlets thousands of classified documents which he had acquired while working for the American consulting firm Booz Allen Hamilton. The American Department of Justice subsequently charged Snowden with espionage but he remains outside their reach – for now – in Russia, where he has been granted temporary asylum. Snowden's leaked documents uncovered the existence of numerous global surveillance programmes and the NSA's monitoring of 122 world leaders (Aljazeera America, 2014). Further revelations have been made by others about surveillance programmes since his disclosure.

6   Manning, who was deployed as an intelligence analyst at an American Army unit near Baghdad in Iraq, was convicted in July 2013 under the Espionage Act to 35 years' imprisonment for leaking classified military and diplomatic records to Wikileaks, an international, non-profit organisation founded by Julian Assange in 2006 that publishes secret information, news leaks and classified media from anonymous sources (Sledge, 2013).

When reporting on someone with whom the employee is in contact with on a fairly regular basis in the same workplace, it often feels too close for comfort.

The reluctance to report based on fear of retribution translates into low levels of effectiveness of an internal hotline or employee reporting system. This is echoed in PwC's *2014 Global Economic Crime Survey*, which identifies a downwards trend in the effectiveness of whistleblowers in reporting crime. The survey found that while more than six in ten companies report having a whistleblower mechanism in place, and half describe their programme as being either effective or very effective, only 5% of all companies reported that their whistleblowing system was the mechanism by which they uncovered fraudulent events (PwC, 2014:43).

Optimising the effectiveness of an ethics reporting system

It is obviously ideal to increase the effectiveness of ethics reporting systems.

In the United States of America financial incentives are used by the Securities and Exchange Commission (SEC) to promote whistleblowing. The SEC set up the Office of the Whistleblower (OWB) in August 2011 with the aim of protecting investors from securities fraud. The 2013 OWB report announced that the number of whistleblower tips it received increased from 3 001 in 2012 to 3 238 in 2013, and that the Office paid whistleblowers a total of over $14 million in 2013 in recognition of their contributions to the success of preventing securities fraud (SEC, 2013:1). While the success of the OWB clearly rests on the "encouragement" the financial reward offers, they also protect the identity of whistleblowers, for example, by allowing information to be submitted via the whistleblower's attorney (SEC, 2013:2).

The American Internal Revenue Service (IRS) also pays whistleblowers for valuable information. An interesting 2012 case involved Bradley Birkenfeld, a former banker at UBS, the Swiss global financial services company. First the government imprisoned Birkenfeld for helping a former client at UBS to hide his wealth from the IRS. Then the IRS paid him a record $104 million reward for providing information on the firm's widespread tax evasion scheme for its wealthy Americans clients (which led to a 2009 settlement between the American government and UBS in terms of which the bank agreed to pay $780 million in penalties and turn over the account information of thousands of American clients) (Dinan, 2012).

Financial incentives are, however, rarely used in the corporate world. To optimise the effectiveness of an ethics reporting system within organisations, a number of other factors need to be addressed.

The organisational culture needs to be conducive to reporting misconduct and employees should be encouraged to raise concerns. High levels of ethical awareness and transparency can contribute to such an environment. If this is absent, a situation can arise such as at Société Générale in 2007: trading irregularities were not reported to bank management by employees who noticed them because, as a report by the bank's own investigators noted, "this was not specifically part of their job description" (Rosenoer & Scherlis, 2009:26).

A perspective that erodes the effectiveness of this type of ethics reporting is that not everyone views it with approval. Instead of being seen as a loyal employee speaking out for the benefit of the organisation, the whistleblower is sometimes treated with hostility as an informer. Decreasing the stigma of the "snitch" through education and raising of awareness is also proposed as a solution by Alison Tilley, the head of advocacy and special projects at the Open Democracy Advice Centre, a South African not-for-profit organisation aimed at promoting democracy and accountability and assisting people to realise their human rights (Tilley, 2014).

The discrimination that is associated with whistleblowers was evident in the recent case in the Irish police force – although this time, with a positive outcome. Two officers brought concerns about flaws in the penalty points system to the attention of the Public Accounts Committee of the parliament of the Republic of Ireland. The concern centred on senior police officers inappropriately wiping the penalty points from the driving licences of well-connected offenders. The head of the Irish police force, Garda Commissioner Martin Callinan, told a parliamentary committee that the actions of the two whistleblowers were "disgusting". However, subsequently, the claims of misconduct were found to be true, and the Commissioner tendered his resignation (BBC, 2014).

The effectiveness of an ethics hotline also depends on the action that follows the information. It often takes real courage to speak out, so if no constructive action follows, employees are less likely to report anything again.

Who takes such action depends on where this function has been delegated in the organisation. If the company has an ethics officer, he/she would deal with it, or it may be assigned to the social and ethics committee, who receive and manage ethics reports. If not those, the reports should be dealt with by the senior management team (such as an executive committee). Charges against management should be directed to the board, who may choose to have the issue investigated by a suitable external company.

What action is taken – a forensic audit, an investigation by an external consultant, a revision of procedures or an internal audit – depends on the nature of the issue and needs to be appropriate for the charge. The action must also balance the importance of the charge with the legal principle of "innocent until proved guilty" relative to the accused – which raises the dark side of ethics reporting.

An additional and crucial factor is accurate and truthful reporting. The anonymity that offers protection and security for the honest reporter can also create opportunities for false or malicious reporting. Whoever reviews the ethics reports, be it the ethics officer or the social and ethics committee, needs to be aware of the potential for abuse or inaccuracy, but without allowing suspicion to undermine or discredit accurate reports received. Creating a responsible review system, which includes a process for verifying the facts, is essential to protect people from false accusations.

Using this approach to reduce unethical behaviour warrants constantly bearing in mind that it takes courage not only to speak out, but also to listen. Those tasked with this job may have to face things they really do not want to hear and do not want to believe. It is therefore a system that should be used with circumspection and discernment.

5.7 BUSINESS ETHICS REPORTING: WHAT SHOULD YOU TELL?

Business reporting is intended to provide meaningful information to stakeholders so that they can get an accurate picture of the organisation and can accordingly make well-informed decisions relative to the business. The focus is therefore on what should be reported (and what should not be omitted) and how clearly that is shared. Paraphrasing the quotation about statistics attributed to Professor Aaron Levenstein, retired associate professor emeritus of business at Baruch College in New York City, illustrates what should **not** happen: "Corporate reporting is like a bikini. What it reveals is interesting, but what it conceals is vital."

The requirements and rationale for corporate ethics reporting

Organisations generally have a number of reporting obligations, many of them in accordance with the law, such as those required of public companies to their shareholders. In the specific area of ethics reporting, there are a number of sources that address the reporting of ethics or governance or facets thereof.

The Companies Act 71 of 2008 added ethics to legal reporting requirements with the mandate that all organisations except small companies should establish a social and ethics committee. The committee's functions include monitoring that the company acts as a good corporate citizen by following a triple bottom line approach encompassing social and environmental dimensions, and its ethical duties include the prevention of unfair discrimination and the reduction of corruption. Accordingly, the committee's duty to report should reflect these issues, among others. However, for some organisations, this legal requirement may not be sufficiently compelling and their committees may amount to only "tick-box" exercises and minimalist reporting.

Beyond the strictly legal requirements, ethics reporting is also recommended by *King III*. Its focus on ethical leadership and the management of ethics specifically includes the reporting and disclosure of an organisation's ethical performance to the board, management and external stakeholders, which is considered "necessary to provide the board and management with relevant and reliable information about the achievement of ethics objectives, the outcome of ethics initiatives and the quality of the company's ethics performance" (IoDSA, 2009:27). As for the assessment of ethics, *King III* recognises that reporting serves the ultimate objective of improving the company's ethical culture by enhancing its ethical performance (IoDSA, 2009:27).

A facet of ethics reporting, specifically the organisation's ethical boundary that reflects the inclusion or exclusion of the interests of stakeholders and the social and environmental responsibilities of the triple bottom line, is also addressed in other mechanisms. The JSE's Socially Responsible Investment (SRI) Index is a measure of the triple bottom line performance of companies listed on the exchange. The Code for Responsible Investing in South Africa (CRISA) gives guidance on how the institutional investor should execute investment analysis and investment activities and exercise rights so as to promote sound governance. First among the five principles is the requirement that "an institutional investor should incorporate sustainability considerations, including environmental, social and governance, into its investment analysis and investment activities as part of the delivery of superior risk-adjusted returns to the ultimate beneficiaries" (IoDSA, 2011:3). The principles espoused by CRISA are also supported by the Financial Services Board and the JSE.

The rationale for ethics reporting is arguably best captured in *King III*'s requirement of integrated reporting, in which ethics is primarily addressed under the banner of sustainability, which is core to business ethics and good corporate citizenship. *King III* defines integrated reporting as "a holistic and integrated representation of the company's performance in terms of both its finance and its sustainability" (IoDSA, 2009:108). In effect, this means that corporates should provide material financial and non-financial information about their strategy, governance, performance and prospects in the context of its material social and environmental issues in a clear, concise and comparable format. *King III* acknowledges two particular benefits of reporting effectively about the goals and strategy of the company, as well as its performance with regard to economic, social and environmental issues: that it serves "to align the company with the legitimate interests and expectations of its stakeholders" and that it gains stakeholder buy-in and support for the objectives that the company is pursuing, which "can prove to be invaluable during difficult times, for instance when the company needs certain approvals and authority, or when it needs and relies on the confidence and loyalty of customers" (IoDSA, 2009:108).

Adding a further benefit, ethics reporting as a key facet of a comprehensive ethics management system also supports the maintenance of an ethical culture via the focus and attention that is achieved by sharing the organisation's ethics performance with others.

Despite the requirements for and benefits of clear, holistic reporting, much corporate reporting still amounts to "compliance reporting" that does not extend beyond a minimalist approach, generally falling far short of meaningful disclosure based on the choice to be open and transparent.

The most recent Africa ESG Investment Forum, Africa's leading event on environmental, social and governance (ESG) issues, held in Johannesburg in 2012, acknowledged that the paucity of information about environmental, social and governance issues (all of which are facets of business ethics) compromised investors' ability to make informed decisions (Blaine, 2012).

Sound ethics reporting

Although the initiatives mentioned are very noteworthy (the social and ethics committee set up in terms of the Companies Act, *King III* and integrated reporting, SRI and CRISA), they have insufficient guidelines about the information that would afford stakeholders better insight into an organisation's ethics. Ideally, companies need to show through their own reporting that they are working to ethical standards.

Writing for *Guardian Sustainable Business*, an initiative of *The Guardian* newspaper, Tim Melville-Ross CBE, president of the British Institute of Business Ethics, states that businesses cannot just say that they are ethical. Acknowledging that there was a time when business leaders could just tell the public "trust me to do the right thing" and they would, he recognises that corporations have entered a new era, the "prove to me" era, which requires that something more is required for society's trust in business to be restored. They need to prove they have embedded ethical values (Melville-Ross, 2013).

The key criteria that would achieve this are the following:

Ideally, ethics reporting should take the form of quantitative measures, not least because it allows results to more easily be compared, for example, to reflect improvements relative to previous ethics performance and to provide a measure of the success of interventions to increase ethical behaviour or remedy ethical breaches.

The list of stakeholders to whom this information should be accessible includes those closely associated with the company, such as employees, labour unions and shareholders, as well as stakeholders who are affected by the organisation's operations, such as communities in the vicinity of the business and lobby groups.

An ethics report should reveal the following as clearly as possible (which echoes the recommended outcomes of assessment per *King III*):

1   An outline of the ethics management system that shapes the company's management of ethics

2   The specific ethics initiatives that were undertaken in the reporting period and what they have achieved

3   The outcome or progress made relative to ethics initiatives in the previous reporting period

4   The organisation's current ethics rating as an indicator of its ethical status and the overall quality of its ethical performance

5   The organisation's ethical strengths

6   The organisation's current ethical weaknesses or areas of concern and how these will be remedied

7   The degree of ethical behaviour or ethical maturity, which should provide insight into employees' commitment to the organisation's values, the extent to which leaders are seen to live the organisation's values and the effectiveness of the factors that drive and improve ethical behaviour in the organisation

8   The levels of unethical behaviour, which should quantify the incidence of specific unethical behaviours and indicate the effectiveness of the factors that reduce or prevent unethical behaviour

9   The degree of inclusiveness or exclusiveness of the company's ethical boundary, which should encompass the extent to which:

   a   the organisation's values apply to different stakeholder groups

   b   the organisation values its employees

   c   the organisation pursues the wider social and environmental interests represented by the triple bottom line.

The benefits of comprehensive ethics reporting are significant. The assurance it offers external stakeholders, such as investors, can improve stakeholder confidence and boost the organisation's reputation and it can also position the organisation as an employer of choice. Its success should be – and the ideal would be – that organisations' own ethics reporting avoids their most vocal ethics reports being negative press reports.

5.8   SAMPLE ETHICS REPORT: EXECUTIVE SUMMARY OF ETHICS MONITOR SURVEY RESULTS

This report is an executive summary of the results of a company's Ethics Monitor survey results (appropriately anonymised). It illustrates what should be reported in order to provide meaningful insight into the organisation's ethical performance.

Purpose of the report

The purpose of the Ethics Report is to provide the social and ethics committee with the information necessary to understand the company's ethical status, encompassing its ethical behaviour and practices, and to be able to report accurately on the company's ethics.

Rationale and compliance

The ethics initiatives described below comply with the requirements of the social and ethics committee in terms of the Companies Act 71 of 2008 and with the recommendations of *King III* (*2009 King Report on Corporate Governance*) as regards the assessment, monitoring and reporting of ethics.

Beyond mere compliance, the company is committed to the proactive management of ethics and to maintaining the highest standards of ethical behaviour relative to all its business practices and relationships.

Methodology

The Ethics Monitor, a confidential web-based ethics survey, was used to assess the company's ethical status and its ethics in relation to stakeholders, including employees, external stakeholders and the environment. This echoes the two key focus areas of the social and ethics committee in the Companies Act, namely ethics and stakeholder management.

The survey was customised according to the organisation's branches, departments and work levels. It also included the organisation's values and company-specific questions to test issues of concern.

Survey results and findings

The survey was conducted in March 2014. Of a total of 525 employees, 77% completed the survey, which means that the results can be viewed as a credible and representative account of the company's current ethical standing.

Ethics rating

The company's ethics rating was A on a scale from AAA to D, where AAA represents the most ethical status and D the least ethical.

The detailed results provided insight into ethical behaviour, unethical behaviour and the company's ethical boundary, which measures inclusiveness or exclusiveness relative to stakeholders and the triple bottom line. These results are for the organisation as a whole and for all its branches, departments and work levels.

Ethical behaviour

The overall score for ethical behaviour was 8.12, which is very positive, given that 10 represents being perfectly ethical. Employees reflected a strong commitment to ethics and leaders were perceived to live the values well, scoring 7.23 on a scale of 0 to 10. The strongest value was honesty / integrity for both employees and leaders. The company's values were shown to be the most effective factor as regards improving ethical conduct, which is a sound (and desired) reflection of their relevance and impact. That the behaviour of colleagues was the second most influential factor offers a very encouraging picture of the quality of workplace relationships.

Unethical behaviour

There were four factors that emerged as being the most effective at reducing unethical behaviour: the company's code of conduct, rules and regulations, disciplinary measures, and policies and procedures. These mechanisms are exactly those that should be effective and the results indicate the associated effectiveness of the company's HR practices. The company's ethics hotline was notably ineffective.

The incidence of unethical conduct was generally very low. The two highest factors were unfair allocation of rewards and discrimination, which scored 3.2 and 3.12 respectively on a scale of 1 to 10, where 0 represents no incidence of misconduct. The occurrence of misconduct by department and work level did not reveal any noteworthy differences, except for the Cape Town branch, where discrimination was somewhat lower than elsewhere in the company.

Ethical boundary

The company's ethical boundary includes the assessment of the extent to which employees feel valued. The score of +4.72 on a –10 to +10 scale is reasonable, although the detailed results showed that directors, executives, HODs and managers held more a positive view than employees. The extent to which the company's values were perceived to apply to stakeholders groups was good: customers +6.13; investors/shareholders +6.01; and suppliers/service provider +5.99, all on a scale of –10 to +10, where +10 is optimal. As regards the company's social and environmental responsibilities, these scores were quite low, averaging +3.4, where +10 is the highest score.

Conclusions and recommendations

The survey results are sound and reveal no major ethical risks. However, the company could strengthen its ethical status, for example, by striving to achieve an AA rating by leveraging the company's values further to shape behaviour. The result for the unfair allocation of rewards warrants that communication regarding remuneration is reviewed to ensure that it is adequate. It is recommended that a more effective and secure (confidential) ethics hotline is implemented to enable the company to benefit from employees' knowledge of misconduct. This could be used to bring to the surface further information about the unfair allocation of rewards and discrimination. The company also needs to improve its social and environmental activities and/or better communicate those that are taking place, which would also contribute to realising an AA rating.

 *WORKPLACE DISCUSSION*

Do you know how ethical your organisation really is?

Is ethics in your organisation viewed as a luxury you can't afford? Is it just an illusion (spoken about but not acted on), or is it recognised as a necessity? Is ethics valued to its full extent?

Consider the following:

- Does your company assess and monitor its ethics?

- Is this adequate? For example, does it provide reliable, representative results for the organisation's ethical performance? Does your monitoring provide meaningful management insight that serves as a sound basis for focused action to improve ethics?

- What could be done to quantify your ethics better or more accurately?

- Does your organisation report on its ethics and ethical performance? Does this include accurate, credible information? For example, does it represent the experiences and perceptions of the majority of the organisation's employees, does it include key external stakeholders, or does it reflect the views of only a select group of directors and executives?

CHAPTER 6

ETHICAL DECISIONS AND DILEMMAS

INTRODUCTION

Ethical decision making is the focus of this chapter.

The chapter addresses the area of ethical decisions and choices that involve right versus wrong situations. This includes considering the effect of self-interest as a decision criterion, the crucial issue of who knows, and hence decides, what is right, and the question of "dirty hands", the concept that questions whether those in power can govern innocently. Ethical dilemmas, the far more difficult decisions that involve right versus right choices, are discussed and the five primary sources of such dilemmas are examined. To address the challenge of resolving or reconciling ethical choices and dilemmas, various decision making approaches and methodologies are shared.

The chapter also includes a recommended case study that explores the clash between personal ethics and the ethics in a developing country and further reading on the topic of right versus right dilemmas.

6.1 ETHICAL DECISION MAKING

Decision making is a core feature of every organisation. So, too, are choices central to the workplace, with the many variables in each situation often giving rise to a multitude of options. A distinction can be made between decisions and choices based on the etymology of the words. For example, choice can be seen to be about possibilities or a selection from various options, while a decision is about direction (Strauss, 2008). Similarly, they may be distinguished by placing one as subject to another: that decisions follow choices, or *vice versa*. However, in the workplace, they are normally used interchangeably: a decision would as easily be considered to entail a choice as a choice would encompass a decision (which is how they have been treated here). The greater focus in the workplace is instead likely to be on decisions and choices as drivers of action, given that action is key to implementation.

Jeffrey Pfeffer, Professor of Organisational Behaviour at Stanford University's Graduate School of Business, captured the implication of this point well. Interviewed about *The Knowing-Doing Gap: How Smart Companies Turn Knowledge Into Action*, which he co-wrote with fellow Stanford Professor Robert

Sutton, he makes the point that "a decision by itself changes nothing. A decision is the beginning of the process of doing, not the end of that process" (in Webber, 2000).

Ethical decisions: choosing between right versus wrong

Decisions as a starting point also apply to ethical decision making. The choice between good or right versus bad or wrong is a central defining feature of ethics. It is important to recognise that this means that ethical decision making is, in effect, synonymous with being ethical, since ethics involves not only doing the right thing, but also determining what the right thing is in the face of competing criteria. Ethics amounts to a "choice with consequences", as the choices that are made will shape whether the resulting behaviour is ethical or unethical.

Ethical decisions and choices are, however, subject to many factors that can divert their path from an ethical outcome. David Gebler, author of *The 3 Power Values,* recognises three ethical traps to sound choices.

1   Employees lie to themselves, for example, to convince themselves that the situation or choice is not really that bad.

2   Employees rationalise their ethical choices. This can be based on an assumed good reason, on the claim that it is standard practice or that other people are doing the same things, or on the view that it is not so serious.

3   Employees disengage, adopting an attitude that it is neither their problem nor their responsibility (in Executive Leadership, 2012).

To these factors can be added the tendency to seek out information that supports one's choice or point of view and to ignore information that contradicts it.

Among these factors, rationalisation is especially problematic because it rests on the employee knowing what is right but finding a reason or circumstance to justify why other (unethical) action is acceptable. It is compounded by the fact that the rationalisation is also often used to reduce the guilt associated with the unethical choice or action. The guilt is generally transferred elsewhere: I stole the company's property because I am not paid well is an example of the flawed logic of rationalisations.

Faced with such responses, it is important that leaders or managers address the problem. This illustrates an important facet of ethics for people in management positions, namely that ethical decision making does not extend only to their choosing between what is right and wrong; it also entails addressing issues and guiding others to ensure that they too make sound ethical choices.

Who knows – and hence decides – what is right?

The basis for decision making, such as choosing right above wrong or good above bad, appears to present a straightforward choice. However, this crucially needs to take into account a core feature of ethics, namely that ethics involves not only oneself but also those others who are affected by the decision and consequent action.

Margaret Thatcher, in a speech at Monash University in Melbourne in 1981, illustrated the opposite. She stated that she operated on the basis of conviction, adding that neither pragmatism nor consensus was enough. Her views on consensus are noteworthy:

> To me consensus seems to be ... the process of abandoning all beliefs, principles, values and policies in search of something in which no-one believes, but to which no-one objects ... the process of avoiding the very issues that have to be solved, merely because you cannot get agreement on the way ahead. What great cause would have been fought and won under the banner "I stand for consensus"? (Thatcher, 1981)

While her words may read well, the underlying message should not be ignored: that decision making by leaders on the basis of their personal conviction, opinion or belief without taking the views of others into account or without allowing others to be part of the decision making process can easily amount to arbitrary or unjust action.

In the same speech, Margaret Thatcher quoted the Roman jurist, Julius Paulus: "What is right is not derived from the rule, but the rule arises from our knowledge of what is right" (1981).

The key question this illustrates is who defines what is right. When people believe that they know definitively what is right, making decisions in that regard is, of course, very easy. That apparent absolute knowledge means not only that the decisions that follow are right, but that the consequent actions are also right. But the implications can be dangerous and damaging. Many dictatorial leaders – Adolf Hitler, Joseph Stalin and others – believed they knew what was right and their actions in following suit had hugely destructive consequences.

The question of knowledge and certainty, and specifically whether knowledge can provide certainty, is well portrayed in the film written and narrated by Jacob Bronowski, *The Ascent of Man*. In the episode on Knowledge or Certainty which explores the achievements of 20th-century physics, he stresses that absolute certainty is beyond the grasp of humans. Filmed standing ankle-deep in a pond in Auschwitz, he concludes as follows:

> Into this pond were flushed the ashes of some four million people. And that was not done by gas. It was done by arrogance. It was done by dogma. It was done by ignorance. When people believe that they have absolute knowledge, with no test in reality, this is how they behave. This is what men do when they aspire to the knowledge of gods (Bronowski, 1973).

The conclusion for decision making in the workplace is not simply that arrogance is bad. Nor is it that decisions should never be made in case not everything is known or in case the decision is wrong. The lesson, instead, is that leaders should consciously strive to ensure that humility counteracts arrogance and that they should always remember that ethics and being ethical encompasses making decisions – whether via consensus, consultation or any other means – that gives consideration to all those who will be affected by the decisions or choices made.

What is right and what works?

In making decisions in the workplace, the focus is likely to not only to be on what is right, but also on what works. Carl Sagan, the American astronomer and astrophysicist, recognised that there is "a tension between what we call ethical and pragmatic. If, even in the long run, ethical behaviour was self-defeating, eventually we would not call it ethical, we would call it foolish". He adds that in such a circumstance while we might claim to respect the ethical behaviour in principle, we would ignore it in practice (Sagan, 1998:187).

Decision making on the basis of what is practical as opposed to what is right or true was also addressed by the Harvard economist, John Kenneth Galbraith. In his 1958 book *The Affluent Society*, he used the phrase "conventional wisdom", which he considered "simple, convenient, comfortable, and comforting, although not necessarily true". He did not use the term as a compliment, acknowledging that "we associate truth with convenience, with what mostly accords with self-interest and personal well-being or promises best to avoid awkward effort or unwelcome dislocation of life. We also find highly acceptable what contributes most to self-esteem" (in Levitt & Dubner, 2005:79–80).

Carl Sagan also acknowledged that choices and decisions are "partly determined by our perceived self-interest" (Sagan, 1998:187).

The tragedy of the commons

Self-interest as a criterion for decision making is at the heart of many ethical scandals, which describe the actions and choices of those who ignored or neglected the well-being of society, the organisation, its employees or its customers in the pursuit of personal gain. The problem was especially well articulated by Garrett Hardin, an American ecologist, in his 1968 article "The Tragedy of the Commons". In this, he explains the dilemma arising from a situation in which individuals with access to a common resource – be it grazing land, the atmosphere, oceans, rivers or national parks – ride roughshod over the interests of others, failing to care for the sustainability of the common resource in pursuit of their own self-interest. Such rampant self-interest has the effect of depleting, polluting, damaging or destroying the shared resource, even though it is clearly in nobody's long-term interest to do so (Hardin, 1968:1243–1246).[1]

Adding to this negative outcome is the fact that while individuals intent on self-gain are able to maximise their own benefit, they do not get to carry the full negative costs of their conduct. These are effectively shared by the whole group. Therefore, the company that pollutes the river reaps the benefit of the lower cost associated with not managing their waste appropriately, but the whole community that uses the river water suffers the cost of the poor water quality. This issue of "shared costs" being borne by those who are innocent of the misconduct adds enormously to public outrage and can exacerbate the reputational damage for the company involved.

Privatisation has been put forward as a partial solution to this problem (the tragedy of the commons), although there is no one simple solution. Nor is there the likelihood that self-interest will abate; it is likely to continue to be part of every facet of society. In the context of the workplace, leaders and managers need to be alert to the potentially destructive impact of self-interest and not only guard against it, but also act against it.

Dirty hands: can you govern innocently?

A further challenge to ethical decision making is whether organisations, leaders and employees can always live up to their values and principles and, if compromises are made, whether they can be justified. Such a situation is often viewed in terms of the concept of "dirty hands".

The term derives from a play by that name written in 1948 by Jean-Paul Sartre, the French existentialist philosopher and novelist. The story takes place in the fictional eastern European country of Illyria in the latter stages of World War II. It centres on the conflict between a young, zealous Communist party member and his older leader, which is based on the young man's view that his leader has betrayed the party's ideals by making compromises with other political groups. Instead of adhering to morally right decisions and the party's principles, he has made expedient political alliances to avoid further problems and hardships for their communities. The older leader answers the accusation, saying:

> How you cling to your purity, young man! How afraid you are to soil your hands! All right, stay pure! What good will it do? Why did you join us? Purity is an idea for a yogi or a monk ... To do nothing, to remain motionless, with your arms at your side, wearing kid gloves. Well, I have dirty hands. Right up to the elbows. I have plunged them in filth and blood. But what do you hope? Do you think you can govern innocently? (Sartre, 1989:218).

---

1   The prioritisation of self-interest mirrors the ethical concept of an ethical boundary, in this instance a very limited, exclusive ethical boundary that does not accommodate the interests of others.

The older leader's view is that people with power over others will almost certainly get their hands dirty in the sense of compromising their moral values: that pragmatic political action sometimes conflicts with moral norms.

The question this poses – whether or not one can govern innocently – applies to business leaders as well as politicians.

Doctors Without Borders / Médecins Sans Frontières (MSF) provides an interesting real example of grappling with this question in a non-governmental organisation. MSF is an international medical humanitarian organisation created by doctors and journalists in France in 1971. It provides independent, impartial assistance in more than 60 countries to those in need, primarily owing to armed conflicts, epidemics, malnutrition or natural disasters. The book *Humanitarian Negotiations Revealed: The MSF Experience*, authored by MSF veterans, explores the practical realities of humanitarian crises through their experience in 11 complex situations: Ethiopia, Yemen, Gaza, South Africa, Somalia, Sri Lanka, Myanmar, Afghanistan, Pakistan, France and Nigeria (Magone, Neuman & Weissman, 2012).

Despite the obvious value of their work (MSF received the Nobel Peace Prize in 1999), they acknowledge the problem of dirty hands. In their book they pose the questions: Do we – can we – always live up to our principles? Are the struggles and compromises we make to reach people in need in places such as Somalia and Myanmar so different from those we faced in the Democratic Republic of Congo (then Zaire) following the Rwandan genocide or in Ethiopia during the 1984 famine (Magone, Neuman & Weissman, 2012)?

In the introduction, aptly entitled "Acting at Any Price?", written by Marie-Pierre Allié, President of MSF France, she acknowledges that they face compromises arising from opposing and convergent interests. Her question, "How can we judge whether a compromise is acceptable?" recognises that they are criticised for accepting that "everything is open to negotiation". Answering her own question, she writes that compromises are considered acceptable if they "reduce the number of deaths, the suffering and the frequency of incapacitating handicaps within groups of people who are usually poorly served by public health systems." Justifying the organisation's choices, she writes: "It seems to us that MSF can only justify its compromises to itself in an ethics of action founded on a principle of medical effectiveness and a refusal to be party to policies of domination" (Allié, 2011).

Fiona Terry, Director of Research at MSF in Paris, adds to this debate in her book *Condemned to Repeat? The Paradox of Humanitarian Action*. Speaking to the common dictum among aid organisations, "Do no harm", she raises the issue that one cannot just assume that aid is intrinsically "good". If, for example, aid benefits the oppressor rather than the victim, then such improvements are actually counterproductive. Terry acknowledges that it is an illusion to assume that no harm is done, claiming that "the best aid organisations can hope to do is minimise the negative effects of their action" (Terry, 2002:224). She concludes that "this inevitability provides an ethical imperative for vigilance in humanitarian organisations" (2002:245).

The paradoxes of humanitarian action – when doing good can also cause harm – and the challenges in the political arena associated with "dirty hands" may not present themselves quite as starkly in the workplace. But similar scenarios can arise, such as when doing the right thing, "doing good", for shareholders entails closing an unprofitable operation, which would cause harm to the affected employees. The problem of "dirty hands" can also occur in business when compromises are made with good intentions in pursuit of a better outcome for the people involved. As to the older Communist leader's question as to "what good will it do?" to make ethical choices and govern with ethics, the added question to be considered is "what bad will it do?". Leaders need to bear in mind that if, in pursuit of a good or more favourable outcome, bad or unethical decisions are made, it still represents a breach of ethics. A variation on the previous example would be altering the business unit's financials and presenting a false picture of its financial health to shareholders and the board to allow the management team time to turn the situation around so as to save the employees' jobs. The intention is sound, but the board and the shareholders would unquestionably view this as being unethical. The tendency to overvalue outcomes can, in the extreme, lead to "results at any cost", which is a serious threat to ethical choices and consequent conduct.

In the sphere of right versus wrong ethical decision making, while many situations may be clear-cut and uncomplicated, these are also complex challenges and choices. Business leaders therefore need to be attentive to the impact of their decisions and make those choices with wisdom, care and integrity.

6.2   WHY IT IS SOMETIMES HARD TO DO WHAT IS RIGHT

In situations that present right versus wrong choices, most people would know what the right thing to do is, even if they do not act on that knowledge. This holds true in the workplace, where unethical conduct is very rarely because the employee did not know the difference between right or wrong: deciding to act unethically generally represents a deliberate choice to act against what would be considered ethical.

A contrary view is presented in the film *The Confession*, an ethical drama about a father who loses his son, which is played out against a parallel story of business misconduct. The father, guilty of killing the three people he holds responsible for his son's death, explains to his attorney that "it's not hard to do the right thing; It's hard to **know** what the right thing is" (Bridge Pictures, 2001). His view highlights the fact that, in addition to right versus wrong choices, there is also a class of decisions that involve right versus right choices.

Ethical dilemmas: choosing between right versus right

Right versus right choices are not focused on the "rights" that are, for example, recognised in South Africa's Constitution. While the rights recognised and protected in the Bill of Rights – "[i]t enshrines the rights of all people in our country and affirms the democratic values of human dignity, equality and freedom" (South Africa, 1996:2.7.(1)1245) – are right in the sense of being correct and sound and are based on sound moral values, they nonetheless amount to an entitlement.

Right versus right decisions and choices instead focus on circumstances that entail two desirable but mutually incompatible "rights", which can make it hard to know which is the right choice. This can occur as a conflict between two ways of resolving a problem, where each option represents a right thing to do; or deciding between valid competing interests. It can also encompass a conflict between personal values and consistency with company policies and can include the allocation of limited resources.

The ethics of right versus right choices is often ignored in the face of more frequent right versus wrong issues. However, it warrants particular attention for two reasons: because right versus right issues are likely to be the hardest ethical decisions to make, and because ethical dilemmas are likely to exert a significant influence on the organisation and the individuals involved.

Joseph Badaracco, Ethics Professor at Harvard Business School, views right versus right choices as "defining moments" with three basic characteristics: They reveal the individual's or the organisation's basic values; they test the strength of the individual's commitment or the commitment the organisation has made; and they shape the individual's or the organisation's character into the future (Badaracco, 1997:6–7).

Rushworth Kidder, founder of the American-based Institute for Global Ethics, differentiates in his book *How Good People make Tough Choices* between "moral temptations", which he views as easier right versus wrong choices, and ethical dilemmas that involve right versus right choices (1995:13–14). The conflict and difficulty inherent in these dilemmas are that both options and choices are grounded on core values and therefore decision making pits one value against another.

The sources of ethical dilemmas

In order to manage right versus right dilemmas, it is important to understand under what circumstances these could arise or how they could present themselves.

Kidder recognises four types of ethical dilemma: short-term versus long-term, individual versus community, truth versus loyalty, and justice versus mercy. In addition, the triple bottom line represents a fifth source of ethical dilemmas. Understanding these dilemmas can help leaders to make better ethical decisions.

Short term versus long term

The tension between short-term and long-term goals and priorities is a long-standing strategic challenge within organisations. This does not include a situation where a business leader has focused on short-term results for personal gain, for example, to boost a performance bonus. That is not a right versus right situation. Instead the conflict between short term and long term rests on both being right choices. Short-term results are crucial to ensure the ongoing viability of the business, while long-term results are important for the organisation's sustainability. Consequently this warrants an "and" approach, rather than an "either/or" approach.

However, balancing the short-term against the long-term is often made more difficult by the pressure to achieve good results in the current period. A common form of pressure is from analysts and investors, whose views and actions can affect the organisation's share price if its immediate results are unsatisfactory. The extent of the short-term pressure that executives face is reflected in the findings of the 2013 *McKinsey Quarterly Survey* among more than 1 000 board members to assess their progress in taking a longer-term approach. The survey found that:

1   63% of respondents said the pressure to generate short term results had increased over the previous five years.

2   79% said that they felt pressurised to produce strong financial results in a period of just two years or less.

3   86% said that using a longer time horizon to make business decisions would positively affect corporate performance, for example, strengthening financial returns and increasing innovation (Barton & Wiseman, 2014:46).

Dominic Barton, Global Managing Director of McKinsey & Company, and Mark Wiseman, President and CEO of the Canada Pension Plan Investment Board (CPPIB), acknowledge the growing movement to reduce the focus on "quarterly capitalism" in favour of a true long-term mind-set. They believe that big investors have an obligation "to end the plague of short-termism" and suggest that the best approach to reverse this destructive trend is to change the investment strategies and approaches of the big asset owners. They advocate four approaches to focus capital more on the longer term:

1   Invest the portfolio after defining long-term objectives and risk appetite.

2   Unlock value through engagement and active ownership.

3   Demand long-term metrics from companies to change their investor-management conversation.

4   Structure institutional governance to support a long-term approach (Barton & Wiseman, 2014:45–51).

Individual versus group

The issue of individual versus group rights is relevant in most workplaces. In this context, it does not address questions such as whether groups or individuals are better at performing tasks, but rather centres on decisions that pitch the interests or well-being of an individual versus a group. This dilemma can also be viewed in terms of us and them, self versus other, the smaller group versus the bigger group, and other such variations.

Even in an apparently homogeneous workforce there are gender, cultural and religious differences and groups with diverse, often conflicting demands that need to be balanced against each other. An example of different rights for different groups applies in the form of affirmative action to citizens classified as previously disadvantaged. In South Africa the Employment Equity Act 55 of 1998 aims to address this historical imbalance.

A particular facet of this dilemma that is an area of concern is the divide between the "haves" and the "have-nots".

In November 2013, the World Economic Forum released its *Outlook on the Global Agenda 2014*, in which it ranked widening income disparities as the second greatest worldwide risk in the coming 12 to 18 months (WEF, 2013:9). Adding to this, the Oxfam paper by Ricardo Fuentes-Nieva and Nicholas Galasso, *Working for the Few*, which was released in January 2014 on the eve of the World Economic Forum in Davos, has captured much attention for its research into the increasing wealth gap in the world. It reveals that:

1   Almost half the world's wealth is owned by 1% of the population.

2   The wealth of 1% of the richest people in the world amounts to $110 trillion, which is 65 times the total wealth of the bottom half of the world's population.

3   Just 85 individuals have amassed fortunes that equal the capital of half the entire world's population (Fuentes-Nieva & Galasso, 2014:2).

The Oxfam paper acknowledges that the wealth gap is not all bad: "some economic inequality is essential to drive growth and progress, rewarding those with talent, hard earned skills, and the ambition to innovate and take entrepreneurial risks" (Fuentes-Nieva & Galasso, 2014:2). However, they also outline the "reinforcing cycles of advantage" that serve to entrench an imbalanced society. For the wealthy, this includes increased access to business opportunities, superior education, better access to services such as health care and, in some instances, favourable economic policies. This unequal environment is further sustained by the tendency for wealth to be self-supporting and the limited social mobility among the poorest in a society (Fuentes-Nieva & Galasso, 2014:2–27). Thus as wealth begets wealth, so the poor remain poor.

The Oxfam paper makes a number of sound recommendations to address this that can be followed by most organisations. It advocates that wealthy individuals and corporations do not dodge taxes, do not use their wealth to seek political favours, support progressive taxation, demand a living wage for workers and challenge governments to use their tax revenues to provide healthcare, education and social protection to all its citizens (Fuentes-Nieva & Galasso, 2014:2–27).

Truth versus loyalty

Both truth or honesty and loyalty are well understood in the workplace. Most people are familiar with the courtroom question: "Do you swear to tell the truth, the whole truth and nothing but the truth?" – probably not personally but definitely via TV programmes – and would know that being truthful or honest implies conforming to the facts and reality, with "telling it as it is". Loyalty entails fidelity or faithfulness, and would be viewed as an allegiance to someone or something, be that a friend or an ideal.

The choice between truth or honesty on the one hand and loyalty on the other can occur at a personal level to anyone within a workplace. It may not, at first sight, appear to be a difficult ethical dilemma because, for many people, honesty is the stronger value. Also, loyalty is arguably a less relevant value in the workplace as a result of changes in employment practices away from the security of the life-long career. Lynda Gratton, Professor of Management Practice at London Business School, claims that loyalty is dead, killed off through shortening contracts, outsourcing, automation and multiple careers (Kandola, 2011). This is illustrated by the colloquial retort to the question of workplace loyalty, which is "if you want loyalty, get a dog".

Much as loyalty to companies may have declined, loyalty can present a hard choice when bonds among colleagues are strong. When, for example, people have shared a profound experience – as those who were part of the struggle for freedom in South Africa – it builds extraordinary bonds of loyalty. This can present a choice between supporting a long-standing friend or comrade who is guilty of misconduct in the name of loyalty, and reporting them to the authorities for a breach of ethics in the name of honesty. While the choice of loyalty may be understandable, it can nonetheless serve to condone unethical behaviour.

This is a topic that should be included in the organisation's ethics training. Not because there is a simple answer, but rather to create an awareness of the potential for an ethical clash and thereby equip employees to manage it better.

A perversion of this dilemma would be to argue that nepotism or cronyism is acceptable because they too are simply placing loyalty to family or friends first. This would, however, be avoiding the second part of the dilemma, that is, honesty. If, for example, appointing a family member or friend to a position of authority is done regardless of the qualifications associated with the job or contrary to fair and correct recruitment procedures, it does not amount to honest behaviour. If the appointment was done correctly and in accordance with the principle of meritocracy, then the dilemma does not apply: both values can be satisfied.

Justice versus mercy

Justice versus mercy contrasts, on the one hand, fairness, impartiality, equity, and the even-handed application of applicable law, rules, codes or policies, with compassion, understanding, empathy and clemency on the other. Situations where justice conflicts with mercy mostly stem from the need to deal with a wrongdoing. The wrongdoing is not ignored in viewing this as a right versus right issue. Instead, this ethical dilemma focuses on managing the consequences or punishment of the unethical behaviour.

Labour law would generally provide guidance on the justice side of the decision. The choice to act mercifully, however, needs to be balanced against the risk that such a decision could set a precedent in the organisation or send the wrong message – for example, that misconduct is not viewed seriously or treated consistently.

A scenario where this conflict could occur would be, for example, when an employee has been found guilty of theft that was motivated by trying to provide for his/her extended family who are unemployed or incapacitated by illness, or for reasons that are even more compelling of one's sympathy and understanding. However, irrespective of the reason, it does not right the wrong of the theft – but it may well act as a mitigating factor to reduce the punishment. While the principle of mitigating factors is well recognised in the law, the organisation still needs to ensure that such a decision is not misunderstood by their employees. Transparency about disciplinary issues can help to avoid speculation and reduce perceptions of unfairness or favouritism when the company has chosen a more merciful approach. A proactive approach to minimising situations like this is to provide an employee assistance programme that can help employees to cope with situations of great need or desperation.

A noteworthy example of justice versus mercy in South Africa was the Truth and Reconciliation Commission (TRC), a body established in terms of the Promotion of National Unity and Reconciliation Act 34 of 1995 under the chairmanship of Archbishop Desmond Tutu to help deal with what happened under the apartheid regime. Dullah Omar, former Minister of Justice, stated that "a commission is a necessary exercise to enable South Africans to come to terms with their past on a morally accepted basis and to advance the cause of reconciliation" (TRC, 1995). While the commission's name does not speak to justice or mercy, a very significant feature of the commission was that it was empowered to grant amnesty from both civil and criminal prosecution to those who committed abuses during the apartheid era as long as the crimes were politically motivated, proportionate, and there was full disclosure by the person seeking amnesty. In legal terms, the democratic government embraced the legal principle of "restorative justice" instead of the "retributive justice" embodied in a Nuremberg-style trial. In human terms, it was an extraordinary demonstration of mercy and forgiveness when the law could have been pursued to take the full course of justice.

Triple bottom line dilemmas

In addition to the four types of ethical dilemma identified by Rushworth Kidder, there is a fifth dilemma. In the realm of the triple bottom line, right versus right dilemmas can arise when economic, social and environmental interests conflict with each other.

The social dimension includes, among many other factors, sound stakeholder relationships, a goal supported by corporate governance guidelines and the mandate of the social and ethics committee. However, the inclusiveness which this implies is not always practised, for example, when the local communities' interests are not taken into account. The organisation that claims a commitment to the environment needs supporting actions that extend beyond paper recycling bins in the office.

Given the increasing focus – and expectation – that organisations should pursue a path of good citizenship and embrace a triple bottom line, this is likely to the most visible area among the five ethical dilemmas. Right versus right conflicts can arise among any of the three bottom lines, including the economic bottom line, which is not only as valid and "right" as the other two, but is also essential for the ongoing operation of the business.

Of the examples of potential conflicts, one of the core ones is likely to be between conservation and development, that is, between protecting the environment and fostering social development. This can arise when business development damages the environment but creates employment and training opportunities for local communities. In the same way, cheap imports can support customers by offering more affordable goods, but could mean sacrificing the benefits of local production and the habit of buying products manufactured at home.

Reconciling these conflicts successfully will continue to become more important given that the overarching issue of sustainability is pertinent to all three areas: economic, social and environmental.

Communicating right versus right decisions

In making decisions related to these ethical dilemmas, organisations need to recognise that their decision may not be shared by other stakeholders who perhaps interpret the situation differently. This means that the company has to improve its communication about such choices. It may not persuade everyone to its view but, in the absence of its own explanation, even fewer people may understand the choice. This kind of communication can also serve as a check and balance as to whether the reasoning and choice will hold up to scrutiny. If the organisation is uncomfortable about having its choice made public, the choice could be a bad one.

In conclusion, the many aspects of right versus right decisions reflect that it may often be hard to know what the right choice or decision is. But these choices and decisions will still need to be made. It is hoped that with insight and a focus on others, these dilemmas will not amount to a zero sum game, where one value must "lose" or be sacrificed for the other to "win", but will increasingly be reconciled to achieve innovative "win–win" solutions that accommodate both desirable ends.

6.3   DECISION-MAKING METHODOLOGIES

It is self-evident that an ethical organisation should be synonymous with ethical decision making. To realise an ethical outcome to those decisions or choices, the decision-making process is important as it can aid positive outcomes and avert negative or less ethical results.

Decision-making procedures

A checklist of questions is a useful tool that can be used to disclose an organisation's ethics relative to specific issues or actions. Its usefulness rests on it being easy to apply and on the questions being based on common sense and framed in straightforward language. It can be an effective part of a decision making process that ensures the organisation looks beyond both the short-term implications of the issue and its own interests in the matter.

1   How did the ethical issue occur in the first place, and has the problem been properly defined?

2   How would the issue be defined or viewed from the opposite perspective, that is, from the standpoint of those whom the decision affects?

3   Which stakeholders would be affected by the decision, and what would the impact be for each of them?

4   What is the intention in making this ethical decision, and how does this intention align with the organisation's values and its profit motive?

5   What is the probability that the affected parties may misunderstand the intention of the decision? If so, what can be done to minimise this?

6   Would the decision stand the test of time: that is, would it be as valid in the long-term as it is in the short-term?

7   Could the ethical decision be shared without shame or guilt with the board of directors, one's family or with the media? If not, it suggests that the decision may be ethically suspect.

8   Does the decision set a precedent for the future? If so, is this a suitable guide for decisions that will follow?

Stephen Goldman, a lawyer and Distinguished Lecturer at Catholic University's Columbus School of Law, is the author of *Temptations in the Office: Ethical Choices and Legal Obligations*. He adopts a legal approach to the application of ethics that includes a procedure to aid managers through the complexity of ethical decisions in the workplace: the Foursquare Protocol. This tool uses a four-step process to help managers to make ethical decisions by determining what is truly relevant and significant in a situation. Goldman applies his proposed protocol to the main areas where he considers ethical problems are found: sexual harassment, conflict of interest, executive compensation, corner-cutting, and the abuse of power (Howes, 2008).

The steps are:

1   Bring to the surface as many facts about the situation as possible.

2   Gauge similarities with past situations, for example, how were previous ethical decisions arrived at? Also examine individual reactions to past solutions, for instance, how were similar decisions generally received by employees? Goldman observes that managers often handle ethical problems by following their "intuition", which can lead to the perception of unfairness and inconsistency, thereby compounding the original problem. This second step is intended to address this by tapping into the "organisational memory" for further insight (Goldman, 2008:65).

3   Clarify the relevant similarities and dissimilarities between those past situations and the present one.

4   Analyse the decision making situation based on an honest assessment of any personal or organisational interests, biases or conflicting interests that may impair the proper treatment of the problem (Howes, 2008).

Goldman stresses that early diagnosis of a problem's ethical core is the key to solving it. But he recognises that this necessitates that the people involved are open to pursuing an ethical path. He identifies people who refuse to acknowledge the ethics of the situation or to pursue an ethical approach as "Ethically Indifferent Persons" or EIPs, and offers advice to those who seek to achieve an ethical outcome but have an EIP as a boss: the employee needs to frame the issue for the boss in terms of business issues or the bottom line rather than from a value-based perspective (Goldman, 2008:13–14, 38–40).

The resolution principles in moral philosophy

However, a checklist or procedure (such as those above) may not always be sufficient when a decision involves right versus right issues. While the questions and steps outlined above are relevant, there are other approaches for dealing with ethical dilemmas that may be more helpful. This also warrants a review of the moral philosophical theories that underpin those processes for resolving the dilemma.

The standard inspirational answer to "do the right thing" offers little help when a really difficult right versus right management choice has to be made. Rushworth Kidder suggests resolving ethical dilemmas on the basis of three principles drawn from moral philosophy, approaches that he calls ends-based thinking, rule-based thinking, and care-based thinking.

Utilitarianism or "ends-based thinking"

"Ends-based thinking" is Kidder's term for what moral philosophers call utilitarianism (1995:24). Utilitarianism forms a sub-category of theories known as consequentialism and is distinguished from other theories in this group by focusing on the relative consequences – the relative amount of happiness or pain – brought about by the decision or action. The primary contributors to this theory are Jeremy Bentham (1748–1832) and John Stuart Mill (1806–1873). The three claims that are central to utilitarianism are:

1   Actions are to be judged as right or wrong solely by virtue of their consequences. Nothing else matters.

2   In assessing consequences, the only thing that matters is the amount of happiness or unhappiness that is created. Everything else is irrelevant.

3   Each person's happiness counts the same. Thus, right actions are those that produce the greatest balance of happiness over unhappiness, with each person's happiness counted equally important (Rachels & Rachels, 2010:109).

The central principle of choosing whatever produces the greatest good for the greatest number can be viewed as a form of cost–benefit analysis. While the theory has many detractors, it serves a purpose in the public and private sector. Public policy, for example, would often be based on the public interest or on the greatest benefit for the citizens. Many businesses use a utilitarian approach in determining how to treat the environment to achieve the greatest good for everyone involved. Norman Bowie and Meg Schneider, authors of *Business Ethics for Dummies*, point out that utilitarianism can also help to determine the least harm to the smallest number of people, for example, when cutting costs or retrenching employees – which, in the longer term, may be considered to benefit more parties (Bowie & Schneider, 2011:60–63).

Kantian deontology or "rule-based thinking"

Another influential moral theory is Kantian deontology – what Kidder refers to as "rule-based thinking" (Kidder, 1995:24) – which draws on the work of the 18th-century German philosopher, Immanuel Kant (1724–1804). Anton van

Niekerk, Professor of Philosophy and Director of the Centre for Applied Ethics at Stellenbosch University explains that an alternative name for this approach is "rule morality" since it emphasises the role of strict rules of behaviour in conferring moral status on actions. In direct opposition to utilitarianism, deontology holds that actions have an inherent moral worth and that unethical actions are in themselves wrong, irrespective of their consequences (van Niekerk, 2011:25). In terms of Kantian deontology, "we act morally when we act on the right motive, and that motive must always be to do one's duty" (van Niekerk, 2011:26). This rule-based approach is firmly based on duty, on what one ought to do.

The core principle of this moral theory is the "categorical imperative", which Kidder summarises as implying that one should act "in such a way that your actions could become a universal standard that others ought to obey" or that one should "follow only the principle that you want everyone else to follow" (Kidder, 1995:24). Kantian ethics recognises a number of actions as universally unacceptable: lying and deception, stealing, laziness and lack of charity (Bowie & Schneider, 2011:51).

Bowie and Schneider highlight the fact that the categorical imperative is easier to apply in business than in other aspects of life, as reasonable people would agree that, for example, committing fraud or treating workers poorly should not happen (2011:52). They also acknowledge that Kantian theory – which requires companies to treat their employees as independent agents, that is, not simply as a means to an end, but as an end in itself – is well suited to dealing with human resource issues (2011:63).

However, for this theory, too, there are limitations. The question of which moral rule should apply is highlighted by Anton van Niekerk. He uses a medical example of an HIV-positive patient who refuses to inform his partner about his status and, under the banner of doctor-patient confidentiality, will not allow the doctor to inform the partner. In this case, what rule should the doctor follow: do not harm, or doctor-patient confidentiality, both of which are core moral rules in the medical profession? (van Niekerk, 2011:29)

The golden rule or "care-based thinking"

"Care-based thinking" is Kidder's term that reflects the golden rule to do unto others as you would like them to do unto you (Kidder, 1995:25). It echoes a philosophy of reversibility, which entails testing actions by imagining oneself in the other person's position and assessing the situation from that perspective. It also requires the same weight to be given to the interests of others as to one's own.

While this theory has the advantage of being a well-recognised approach and a principle at the centre of most religions, it is also subject to criticism. Carl Sagan explores the golden rule and its variations. As regards doing unto others as you would have them do unto you, he points out that, for example, turning the other cheek is just a guarantee for more suffering if it involves a heartless adversary (Sagan, 1998:188).

Sagan describes the "silver rule" as embodying that one should not "do unto others what you would not have them do to you". He recognises this as being at the heart of non-violent civil disobedience such as advocated by Mahatma Gandhi and Martin Luther King Jr, which is an approach that has effected notable political change (1998:188).

The "brass rule", to "do unto others as they do unto you", echoes the principle of "an eye for an eye" in the negative and "one good deed deserves another" in the positive. Sagan also acknowledges what he calls the "iron rule", advocating that one "do unto others as you like, before they do it unto you", sometimes formulated as "he who has the gold makes the rules", which is, of course, in direct opposition to the golden rule (1998:188–189).

As to which approach is best, Sagan explores the Prisoner's Dilemma exercise[2] and game theory to conclude by acknowledging the self-defeating nature of envy, the importance of long-term over short-term goals, and dangers of both tyranny and patsy-dom[3] (1998, 195).

Resolving ethical dilemmas

Badaracco, in pursuit of clarifying ways to resolve ethical dilemmas, acknowledges that "in many right versus right dilemmas, the morality of consequences clashes with the morality of rights and duties" and concludes that "managers sense, quite correctly, that what philosophers have failed to resolve in theory, [the managers] must somehow resolve in practice" (Badaracco, 1997:36–37). He acknowledges that moral dilemmas are often likened to "wake-up calls" that highlight more clearly the significance of the issue and the decision. Badaracco also explores the "sleep test" as a route to resolving ethical dilemmas. In the literal version, it connects sound sleep to a good decision and *vice versa*. Defining the sleep test more broadly, Badaracco equates it with the ethics of intuition. This uses physical and emotional distress as indicators of a wrong decision and rests on the premise that you should follow your heart and trust yourself to make the right decision. It requires managers to use this approach thoughtfully and responsibly, however, and also to follow the ancient but difficult advice: "know thyself" (1997:41–42).

---

2   The game commonly referred to as The Prisoner's Dilemma is a classic example used to demonstrate game theory. It is usually explained through the use of a story about two people who are locked up for armed robbery and are not able to consult with each other as regards whether they confess, deny the charges, or blame the other person. The game shows why two individuals might not co-operate, even if it appears that it is in their best interests to do so, and why acting in their own best interest does not result in the ideal outcome.

3   Derived from the word "patsy", meaning someone who is a scapegoat or is easily cheated or victimised.

Kidder proposes nine checkpoints that should be worked through to resolve an ethical dilemma:

1   Recognise that there **is** a moral issue. This serves to exclude issues that have at their base economic or technological issues.

2   Determine the protagonist, not to establish who is involved, but to clarify who is responsible.

3   Gather the relevant facts.

4   Test for right versus wrong issues to establish if the case involves wrongdoing. If it does, it does not warrant this process – in the absence of a moral dilemma, the decision for a right-wrong issue should be clear. Kidder advocates three other tests if it is less obvious whether the decision being made involves a right versus wrong issue:

    a   *The stench test – does it smell?* This relies on moral intuition or gut response.

    b   *The front page test:* How would you feel if this were on the front page of tomorrow newspaper (or on headline TV news)?

    c   *The Mom test:* This asks whether one's mother (or any other admired role model) would do this.

5   Test which right versus right dilemma applies to the situation, that is, one from among the four Kidder identified – honesty versus loyalty, justice versus mercy, long-term versus short-term, or individual versus community – and the triple bottom line.

6   Apply the resolution principles – ends-based thinking, rule-based thinking or care-based thinking – to find the approach that seems most relevant to the issue.

7   Investigate whether there is a "trilemma'" option, a third choice or middle-ground solution that resolves the issue.

8   Make the decision.

9   Revisit and reflect on the decision. The value of this step lies in clarifying lessons, building expertise and embedding new examples for moral discussion. (Kidder, 1995:183–6)

The strength of Kidder's approach[4] (as it is exercised by the Institute for Global Ethics in their work in many places around the world) rests on the moral awareness and the clear definition of the opposing values established by having to explore the issue to establish which right versus right paradigm is applicable. Applying

---

4   The author was fortunate to have the opportunity to invite Rushworth Kidder to South Africa. He facilitated three workshops in 1999 and 2000 with senior executive groups, all of which were extremely successful.

the resolution principles also demands an in-depth focus on quite different approaches and reasoning which achieves a comprehensive ethical analysis of what is most pertinent.

While these resolution approaches combined with the principles of moral philosophy still do not offer an easy solution to manage ethical dilemmas, it should be borne in mind that ethical dilemmas, by their very nature, are complex issues that do not lend themselves to easy answers. The three resolution approaches can be very helpful, not least for the clarity of thought, definition of issues, level of attention and in-depth moral reasoning that they require to be applied to the ethical decision that needs to be made.

RECOMMENDED CASE STUDY AND COMMENTARY

Bodrock, P. 2005. The Shakedown. *Harvard Business Review*, March. HBR Reprint R0503A.

"A young American businessman in a developing country discovers that nothing gets done unless palms are greased. Should he play the game by his personal ethics – or the local rules?"

FURTHER READING

Badaracco Jr, JL. 1997. *Defining Moments: When Managers Must Choose Between Right And Right.* Boston: Harvard Business School Press.

Barton. D & Wiseman, M. 2014. Focusing Capital on the Long Term. *Harvard Business Review*, January-February.

Kidder, RM. 1995. *How Good People Make Tough Choices: Resolving the Dilemmas of Ethical Living.* New York: Fireside.

Magone, C, Neuman, M, & Weissman, F. (eds). 2011. *Humanitarian Negotiations Revealed: The MSF Experience.* London: C Hurst & Co. (Publishers) Ltd.

CHAPTER 7

ETHICS CAN

INTRODUCTION

The reasons organisations should actively pursue an ethical path and the issues to be considered have been outlined in the preceding six chapters. The ways in which an ethical outcome can be achieved has also been addressed, notably via the guidelines of the ethics management system. The immense value of ethical leadership has been recognised, as has the contribution of ordinary individuals to shape their circumstances to be more ethical. The final question is then: to give effect to the statement "ethics can", what else will it take?

There are a few things that warrant mention.

7.1　Responsibility beyond rules

Moving beyond rules and a largely rule-based approach to ethics is an important final take-away.

Among the enormous amount of research into children's development and education by Jean Piaget (1896–1980), a Swiss psychologist and philosopher, he focused on their concepts of right and wrong in his 1932 book *The Moral Judgement of the Child*. In this, he recognised that as children grow older, they move beyond simple obedience to rules to a stage where they recognise that being "good" no longer means just obeying the rules. They come to understand that, in order to achieve a fair and just outcome, it also means that they need to accept and share the responsibility of evaluating and making rules that will be fair to all (Piaget, 1932).

This is a good extension of the roles and responsibilities of being the rule-maker. But it needs to go further. It needs to extend to values, too. Everyone in his/her own capacity and his/her own context can also make the choice to live by values that are fair and just to all. The choice means that one needs to move from being a passive observer to become a teacher, an active participant and a role model for ethics.

7.2 Do something: stand together

Being a conscious role model implies that one acts to support and foster ethical conduct and that one acts against unethical behaviour. However, the impetus to stand up for ethics can be undermined by the extent of misconduct that is evident in virtually every sector and industry. This is where standing together with others is so valuable.

The saying "all that is necessary for the triumph of evil is that good men do nothing" is often attributed to Edmund Burke (1729–1797), the renowned Irish political philosopher. But the correct quote speaks to the point of standing together even better: "When bad men combine, the good must associate; else they will fall one by one, an unpitied sacrifice in a contemptible struggle" (Burke, 1770:i,526). Surrounding and associating oneself with people who are ethical add a great deal to what can be done individually.

Statistics from Transparency International's 2013 Global Corruption Barometer support this view from the perspective of fighting corruption. The survey, which interviewed more than 114 000 people in 107 countries, found that two in three people (67%) believe that ordinary citizens can make a difference in the fight against corruption, with South Africa falling in the 61% to 80% cluster of respondents who felt they could make a difference (Transparency International, 2013:21). It is an encouraging point to remember.

7.3 All that is needed is a tipping point

A last point that should be taken into account to deter the sense that misconduct is so vast that nothing will make a difference is the fact that achieving a change does not necessarily rest on getting the majority of people to change. Tipping point theory recognises that a series of small changes or incidents can become significant enough to cause a larger, more important change.

Malcolm Gladwell, a Canadian journalist, a staff writer for *The New Yorker* and best-selling author, popularised this in his book *The Tipping Point: How Little Things Can Make a Big Difference*. He identified three concepts that contribute to a tipping point: the law of the few, the stickiness factor, and the power of context (Gladwell, 2001:29). The law of the few maintains that before widespread popularity can be attained, a few key people must champion the idea, concept or product before it can reach the tipping point. The stickiness factor is the quality that makes messages and meaning stick, and the power of context reflects the influence of the surrounding circumstances at both a macro and a micro level (2001:15–29).

Applied to ethics, there is a need for people to champion the concept of ethics and the message needs to be persuasive. The message and the focus cannot be just on what is bad: most people are already almost "immune" to being shocked by ethical scandals. Instead the focus should be on growing and highlighting the good as well. It is unlikely that the media will change to run "good news" headlines, but within organisations it is perfectly possible to ensure that what is ethical is recognised and celebrated. As to the context, ironically, each ethical scandal creates a more conducive context for change.

7.4   Ethics can

So, is changing ethics within each workplace really impossible? Can it be done?

Granted, transforming one organisation ethically may not change the industry, the region or the country, but it can make a difference – and not only in the workplace. Wouldn't it be wonderful if the positive impact of ethics on employees was such that they took those ethical lessons back to their homes and communities? What a great achievement it would be to hear an employee standing up for what is right on the basis that "it is not the way we do things where I work".

APPENDIX

---

1 PRACTICAL EXERCISE: TEST YOUR KNOWLEDGE OF BRIBERY, FRAUD AND CORRUPTION

The following selection of questions and answers is a useful exercise to test understanding and knowledge relative to bribery, fraud and corruption. The exercise addresses the dimensions of bribery, fraud and corruption and what it does and does not include, which is based largely on the criteria set out in the Prevention and Combating of Corrupt Activities Act 12 of 2004. It also highlights the many negative consequences and illustrates why the fight against bribery, fraud and corruption is so important.

Although employees may already know the answers to many of the questions below, it is nonetheless a valuable exercise because it acts as a reminder that increases their awareness (high ethical awareness is an effective deterrent of misconduct) and emphasises the company's stance on fraud and fraudulent conduct.

Table 1: Questions to test your knowledge of bribery, fraud and corruption

1. **What is fraud?**	
Which of the following statements are true or false relative to fraudulent conduct in the workplace?	
1. Fraud is characterised by intentional deception or wilful misrepresentation.	
2. Fraud is generally committed for the benefit of the perpetrator.	
3. Fraud can only be committed by people inside the company.	
4. Fraud can involve the falsification or alteration of records or documents.	
5. Fraud includes the misappropriation of any of the company's assets.	

2. What constitutes bribery?	
Indicate if the following examples do or do not constitute bribery.	
1. The employee accepts a R500 donation towards his/her favourite charity from a potential new supplier for ignoring the lack of the necessary documentation in their vendor application.	
2. The manager signs off a fraudulent sick note for a favourite employee.	
3. The procurement official accepts two tickets to a major local sporting event in return for falsifying the BEE credentials for a new supplier.	
4. The recruitment manager's wife is given a R1 000 beauty salon/spa voucher to thank him for giving a friend a job.	
3. What does corruption entail?	
Indicate which statements do or do not define corruption in the workplace.	
1. Corruption is dishonest or fraudulent conduct by those in power.	
2. Corruption applies only to the public sector, for example, government officials who take bribes.	
3. Corruption is the deliberate disregard of legislation, regulations or instructions for personal gain.	
4. Corruption mostly applies to fraudulent tenders.	
5. Corruption includes improper favouritism, for example, among employees.	
6. Corruption is any wilful action that influences or attempts to influence conduct or decisions away from what is fair and equitable.	

4. What behaviours are associated with fraud?

Indicate which of the following behaviours would normally be identified in a fraud prevention policy as wrong or unacceptable.

1. Smoking in non-designated areas	
2. Forgery, for example, recording of transactions without substance	
3. Omission of the effects of a transaction from records or documents	
4. Dishonesty	
5. Theft of company assets	
6. Falsification or alteration of records	
7. Sexual harassment	
8. Intimidation	
9. Accepting a gift that is valued in excess of the company's limit.	

5. What are the consequences of bribery, fraud and corruption?

Indicate which outcomes are or are not likely or possible.

1. Damaged company reputation	
2. A criminal record for the individual involved	
3. A verbal warning	
4. Damaged personal reputation for the employee	
5. A disciplinary hearing	
6. Dismissal	
7. Negative press coverage	
8. Financial loss for the company	
9. No action if you are a senior employee	

10. A written warning	
11. Nothing: it is unlikely that this action would be uncovered	
12. Criminal charges.	

6. Can you do anything to prevent or curb bribery, fraud and corruption?	
Indicate what can or cannot be done.	
1. Yes, I will not personally engage in any fraudulent activities.	
2. No, I cannot make a difference.	
3. Yes, I can ensure that I never accept a gift or a favour that could be viewed as a bribe.	
4. Yes, I can report incidents of bribery, fraud or corruption.	
5. No, it is not my responsibility to do anything about bribery, fraud or corruption.	

7. How does your company score?	
The following are all examples of how companies address fraud and fraudulent activities. Score each factor on a scale of 1 – 10 based on how effective you think it is in your company, using 1 for factors that you think are not at all effective, and 10 for the factors that are the most effective at reducing bribery, fraud and corruption.	
1. Promoting transparency in procedures, for example, for procurement.	
2. Establishing strong financial management systems.	
3. Prohibiting individuals found guilty of bribery, fraud or corruption from doing future business with the company.	
4. Adopting mechanisms for stakeholders or the public to submit complaints or reports of bribery, fraud and corruption.	
5. Co-operating with the relevant authorities investigating cases involving bribery, fraud or corruption, for example, by giving them evidence, documents, records and witness statements.	
6. Establishing accountability and oversight mechanisms, for example, by the compliance function, the internal audit function and external auditors.	

Table 2: Answers to the questions about bribery, fraud and corruption in Table 1

Answers to question 1: What is fraud?

Answers to 1, 4 and 5

These are true. Fraud encompasses a wide range of irregularities, illegal acts and includes all acts of dishonesty. It is characterised by, among other factors:

- Intentional deception or wilful misrepresentation
- The falsification or alteration of records or documents, for example, changing the date of a document and representing it as the correct version, and
- The misappropriation of any of the company's assets.

Answer to 2

Untrue. Fraud is not committed for the benefit of only the perpetrator. It can also be committed to the detriment of the company or even for the benefit of a third party.

Answer to 3

Untrue. Fraud can be committed by people both inside and outside the company.

Useful explanation

Fraud is defined in South African law as the unlawful and intentional misrepresentation of facts (that is, distortion of the truth) intended to cause actual or potential prejudice to another.

Answers to question 2: What constitutes bribery?

Answers to 1 and 3

- The procurement official example is very clear: it is bribery.
- The donation to charity can appear to confuse that scenario. But, while a donation to charity is good, the R500 has been given to influence the employee unduly to act against what is correct and right, that is, to ignore the lack of necessary documentation in the vendor application. As such, this does constitute bribery.
- Both are also subject to disciplinary action. If the employee is found guilty, the likely outcome is dismissal.

Answer to 2

Signing off a false sick note does not represent bribery. However, the falsification and misrepresentation amounts to dishonesty, which is a core facet of fraud.

Answer to 4

While a "thank-you'" gift may be appropriate at times, it risks creating the impression that it was given to create undue influence. In this instance, it would easily be seen to be a bribe in return for giving the friend a job – irrespective of whether the appointment was perfectly fair and in line with company policy and legislation.

Useful explanation

Bribery is regarded as the act of offering, giving, receiving or soliciting money, a gift or something of value for the purpose of influencing the action of another in the discharge of his/her business or public or legal duties.

Answers to question 3: What does corruption entail?

Answers to 1, 3, 5 and 6

These factors all define corruption. Corruption is a broad term that encompasses, among other behaviours:

*   Dishonest or fraudulent conduct by those in power
*   The deliberate disregard of legislation, regulations or instructions for personal gain
*   Improper favouritism, for example, among employees
*   Any wilful action that influences or attempts to influence conduct or decisions away from what is fair and equitable.

Answer to 2

This is incorrect. Corruption is not limited to the public sector. Corruption can occur in organisations of all kinds, such as private sector companies, state-owned companies or not-for-profit organisations.

Answer to 4

Fraudulent tenders are a high profile example of corruption, but corruption includes many other types of illegal and fraudulent actions, including all forms of bribery.

Useful explanation

Corruption includes the following:

*   The private use of public resources, bribery, improper favouritism and the dishonest or fraudulent conduct by those in power.
*   Any wilful action that by means of bribery or attempted bribery, extortion, intimidation, fraud or misinterpretation of facts sways or attempts to sway the natural course of events from open, fair and equitable practices.
*   Wilful disregard of legislation, regulations, instructions or directives for personal gain.

Answers to question 4: What behaviours are associated with fraud?

Answers to 1, 7, 8 and 9

All of these behaviours are not acceptable in the workplace. However, they would generally not fall within a fraud prevention policy, but would usually be addressed in the company's code of conduct or in specific policies, such as:

- The smoking policy

- The sexual harassment policy and procedure

- Intimidation in the disorderly conduct policy

- Gifts in a gift policy.

Answers to 2, 3, 4, 5 and 6

These are correct as all these examples reflect unacceptable behaviours that should be addressed in a fraud prevention or similar policy:

- Forgery, for instance, recording of transactions without substance

- Omission of the effects of a transaction from records or documents

- Dishonesty

- Theft of company assets

- Falsification or alteration of records.

Answers to question 5: What are the consequences of bribery, fraud and corruption?

Answers to 1, 2, 4, 5, 6, 7, 8 and 12

These all represent possible negative consequences of bribery, fraud and corruption.

- It can damage the company's reputation, generate negative press coverage, and cause the company financial loss.

- The employee found guilty of bribery, fraud or corruption will almost certainly go through a disciplinary process and he/she faces dismissal and a damaged personal reputation if found guilty.

- Criminal charges can follow, as many companies reserve the right in incidence of bribery, fraud or corruption to institute legal action, including possible criminal prosecution and civil action for the recovery of losses, often irrespective of the amount involved. The guilty individual could therefore end up with a criminal record.

Answers to 3 and 10

It is extremely unlikely that a sanction as mild as a verbal warning or even a written warning would be given to an employee who is suspected of bribery, fraud or corruption. Since this behaviour is considered very serious, the disciplinary process would probably start at a much higher level. If found guilty, dismissal is almost certainly the outcome for the employee.

Answer to 9

The company should ensure that this does not occur: there should be no exceptions for senior employees, managers, executives or directors. The fraud policy should be applied consistently irrespective of seniority.

Answer to 11

The possibility exists that other employees or stakeholders apart from the perpetrators will know when bribery, fraud or corruption occurs. It is therefore not totally unlikely that the action could be uncovered. Investigative journalists, for instance, have been very effective in uncovering and publicising many instances of misconduct. Regrettably, however, the impunity of many influential individuals and public officials does give credence to the view that there are occasions when nothing will happen.

Answers to question 6: Can you do anything to prevent or curb bribery, fraud and corruption?

Answers to 1, 3 and 4

These answers are correct inasmuch as everyone can make a difference to reduce or prevent bribery, fraud, corruption or any irregular activity by:

- Not engaging in any fraudulent activities.

- Never accepting a workplace-related gift or a favour that could be viewed as a bribe.

- Reporting occurrences of bribery, fraud or corruption.

Answer to 2

This is not true and it is a view that needs to be addressed. Everyone can make a difference if they act on the knowledge or suspicion they have of wrongdoing or possible wrongdoing.

Answer to 5

This is also not true and such lack of responsibility to do anything about bribery, fraud or corruption is a cause for concern. Rather, it is everyone's responsibility to act against illegal and irregular behaviour. Ignoring it and failing to do anything can suggest to others that you condone the activity, which could harm your reputation.

Useful explanations about reporting misconduct

- Reporting bribery, fraud and corruption is a legal duty in South Africa. In terms of the Prevention and Combating of Corrupt Activities Act 12 of 2004 (PCCA), chapter 7, section 34, any person who holds a position of authority and who knows or ought reasonably to have known or suspected that someone has committed a corrupt or fraudulent act involving an amount of R100 000 or more must report that knowledge or suspicion to any police official (South Africa, 2004:32, Ch 7, s 34).

- While employees are encouraged to report misconduct, disciplinary action may be taken against anyone making an allegation that is made frivolously, in bad faith, maliciously or for personal gain.

- Employees who wish to remain anonymous can report misconduct via anonymous ethics hotline (if the company has that facility), which is intended to provide a completely independent, confidential service to provide a safe reporting channel.

Answers to question 7: How does your company score?

All these factors should form part of a company's commitment to reduce and eliminate bribery, fraud and corruption. The scoring of the effectiveness of these mechanisms should be used to provide feedback to the company about what is and is not perceived to be effective in the fight against fraud.

2 PRACTICAL EXERCISE: TEST YOUR KNOWLEDGE OF DISORDERLY CONDUCT

Disorderly conduct can have a negative impact on organisations and its people. It can, for example, create an unpleasant working environment for employees, damage the professional image of the company in the eye of stakeholders who observe unacceptable behaviour, and erode the value of integrity.

The aim of an exercise focused on disorderly conduct – such as the questions and answers below – is to raise the level of awareness of disorderly conduct among employees and ensure that they have a good understanding of what behaviour is not permitted.

Although in many cases employees already know the right answer as to what is or is not acceptable conduct in the workplace, a reminder is nonetheless important. It serves to emphasise the company's stance on disorderly conduct and make desirable behaviour a clear, constant goal.

A policy on disorderly conduct is also a valuable inclusion in a company's code of conduct as it is very wide-ranging. It addresses a host of unacceptable behaviours that are often written up in separate policies, thereby contributing to making the code more succinct.

Table 3: Questions to test your knowledge of disorderly conduct

1	**What constitutes disorderly conduct?**	
Indicate which behaviours do or do not constitute disorderly conduct in the workplace.		
1	Insubordination	
2	Accidental damage to company property	
3	Assault, attempted assault, threats of violence or physical violence	
4	Intimidation	
5	Indecency	
6	Untidiness	
7	Negligence	
8	Occasional late arrival for work	
9	Abusive language	
10	Wilful damage to company property	
11	Racial harassment	
12	Sexual harassment	
13	Sleeping on duty	
14	Consuming alcohol on company premises, being drunk at work or being under the influence of narcotics.	

2	**What is correct as regards absenteeism and sick leave?**	

Indicate if you consider the following statements to be correct or incorrect as regards unauthorised absenteeism and/or sick leave abuse.

1	It shows the employee is lazy.	
2	It erodes productivity.	
3	It can place a greater workload on colleagues who have to do the work of the absent employee.	
4	It indicates that the employee is not enjoying his/her job.	
5	It amounts to theft of the company's time.	
6	It disrupts the company's normal operations.	
7	It risks the offender's job as it can lead to a disciplinary action and dismissal	
8	Employees are entitled to sick leave in terms of South Africa labour law.	
9	It is acceptable to call in sick if the company is unlikely to authorise the time off that an employee needs.	

3	**Understanding disorderly conduct**	

Indicate if you agree or disagree with the following statements.

1	Failure to comply with safety standards should be part of a policy on disorderly conduct and should be treated very seriously.	
2	Reporting disorderly conduct is not the concern of employees. It is for the company to act against misconduct.	
3	The unauthorised entry to the workplace with firearms or other dangerous weapons by employees and/or their visitors should be strictly prohibited.	
4	Victimisation should not be tolerated under any circumstances.	

Table 4: Answers to the questions in Table 3 about disorderly conduct

---

Answers to question 1: What constitutes disorderly conduct?

Answers to 2, 6 and 8

While companies should aim to minimise accidental damage to its property, untidiness and occasional late arrival at work, these behaviours do not amount to disorderly conduct.

Answers to 1, 3, 4, 5, 7, 9, 10, 11, 12 and 13

- Yes, these behaviours constitute disorderly conduct: insubordination, assault or attempted assault, threats of violence or physical violence, intimidation, indecency, negligence, abusive language, wilful damage to company property, racial harassment, sexual harassment and sleeping on duty.

- While the majority of these behaviours are unacceptable under any circumstances, there are some nuances that could be taken into account. For example:

  o Abusive language includes abuse in any language. While abusive language to a fellow employee is totally unacceptable, it may be considered even more severe when it is directed at an external stakeholder, such as a customer or client.

  o Sleeping on duty is unacceptable conduct for an office worker because it reduces productivity and amounts to the "theft" of company time. However, this is much more serious for security staff, for instance, for whom sleeping on duty could lead to serious safety risks.

Answer to 14

Consuming alcohol on company premises, being drunk at work and being under the influence of narcotics at work are all completely unacceptable. However, most companies would include these issues in a policy for substance abuse and dependency rather than in a disorderly conduct policy.

Useful explanations

- Insubordination is the intentional and wilful refusal by a subordinate to obey lawful, legitimate orders given by a superior. However, refusing to perform an action that is illegal is not insubordination.

- Indecency refers to improper or disgraceful conduct, such as indecent exposure.

- Negligence refers to the failure to exercise reasonable care.

- Gross negligence is the conscious disregard of the need to use reasonable care, which is likely to cause foreseeable injury or harm to people, property or both.

Answers to question 2: What is correct as regards absenteeism and sick leave?

Answers to 1 and 4

Absenteeism doesn't necessarily indicate laziness or a lack of job satisfaction. It can arise from many factors. However, the many negative consequences of unauthorised absenteeism make it an offence that is treated very seriously.

Answers to 2, 3, 5, 6 and 7

All of these factors correctly represent the negative consequences of absenteeism. These factors, together with the fact that unauthorised absenteeism and sick leave abuse are often among the highest areas of disorderly conduct, illustrate why it is so serious.

- It erodes productivity.
- It can place a greater workload on colleagues who have to do the work of the absent employee.
- It amounts to theft of the company's time.
- It disrupts the company's normal operations.
- Disciplinary action can be taken against employees who abuse sick leave or are absent without permission, which can include dismissal.

Answer to 8

Section 22 of the South African Basic Conditions of Employment Act 75 of 1997 (as amended by the Basic Conditions of Employment Amendment Act 11 of 2002, among others) provides for time off in the event of ill health. This is, however, not a "right" accorded to employees under other circumstances than those specified in the legislation.

Answer to 9

If an employee tells the employer that he/she is ill when he/she is not, it constitutes being dishonest, which would be included either in the disorderly conduct policy or the bribery, fraud and corruption policy, or both.

Useful explanations

- *Sick leave allowance in South Africa:* Section 22 of the South African Basic Conditions of Employment Act 75 of 1997 provides that workers may take the number of days they would normally work in a six-week period for sick leave on full pay in a three-year period. However, during the first six months of employment, workers are entitled to only one day of paid sick leave for every 26 days worked (South Africa, 1997).

- *Family responsibility leave or compassionate leave in South Africa:* Subject to a few conditions, section 27 of the Basic Conditions of Employment Act provides for three days' paid family responsibility leave during each annual leave cycle for fulltime workers. This is for family matters such as the birth of the employee's child or death of a close relative (South Africa, 1997).

- *"Duvet day":* A "duvet day" is generally a formal allowance of time off given by some employers, most commonly in the United Kingdom and the United States of America. It differs from annual leave in that no prior notice is needed. However, the term is also more loosely used by people who take a day off work for no normally accepted reason, such as because of a grievance.

Answers to question 3: Understanding disorderly conduct

Answers to 1, 2, 3 and 4

1   *Agree:* Failure to comply with safety standards should be include in the disorderly conduct policy. Its severity, however, would be dependent on the nature of the organisation's business and the industry. Thus, for example, safety would feature much more prominently for a mining or construction company than for a legal practice.

2   *Disagree:* Everyone should report disorderly conduct. It allows the company to act against misconduct, and, because reporting can minimise misconduct, it can also create a more pleasant working environment.

3   *Agree:* All organisations should strictly prohibit the unauthorised entry to the workplace with firearms or other dangerous weapons by employees and/or their visitors. Such security infringements are very serious because they can endanger employees' safety and/or the safety of others.

4   *Agree:* The company should not tolerate victimisation under any circumstances. Even if workers have embarked on a legal strike, victimisation is still prohibited.

BIBLIOGRAPHY

INTRODUCTION

Bloomberg Businessweek. 2014. Bloomberg Businessweek's 2014 design issue. *Bloomberg Businessweek*, 20 March. [Online]. Available: http://www.businessweek.com/articles/2014-03-20/businessweeks-2014-design-issue-what-cant-design-do. [Accessed 30 March 2014].

CHAPTER 1

Agency staff. 2014. Court dismisses DA's e-tolling application. *BDlive*, 13 March. [Online]. Available: http://www.bdlive.co.za/business/transport/2014/03/13/court-dismisses-das-e-tolling-application. [Accessed 30 April 2014].

Barford, V & Holt, G. 2013. *Google, Amazon, Starbucks: The rise of tax shaming*. BBC, 21 May. [Online]. Available: http://www.bbc.com/news/magazine-20560359. [Accessed 30 March 2014].

Bowie, NE & Schneider, M. 2011. *Business ethics for dummies*. Hoboken, NJ: Wiley Publishing.

Clayton, S. 2012. Amendment to the Foreign Corrupt Practices Act – Another perspective. *FCPA compliance and ethics blog*, 3 July. [Online]. Available: http://tfoxlaw.wordpress.com/2012/07/03/amendment-to-the-foreign-corrupt-practices-act-another-perspective/. [Accessed 29 March 2014].

de Vos, P. 2013. E-toll civil disobedience reveals lack of respect for democracy. *Constitutionally Speaking*, 22 November. [Online]. Available: http://constitutionallyspeaking.co.za/e-toll-civil-disobedience-reveals-lack-of-respect-for-democracy/. [Accessed 30 April 2014].

Denning, S. 2013. The origin of the world's dumbest idea: Milton Friedman. *Forbes*, 26 June. [Online]. Available: http://www.forbes.com/sites/stevedenning/2013/06/26/the-origin-of-the-worlds-dumbest-idea-milton-friedman/. [Accessed 1 April 2014].

Domscheit-Berg, D. 2014. Edward Snowden, Time 100 pioneers (the 100 most influential people) *Time*, 23 April. [Online]. Available: http://time.com/70869/jose-mujica-2014-time-100/ (accessed 26 April 2014].

Duvenage, W. 2014. Sanral – critically out of touch with reality? *Daily Maverick*, 27 January. [Online]. Available: http://www.dailymaverick.co.za/opinionista/2014-01-27-sanral-critically-out-of-touch-with-reality/#.U2FRGvmSzYs. [Accessed 30 April 2014].

Elkington, J. 1999. *Cannibals with forks: The triple bottom line of 21st century business*. Oxford: Capstone Publishing Ltd.

Franklin, B. 1789. *Letter to Jean-Baptiste Leroy*. UShistory.org, 13 November. [Online]. Available: http://www.ushistory.org/franklin/quotable/quote73.htm. [Accessed 30 March 2014].

Freemantle, A & Rockey, N. (eds). 2004. *The good corporate citizen – pursuing sustainable business in South Africa*. Cape Town: Trialogue.

Friedman, M. 1970. The social responsibility of business is to increase its profits. *The New York Times Magazine*, 13 September. [Online]. Available: http://www.colorado.edu/studentgroups/libertarians/issues/friedman soc resp business.html. [Accessed 31 March 2014].

Fuentes-Nieva, R & Galasso, N. 2014. *Working for the few: Political capture and economic inequality, Oxfam Briefing Paper*. Oxfam, 178, 20 January. [Online]. Available: http://www.oxfam.org/sites/www.oxfam.org/files/bp-working-for-few-political-capture-economic-inequality-200114-en.pdf. [Accessed 29 April 2014].

Handy, C. 2002. What's a business for? *Harvard Business Review,* December.

Institute of Directors in Southern Africa (IoDSA). 2009. *King report on corporate governance in South Africa (King III).* Johannesburg: IoDSA.

Irving, J. 1994. *The cider house rules.* London: Corgi Books, Transworld Publishers Ltd.

Judin, M. 2012. Bribe, facilitation fee or commission? Setting the example. *Ethics Monitor,* 5, August. [Online]. Available: http://www.ethicsmonitor.co.za/Article.aspx?AID=63. [Accessed 29 March 2014].

Kidder, RM. 1995. *How good people make tough choices: Resolving the dilemmas of ethical living.* New York, NY: Simon & Schuster.

Neate, R. 2014. GlaxoSmithKline accused of bribing doctors in Poland. *The Guardian,* 14 April. [Online]. Available: http://www.theguardian.com/business/2014/apr/14/gsk-accused-bribing-doctors-poland. [Accessed 18 April 2014].

OECD/AfDB. 2012. Bribery and related offences (Chapter 2). *Stocktaking of business integrity and anti-bribery legislation, policies and practices in twenty African countries.* OECD. Paris: OECD Publishing. [Online]. Available: http://www.keepeek.com/Digital-Asset-Management/oecd/governance/stocktaking-of-business-integrity-and-anti-bribery-legislation-policies-and-practices-in-twenty-african-countries/bribery-and-related-offences_9789264169586-6-en#page5. [Accessed 30 March 2014].

Peters, T & Waterman, RH. 1995. *In search of excellence: Lessons from America's best-run companies.* Glasgow: HarperCollins Publishers.

Ramalho, A. 2012. Bribe, facilitation fee or commission? Setting the example. *Ethics Monitor,* 5, August. [Online]. Available: http://www.ethicsmonitor.co.za/Article.aspx?AID=63. [Accessed 29 March 2014].

SAPA. 2014. E-tolls: Sanral, transport minister admit 'teething' problems. *City Press,* 18 February. [Online]. Available: http://www.citypress.co.za/news/e-tolls-sanral-transport-minister-admit-teething-problems/. [Accessed 30 April 2014].

Schoeman, C. 2012. *Ethics: Giving a damn, making a difference.* Grahamstown: NISC.

Singer, P. 1993. *Practical ethics.* 2nd ed. Cambridge: Cambridge University Press.

South Africa. 1996. Constitution of the Republic of South Africa, 1996. Chapter 2 Bill of Rights, section 15. Pretoria: Government Printer. [Laws]. [Online]. Available: http://www.gov.za/documents/constitution/1996/a108-96.pdf. [Accessed 31 March 2014].

South Africa. 2004. Prevention and Combating of Corrupt Activities Act 12 of 2004. Pretoria: Government Printer. [Laws]. [Online]. Available: http://www.justice.gov.za/legislation/acts/2004-012.pdf. [Accessed 10 April 2014].

South Africa. 2009. Companies Act 71 of 2008. Pretoria: Government Printer. [Laws].

The Economist. 2012. Wake up and smell the coffee. *The Economist,* 15 December. [Online]. Available: http://www.economist.com/news/business/21568432-starbuckss-tax-troubles-are-sign-things-come-multinationals-wake-up-and-smell. [Accessed 30 March 2014].

Thomas, K. 2013. Glaxo says it will stop paying doctors to promote drugs. *New York Times,* 16 December. [Online]. Available: http://www.nytimes.com/2013/12/17/business/glaxo-says-it-will-stop-paying-doctors-to-promote-drugs.html?_r=2&hp=&adxnnl=1&adxnnlx=1387247811-5ZLkdoLSr+BHantpg1+APQ&.. [Accessed 7 March 2014].

Tichy, NM & Sherman, S. 1993. *Control your destiny or someone else will.* New York: HarperCollins Publishers.

World Commission on Environment and Development (WECD). 1987. *Report: Our common future.* WECD. [Online]. Available: http://www.un-documents.net/our-common-future.pdf. [Accessed 1 April 2014].

CHAPTER 2

Adams, S. 1997. *The Dilbert principle*. London: Boxtree.

BizNews. 2013. Why public sector corruption is more worrying than its private sector counterpart. *BizNews.com*, 10 December. [Online]. Available: http://www.biznews.com/cynthia-schoeman-etihicsn-monitor/. [Accessed 27 March 2014].

Corsmeier, JA. 2013. Wisconsin Supreme Court imposes one year suspension on lawyer for greatly inflating his billable hours to qualify for almost $50,000.00 in law firm bonuses. *Lawyer Ethics Alert Blogs*, 9 January. [Online]. Available: http://jcorsmeier.wordpress.com/2013/01/09/wisconsin-supreme-court-imposes-one-year-suspension-on-lawyer-for-greatly-inflating-his-billable-hours-to-qualify-for-almost-50000-00-in-law-firm--bonuses/. [Accessed 27 March 2014].

De Wet, P. 2013. First Strut: 20 years of mega fraud. *Mail & Guardian*, 8 August. Available at http://mg.co.za/article/2013-08-08-00-mind-boggling-fraud-is-one-for-the-books. [Accessed 17 March 2014].

eNCA. 2013a. Madonsela warns SA corruption at crisis levels. *eNCA*, 15 October. [Online]. Available: http://www.enca.com/south-africa/madonsela-warns-sa-corruption-crisis-levels. [Accessed 27 March 2014].

eNCA. 2013b. SA losing battle against corruption. *eNCA*, 3 May. [Online]. Available: http://www.enca.com/south-africa/sa-losing-battle-against-corruption. [Accessed 27 March 2014].

Hall, V. 2009. *The truth about trust in business*. Austin, TX: Emerald Book Company.

Ingram, D & Henry, D. 2014. UPDATE 2-JPMorgan to pay $614 mln in U.S. mortgage fraud case. *Reuters*, 4 February. [Online]. Available: http://www.reuters.com/article/2014/02/05/jpmorgan-settle-idUSL2N0L928N20140205. [Accessed 2 April 2014].

Institute of Directors in Southern Africa (IoDSA). 2009. *King report on corporate governance in South Africa (King III)*. Johannesburg: IoDSA.

James. G. 2014. When leaders cheat, companies lose. *Inc.*, 10 February. [Online]. Available: http://www.inc.com/geoffrey-james/when-leaders-cheat-companies-lose.html. [Accessed 7 April 2014].

Mantshantsha, S & Mungadze, S. 2014. Pinnacle Holdings share dive 'tempts' CEO to buy stock. *BDlive*, 27 March. [Online]. Available: http://www.bdlive.co.za/business/technology/2014/03/27/pinnacle-holdings-share-dive-tempts-ceo-to-buy-stock. [Accessed 10 April 2014].

Muller, J. 2014. Toyota admits misleading customers; agrees to $1.2 billion criminal fine. *Forbes*, 19 March. [Online]. Available: http://www.forbes.com/sites/joannmuller/2014/03/19/toyota-admits-misleading-customers-agrees-to-1-2-billion-criminal-fine/. [Accessed 2 April 2014].

Public Service Commission. 2013. *Fact sheet on finalised cases of financial misconduct for the 2011/2012 financial year*. February. Public Service Commission. [Online]. Available: http://www.psc.gov.za/documents/2013/Factsheet%20Finalised%20Cases%20of%20Financial%20Misconduct%202011-12.pdf. [Accessed 27 March 2014].

PwC, 2014. *Global economic crime survey. Economic crime: A threat to business globally*. PwC. [Online]. Available: http://www.pwc.com/gx/en/economic-crime-survey/. [Accessed 12 April 2014].

Saint-Onge, H. 1997. *The principles of leadership: Creating competitive advantage in the knowledge era*. Presentation at the Global Leadership Development Conference, Brussels, 22 May.

Sedutla, M. 2014. 2014 – year of the morally ethical lawyer. *De Rebus*, January/February.

Solis, B. 2012. Survival of the fitting: 10 important trends to survive digital Darwinism. @ *BrianSolis*, 29 March. [Online]. Available: http://www.briansolis.com/2012/03/10-tenets-to-survive-digital-darwinism/. [Accessed 4 April 2014].

South Africa. 2004. Prevention and Combating of Corrupt Activities Act 12 of 2004. Pretoria: Government Printer. [Laws]. [Online]. Available: http://www.justice.gov.za/legislation/acts/2004-012.pdf. [Accessed 10 April 2014].

South Africa. 2009. Companies Act 71 of 2008. Pretoria: Government Printer. [Laws].

Swift, A. 2013. Honesty and ethics rating of clergy slides to new low. *Gallup Politics*, 16 December. [Online]. Available: http://www.gallup.com/poll/166298/honesty-ethics-rating-clergy-slides-new-low.aspx. [Accessed 27 March 2014].

Transparency International. 2012. *Corruption perceptions index 2012*. Transparency International. [Online]. Available: http://www.transparency.org/cpi2012/results. [Accessed 27 March 2014].

Transparency International. 2013a. *Corruption perceptions index 2013*. Transparency International. [Online]. Available: http://www.transparency.org/cpi2013/results. [Accessed 27 March 2014].

Transparency International. 2013b. *Global corruption barometer 2013*. Transparency International. Available on: http://www.transparency.org/whatwedo/pub/global_corruption_barometer_2013. [Accessed 27 March 2014].

Vegter, I. 2013. Do we tolerate private sector corruption? *Daily Maverick*, 25 November. [Online]. Available: http://www.dailymaverick.co.za/opinionista/2013-11-26-do-we-tolerate-private-sector-corruption/#.UzQ4QvmSzYs. [Accessed 27 March 2014].

Williams, DK. 2013. The most valuable business commodity: Trust. *Forbes*, 20 June. [Online]. Available: http://www.forbes.com/sites/davidkwilliams/2013/06/20/the-most-valuable-business-commodity-trust/. [Accessed 4 April 2014].

CHAPTER 3

Association of Certified Fraud Examiners (ACFE). 2012. *2012 Report to the nations on occupational fraud and abuse*. ACFE. [Online]. Available: http://www.acfe.com/uploadedFiles/ACFE_Website/Content/rttn/2012-report-to-nations.pdf. [Accessed 13 April 2014].

Block, P. 1993. *Stewardship: Choosing service over self-interest*. San Francisco, CA: Berrett-Koehler Publishers.

Bulawayo24 staff reporter. 2014. Shocking recruitment corruption at Gwanda School of Nursing. *Bulawayo24*, 18 February. [Online]. Available: http://bulawayo24.com/index-id-news-sc-regional-byo-43026.html#sthash.4Bv2LTu9.dpuf. [Accessed 21 March 2014].

Bussin, M. 2014. *Remuneration and talent management: Strategic compensation approaches for attracting, retaining and engaging talent*. Johannesburg: Knowres Publishing (Pty) Ltd.

Catalyst. 2014a. Statistical overview of women in the workplace. *Catalyst*, 3 March. [Online]. Available: http://www.catalyst.org/knowledge/statistical-overview-women-workplace. [Accessed 12 April 2014].

Catalyst. 2014b. Women CEOs of the Fortune 1000. *Catalyst*, 15 January. [Online]. Available: http://www.catalyst.org/knowledge/women-ceos-fortune-1000. [Accessed 12 April 2014].

Claassen, RD. 2013. *Dictionary of legal words and phrases*. Durban: Butterworth Publishers (Pty) Ltd (an imprint of Lexis Nexis).

Cooper, M. 2013. For women leaders, likability and success hardly go hand-in-hand, *Harvard Business Review HBR Blog Network*, 30 April. [Online]. Available: http://blogs.hbr.org/2013/04/for-women-leaders-likability-a/. [Accessed 12 April 2014].

Corruption Watch. nd. Conflict of interest. *Corruption Watch*. [Online]. Available: http://www.corruptionwatch.org.za/sites/default/files/conflict-of-interest-corruption-watch.pdf. [Accessed 12 April 2014].

Dannhauser, R. 2012. Can investment management ethics be taught? *CFA Institute*. [Online]. Available: http://www.cfainstitute.org/ethics/Documents/cfa_ethics_article.pdf. [Accessed 15 April 2014].

Dlamini, P. 2014. Millions paid to 'ghosts'. *Times Live*, 6 March. [Online]. Available: http://m.timeslive.co.za/thetimes/?articleId=11210898. [Accessed 12 April 2014].

Drucker, P. 1996. Introduction: Not enough generals were killed. In F Hesselbein, M Goldsmith & R Beckhard (eds). *The leader of the future*. San Francisco, CA: Jossey-Bass Publishers.

eNCA. 2014. Institute calls for South African code of ethics. *eNCA*, 21 February. [Online]. Available: http://www.enca.com/money/institute-calls-south-african-code-ethics. [Accessed 7 March 2014].

Ethics Resource Center. 2013. *National business ethics survey of the US workforce*. Ethics Resource Center. [Online]. Available: http://www.ethics.org/downloads/2013NBESFinalWeb.pdf. [Accessed 15 April 2014].

Greenleaf, RK. 1977. *Servant leadership: A journey into the nature of legitimate power and greatness*. New York, NY: Paulist Press.

Hannon, K. 2013. Sheryl Sandberg's 5 best lean in tips for women. *Forbes*, 3 March. [Online]. Available: http://www.forbes.com/sites/nextavenue/2013/03/13/sheryl-sandbergs-5-best-lean-in-tips-for-women/. [Accessed 12 April 2014].

Hofmeyr, J & Nyoka, A. 2013. *Transformation audit 2013: Confronting exclusion*. Cape Town: The Institute for Justice and Reconciliation. [Online]. Available: http://ijr.org.za/publications/ta2013.php. [Accessed 12 April 2014].

Hymowitz, C & Daurat, C. 2013. Best-paid women in S&P 500 settle for less remuneration. *Bloomberg*, 13 August. [Online]. Available: http://www.bloomberg.com/news/2013-08-13/best-paid-women-in-s-p-500-settle-for-less-with-18-gender-gap.html. [Accessed 12 April 2014].

Institute of Directors in Southern Africa (IoDSA). 2009. *King report on corporate governance in South Africa (King III)*. Johannesburg: IoDSA.

International Labour Office (ILO). 2012. *Decent work country profile: South Africa*. Geneva: International Labour Office (ILO). [Online]. Available: http://www.ilo.org/wcmsp5/groups/public/---dgreports/---integration/documents/publication/wcms_180322.pdf. [Accessed 16 June 2014].

IOL staff reporter. 2013. Unisa swoops on fraudulent certificates. *IOL News*, 27 June. [Online]. Available: http://www.iol.co.za/news/crime-courts/unisa-swoops-on-fraudulent-certificates-1.1538445#.UywvtPmSzYs. [Accessed 21 March 2014].

Kidder, RM. 1995. *How good people make tough choices: Resolving the dilemmas of ethical living*. New York, NY: Simon & Schuster.

Legalbrief Today. 2013. Finance Committee adopts Banks Amendment Bill. *Legalbrief Today*, 14 August. [Online]. Available: http://www.legalbrief.co.za/article.php?story=20130814053127267>. [Accessed 13 April 2014].

Louw, W. 2013. *Sexual offences in South Africa*. 25 April. Helen Suzman Foundation. [Online]. Available: http://hsf.org.za/resource-centre/hsf-briefs/sexual-offences-in-south-africa. [Accessed 12 April 2014].

Mabuza, E. 2013. Lesotho denies women right to be chiefs. *BDlive*, 17 May. [Online]. Available: http://www.bdlive.co.za/africa/africannews/2013/05/17/lesotho-denies-women-right-to-be-chiefs. [Accessed 12 April 2014].

Madison, J. 1941. The Federalist No. 51. In A Hamilton, J Jay & J Madison. *The federalist: A commentary on the Constitution of the United States*. New York, NY: Modern Library.

Mail & Guardian staff reporter. 2013. Zuma addresses gender concerns with appointment of new judges. *Mail & Guardian*, 16 May. [Online]. Available: http://mg.co.za/article/2013-05-16-zuma-congratulates-newly-appointed-jsc-judges. [Accessed 12 April 2014].

Manyathi-Jele, N. 2014. Can ethics be taught? *De Rebus*, April. [Online]. Available: http://www.myvirtualpaper.com/doc/derebus/de_rebus_april_2014/2014032002/#12. [Accessed 15 April 2014].

OECD. 2006. *The OECD fights corruption*. OECD. [Online]. Available: http://www.oecd.org/development/governance-development/37393705.pdf. [Accessed 13 April 2014].

OECD. 2009. *OECD convention on combating bribery of foreign public officials in international business transactions*. OECD. [Online]. Available: http://www.oecd.org/daf/anti-bribery/oecdantibriberyconvention.htm. [Accessed 13 April 2014].

OECD/AfDB. 2008. *Initiative to support business integrity and anti-bribery efforts in Africa*. OECD. [Online]. Available: http://www.oecd.org/daf/anti-bribery/businessintegrityandanti-briberyeffortsinafricaoecdafdbinitiative.htm. [Accessed 13 April 2014].

Pickworth, E. 2014. CEOs address executive remuneration concerns. *BDlive*, 12 February. [Online]. Available: http://www.bdlive.co.za/business/financial/2014/02/12/ceos-address-executive-remuneration-concerns. [Accessed 13 April 2014].

Public Protector (South Africa). 2014a. *Secure in comfort* (Report No. 25 of 2013/4). March. Public Protector South Africa. [Online]. Available: http://www.publicprotector.org/library%5Cinvestigation_report%5C2013-14%5CFinal%20Report%2019%20March%202014%20.pdf. [Accessed 12 April 2014].

Public Protector (South Africa). 2014b. *When governance and ethics fail* (Report No. 23 of 2013/2014). February. Public Protector South Africa. [Online]. Available: http://www.pprotect.org/library/investigation_report/2013-14/WHEN%20GOVERNANCE%20FAILS%20REPORT%20EXEC%20SUMMARY.pdf. [Accessed 18 March 2014].

Raman, AP. 2011. Why don't we try to be India's most respected company? *Harvard Business Review*, November.

Remuneration Committee Forum (RemCo). 2013. *Position paper 2: The remuneration policy*. December. Institute of Directors in Southern Africa (IoDSA), [Online]. Available: http://c.ymcdn.com/sites/www.iodsa.co.za/resource/collection/57F28684-0FFA-4C46-9AD9-EBE3A3DFB101/Remuneration_Policy_December_2013_FINAL.pdf. [Accessed 13 April 2014].

Rossouw, M. 2011. From the presidency to 'ice-cream mission' to Zim. *Mail & Guardian*, 28 February. [Online]. Available: http://mg.co.za/article/2011-02-28-from-the-presidency-to-icecream-mission-zim. [Accessed 11 April 2014].

Rushe, D. 2014. Five former Bernie Madoff aides found guilty of concealing Ponzi scheme. *The Guardian*, 24 March. [Online]. Available: http://www.theguardian.com/business/2014/mar/24/bernie-madoff-five-former-aides-guilty. [Accessed 11 April 2014].

Sundberg, S. 2013. *Woman, Work, and the Will to Lead*. London (UK): Ebury Press/W Allen.

Senge, P. 1996. Introduction. In J Jaworksi (ed). *Synchronicity: The inner path of leadership*. San Francisco (CA): Berrett-Koehler Publishers.

Sky News. 2014. Shock pay statistic on fat cat Wednesday. *Sky News*, 8 January. [Online]. Available: http://news.sky.com/story/1191957/shock-pay-statistic-on-fat-cat-wednesday. [Accessed 13 April 2014].

South Africa. 1996. Constitution of the Republic of South Africa, 1996. Pretoria: Government Printer. [Laws].

South Africa. 1998. Employment Equity Act 55 of 1998. Pretoria: Government Printer. [Laws].

South Africa. 2000. Protected Disclosures Act 26 of 2000. Pretoria: Government Printer. [Laws].

South Africa. 2003. Broad-Based Black Economic Empowerment Act 53 of 2003. Pretoria: Government Printer. [Laws].

South Africa. 2004. Prevention and Combating of Corrupt Activities Act 12 of 2004. Pretoria: Government Printer. [Laws]. [Online]. Available: http://www.justice.gov.za/legislation/acts/2004-012.pdf. [Accessed 26 March 2014].

South Africa. 2009. Consumer Protection Act 68 of 2008. Pretoria: Government Printer. [Laws].

South Africa. 2009. Companies Act 71 of 2008. Pretoria: Government Printer. [Laws].

South Africa. 2011. Companies Regulations (GN R351 in GG 34239, 26 April). Pretoria: Government Printer. [Laws].

The Economist. 2013a. The feminist mystique. *The Economist*, 16–22 March.

The Economist. 2013b. Fixing the fat cats. *The Economist*, 9–15 March.

The Telegraph. 2013. Antony Jenkins to staff: Adopt new values or leave Barclays. *The Telegraph*, 17 January. [Online]. Available: http://www.telegraph.co.uk/finance/newsbysector/banksandfinance/9808042/Antony-Jenkins-to-staff-adopt-new-values-or-leave-Barclays.html. [Accessed 10 April 2014].

Transparency International. 2013a. *Corruption Perceptions Index 2013*. Transparency International. [Online]. Available: http://www.transparency.org/cpi2013/results. [Accessed 27 March 2014].

Transparency International. 2013b. *Global Corruption Barometer 2013*. Transparency International. [Online]. Available: http://www.transparency.org/whatwedo/pub/global_corruption_barometer_2013. [Accessed 27 March 2014].

United Nations Global Compact. 2000. *The ten principles. United Nations Global Compact.* [Online]. Available: http://www.unglobalcompact.org/abouttheGc/TheTenprinciples/index.html. [Accessed 13 April 2014].

University of Pretoria Law Clinic, 2013. *The incidence of and undesirable practices relating to garnishee orders – a follow-up report.* Pretoria: University of Pretoria Law Clinic.

Vaughan, L & Finch, G. 2013. The lie in Libor. *Bloomberg Markets*, March.

Williams, JC & Cuddy, AJC. 2012. Will working mothers take your company to court? *Harvard Business Review*, September.

Williams, L. 2014. Platinum strike could be godsend for South African pgm miners. *Mineweb,10* April. [Online]. Available: http://www.mineweb.com/mineweb/content/en//mineweb-platinum-group-metals?oid–237082&sn–Detail. [Accessed 13 April 2014].

CHAPTER 4

ABC News. 2013. Gillard delivers apology to victims of forced adoption. *ABC News*, 21 March. [Online]. Available: http://www.abc.net.au/news/2013-03-21/gillard-delivers-apology-to-victims-of-forced-adoption/4585972. [Accessed 20 April 2014].

Agence France-Press. 2014. Alexei Navalny placed under house arrest in Russia. *The Guardian*, 28 February. [Online]. Available: http://www.theguardian.com/world/2014/feb/28/alexei-navalny-russia-opposition-leader-house-arrest. [Accessed 19 April 2014].

Allix, M. 2014. Construction collusion 'was almost entrenched'. *BDlive*, 11 March. [Online]. Available: http://www.bdlive.co.za/business/industrials/2014/03/11/construction-collusion-was-almost-entrenched. [Accessed 27 March 2014].

Associated Press. 2014. Why did GM just launch a recall on cars it knew were causing deaths as far back as 2004? *Financial Post,* 12 March. Available on: http://business.financialpost.com/2014/03/12/gm-recall-deaths/. [Accessed 26 March 2014].

Bazerman, MH & Tenbrunsel, AE. 2011. Ethical breakdowns. *Harvard Business Review*, April.

Beard, A & Hornick, R. 2011. It's hard to be good. *Harvard Business Review*, November.

Bruce, M. 2013. Jofi Joseph fired: White House official ousted for snarky anonymous tweets. *ABC News*, 23 October. [Online]. Available: http://abcnews.go.com/blogs/politics/2013/10/white-house-official-fired-for-snarky-anonymous-twitter-feed/. [Accessed 21 April 2014].

Chumley, CK. 2014. Anthony Weiner on his current sexting habits: 'None of your business'. *The Washington Times*, 17 April. [Online]. Available: http://www.washingtontimes.com/news/2014/apr/17/anthony-weiner-his-current-sexting-habits-none-you/. [Accessed 19 April 2014].

Clark, J. 2013. We owe SA an explanation – Murray & Roberts CEO. *Moneyweb*, 11 July. [Online]. Available: http://www.moneyweb.co.za/moneyweb-industrials/we-owe-sa-an-explanation--murray--roberts-ceo. [Accessed 27 March 2014].

CNBC Africa Power Lunch. 2013. SARS & Hawks probing SA cell-phone giants. *CNBC Africa*, 2 December. [Online]. Available: http://www.cnbcafrica.com/video/?bctid=2884284104001. [Accessed 20 April 2014].

Cushman Jr, JH. 1998. Nike pledges to end child labor and apply US rules abroad. *New York Times, International Business*, 13 May. [Online]. Available: http://www.nytimes.com/1998/05/13/business/international-business-nike-pledges-to-end-child-labor-and-apply-us-rules-abroad.html?pagewanted=all&src=pm. [Accessed 20 April 2014].

Deloitte & Compliance Week. 2013. *Compliance trends survey 2013*. Deloitte, August. [Online]. Available:http://deloitte.wsj.com/riskandcompliance/files/2013/09/us_aers_grr_final_deloitte_compliance_week_pdf_080813.pdf. [Accessed 19 April 2014].

De Rebus. 2014. The fight against counterfeiting. *De Rebus*, 14 April. [Online]. Available: http://www.myvirtualpaper.com/doc/derebus/de_rebus_april_2014/2014032002/7.html#6. [Accessed 15 April 2014].

Dolan, D. 2014. Pinnacle director faces bribery charge. *IOL Business News*, 26 March. [Online]. Available:http://www.iol.co.za/business/news/pinnacle-director-faces-bribery-charge-1.1666272#.U1L__vmSzYs. [Accessed 20 April 2014].

Eliseev, A & Whittles, G. 2013. IPID defends low conviction rate. *Eye Witness News (EWN)*,12 April. [Online]. Available: http://ewn.co.za/2013/04/12/Mido-Macia-court-case-to-be-postponed. [Accessed 18 April 2014].

Ernst & Young (EY). 2013. *Navigating today's complex business risks: Europe, Middle East, India and Africa fraud survey 2013*. Ernst & Young. [Online]. Available: http://www.ey.com/Publication/vwLUAssets/Navigating_todays_complex_business_risks/$FILE/Navigating_todays_complex_business_risks.pdf. [Accessed 18 April 2014].

Ethics Resource Center. 2013. *National business ethics survey of the US workforce*. Ethics Resource Center. [Online]. Available: http://www.ethics.org/downloads/2013NBESFinalWeb.pdf. [Accessed 15 April 2014].

Garside, J. 2014. Hewlett-Packard to pay $108m to settle scandal over bribery of public officials. *The Guardian*, 9 April. [Online]. Available: http://www.theguardian.com/business/2014/apr/09/hewlett-packard-108m-corruption-government-it-us-bribery. [Accessed 18 April 2014].

Gentile, MC. 2010. Keeping your colleagues honest. *Harvard Business Review*, March.

Greene, G. 2002. *The quiet american.* London: Vintage.

Hall, V. 2009. *The truth about trust in business.* Austin, TX: Emerald Book Company.

Healy, PM & Ramanna, K. 2013. When the crowd fights corruption. *Harvard Business Review*, January–February.

Heineman Jr, B. 2007. Avoiding ethical landmines. *Harvard Business Review*, April.

Herzberg, F. 1968. One more time: How do we motivate employees? *Harvard Business Review*, January-February. (Reproduced in Business classics: Fifteen key concepts for managerial success, *Harvard Business Review*, 1991.

Holmes, R. 2014. 5 lessons from US Airways' social media scandal. *LinkedIn*, 16 April. [Online]. Available: http://www.linkedin.com/today/post/article/20140416185316-2967511-5-lessons-from-us-airways-social-media-scandal. [Accessed 21 April 2014].

Institute of Directors in Southern Africa (IoDSA). 2009. *King report on corporate governance in South Africa (King III)*. Johannesburg: IoDSA.

IPEC (ILO). 2005. Combating child labour in cocoa growing. *ILO*, February. [Online]. Available: http://thecnnfreedomproject.blogs.cnn.com/category/chocolates-child-slaves/. [Accessed 2 April 2014].

Jones, G. 2014. South Africa neglects alarming effect of cybercrime. *BDlive*, 14 January. [Online]. Available: http://www.bdlive.co.za/business/2014/01/14/south-africa-neglects-alarming-effect-of-cybercrime. [Accessed 21 April 2014].

Katz, C & Lemire, J. 2013. Anthony Weiner bares soul in magazine interview, declares he's weighing run for mayor. *New York Times Daily News*, 11 April. [Online]. Available: http://www.nydailynews.com/new-york/anthony-weiner-weighing-run-mayor-article-1.1313438. [Accessed 19 April 2014].

Kellogg's. 2014. Kellogg announces global commitment to fully traceable sourcing of palm oil. Kellogg Company, 14 February. [Online]. Available: http://newsroom.kelloggcompany.com/2014-02-14-kellogg-announces-global-commitment-to-fully-traceable-sourcing-of-palm-oil. [Accessed 2 April 2014].

Kidder, RM. 1995. *How good people make tough choices: Resolving the dilemmas of ethical living*. New York, NY: Fireside.

Kopecki, D. 2013. JPMorgan's #AskJPM Twitter hashtag backfires against bank. *Bloomberg*, 14 November. [Online]. Available: http://www.bloomberg.com/news/2013-11-14/jpmorgan-twitter-hashtag-trends-against-bank.html. [Accessed 21 April 2014].

Levitt, SD & Dubner, SJ. 2005. *Freakonomics*. London: Penguin Books.

Machanik, W. 2012. I take full responsibility for my actions. *BDlive*, 2 December. [Online]. Available: http://www.bdlive.co.za/business/property/2012/12/02/i-take-full-responsibility-for-my-actions. [Accessed 20 April 2014].

Mail & Guardian reporter . 2014. Malawi in middle of $100m 'cashgate' scandal, *Mail & Guardian*, 14 January. [Online]. Available: http://mg.co.za/article/2014-01-14-malawi-in-midst-of-100m-cashgate-scandal. [Accessed 18 April 2014].

McKenzie, D & Swails, B. 2012. Child slavery and chocolate: All too easy to find. *CNN*, 19 January. [Online]. Available: http://thecnnfreedomproject.blogs.cnn.com/2012/01/19/child-slavery-and-chocolate-all-too-easy-to-find/. [Accessed 2 April 2014].

McLeod, T. 2014. One with the lot. *McLeod Governance: The Weekly Wrap*, 27 March. [Online]. Available: http://www.mcleodgovernance.com/one-lot/?utm_source=McLeod+Governance+Newsletter&utm_campaign=7271812557-McLeod_Governance_News_Test_38 [Accessed 7 April 2014].

Moulton, J. 1924. In RM Kidder (ed). 1995. *How good people make tough choices: Resolving the dilemmas of ethical living*. New York, NY: Fireside.

Mungadze, S. 2014. A need for speed: SA cyber security lags behind its peers. *Financial Mail*, 27 March. [Online]. Available: http://www.financialmail.co.za/features/2014/03/27/sa-cyber-security-lags-behind-its-peers. [Accessed 21 April 2014].

Nestlé. 2012. Nestlé sets out actions to address child labour: Nestlé cocoa plan. *Nestlé*. [Online]. Available: http://www.nestlecocoaplan.com/nestle-sets-out-actions-to-address-child-labour/. [Accessed 2 April 2014].

Nieuwenkamp, R. 2014. Cut and run, or stay and help? *Ethical Corporation*, 5 March. [Online]. Available: http://www.ethicalcorp.com/supply-chains/cut-and-run-or-stay-and-help. [Accessed 20 April 2014].

O'Carroll, L. 2011. Rupert Murdoch's public acts of contrition. *The Guardian*, 16 July. [Online]. Available: http://www.guardian.co.uk/media/2011/jul/16/rupert-murdoch-phone-hacking-apology. [Accessed 20 April 2014].

OECD. 2002. *Supply chains and the OECD guidelines for multinational enterprises: Roundtable on corporate responsibility*. OECD, 19 June. [Online]. Available: http://www.oecd.org/corporate/mne/roundtableoncorporateresponsibilitysupplychainsandtheoecdguidelinesformultinationalenterprises.htm. [Accessed 2 April 2014].

OECD/AfDB. 2012. Bribery and related offences (Chapter 2). *Stocktaking of business integrity and anti-bribery legislation, policies and practices in twenty African countries*. OECD. Paris: OECD Publishing. [Online]. Available: http://www.keepeek.com/Digital-Asset-Management/oecd/governance/stocktaking-of-business-integrity-and-anti-bribery-legislation-policies-and-practices-in-twenty-african-countries/bribery-and-related-offences_9789264169586-6-en#page5. [Accessed 30 March 2014].

Parloff, R. 2006. Not exactly counterfeit. *Fortune*, 26 April. [Online]. Available: http://money.cnn.com/magazines/fortune/fortune_archive/2006/05/01/8375455/index.htm. [Accessed 2 April 2014].

Paton, G. 2014. Teachers 'cheat' to hit exam targets. *The Telegraph*, 13 April. [Online]. Available: http://www.telegraph.co.uk/education/educationnews/10763017/Teachers-cheat-to-hit-exam-targets.html. [Accessed 17 April 2014].

Perkins Coie LLP. 2014. Top 10 Compliance trends for the new year. *Perkins Coie LLP*. [Online]. Available: http://ethisphere.com/wp-content/uploads/2014/02/perkins-coie-compliance-trends-2014.pdf. [Accessed 20 April 2014].

Puzzanghera, J. 2014. Bank of America to pay $772 million for illegal credit card practices. *Los Angeles Times*, 9 April. [Online]. Available: http://www.latimes.com/business/money/la-fi-mo-bank-of-america-credit-card-consumer-financial-protection-bureau-20140409,0,1935530.story#ixzz2z7cD5Odm. [Accessed 18 April 2014].

PwC. 2014. *Global economic crime survey. Economic crime: A threat to business globally*. PwC. [Online]. Available: http://www.pwc.com/gx/en/economic-crime-survey/. [Accessed 21 April 2014].

Radcliffe, S. 2013. The origins of that hummingbird. *Biz Community*, 23 October. [Online]. Available: http://www.bizcommunity.com/Article/196/182/102342.html. [Accessed 21 April 2014].

Rehak, J. 2002. Tylenol made a hero of Johnson & Johnson: The recall that started them all. *New York Times*, 23 March. [Online]. Available: http://www.nytimes.com/2002/03/23/your-money/23iht-mjj_ed3_.html. [Accessed 20 April 2014].

Reuters. 2013. Pasta maker Barilla tries to make amends after chairman's anti-gay remarks. *NY Daily News*, 4 November. [Online]. Available: http://www.nydailynews.com/life-style/eats/barilla-fix-anti-gay-scandal-article-1.1506397. [Accessed 20 April 2014].

Riley, M, Elgin, B, Lawrence, D & Matlack, C. 2014. Missed alarms and 40 million stolen credit card numbers: How Target blew it. *Bloomberg Businessweek*, 13 March. [Online]. Available: http://www.businessweek.com/articles/2014-03-13/target-missed-alarms-in-epic-hack-of-credit-card-data. [Accessed 21 April 2014].

Rossouw, D. 2002. *Business ethics in Africa*. Cape Town: Oxford University Press.

SAPA. 2009. UK imposes visa restrictions on South Africans. *Politicsweb*, 9 February. [Online]. Available: http://www.politicsweb.co.za/politicsweb/view/politicsweb/en/page72308?oid=117065&sn=Marketingweb%20detail. [Accessed 2 April 2014].

SAPA. 2013a. Interpol seizes 100 tons of illicit medicines. *eNCA*, 11 October. [Online]. Available: http://enca.com/south-africa/interpol-seizes-100-tons-illicit-medicines. [Accessed 2 April 2014].

SAPA. 2013b. Fake driver's licence racket bust. *City Press*, 24 January. [Online]. Available: http://www.citypress.co.za/news/fake-drivers-licence-racket-bust/. [Accessed 2 April 2014].

SAPA. 2014. Take corrupt politicians to task. *IOL News*, 25 March. Available on: http://www.iol.co.za/news/crime-courts/take-corrupt-politicians-to-task-1.1666210. [Accessed 26 March 2014].

Schuitema, E. 1998. *Leadership*. Cape Town: Ampersand Press.

Sellers, P. 2005. Remodeling Martha. *Fortune* (Europe edition), 14 November.

Shirky, C. 2010. *Cognitive surplus: Creativity and generosity in a connected age*. New York, NY: The Penguin Press.

Shuibo, X. 2011. The experts respond. In K Xin & W Haijie. Culture Clash in the Boardroom. *Harvard Business Review*, September.

Simonian, H. 2011. UBS chief resigns over rogue trader affair. *Financial Times (ft).com*, 24 September. [Online]. Available: http://www.ft.com/intl/cms/s/0/ce67a8ca-e697-11e0-8c5e-00144feab49a.html#axzz2zNwF3LW9. [Accessed 20 April 2014].

Singer, P. 1993. *Practical ethics*. 2nd ed. Cambridge: Cambridge University Press.

South Africa. 2002. Electronic Communications and Transactions Act 25 of 2002. Pretoria: Government Printer. [Laws].

South Africa. 2004. Prevention and Combating of Corrupt Activities Act 12 of 2004. Pretoria: Government Printer. [Laws]. [Online]. Available: http://www.justice.gov.za/legislation/acts/2004-012.pdf. [Accessed 26 March 2014].

South Africa. 2009. Companies Act 71 of 2008. Pretoria: Government Printer. [Laws].

Spoor & Fischer. 2013. Social media in the workplace – employer's or employee's? *Point*, (5), November. [Online]. Available: http://www.spoor.com/home/25/files/Point2013/PointNovember2013_1_Social_Media.pdf. [Accessed 21 April 2014].

Stout, H, Vlasic, B, Ivory, D & Ruiz, R. 2014. General Motors misled grieving families on a lethal flaw. *The New York Times*, 24 March. Available on: http://www.nytimes.com/2014/03/25/business/carmaker-misled-grieving-families-on-a-lethal-flaw.html?_r=0. [Accessed 26 March 2014].

The Economist. 2013. The digital arms trade. *The Economist*, 30 March–5 April.

The Economist. 2014. Hacking back: Bankers go undercover to catch bad guys, *The Economist*, 5 April. [Online]. Available: http://www.economist.com/news/finance-and-economics/21600148-bankers-go-undercover-catch-bad-guys-hacking-back. [Accessed 21 April 2014].

The Ethisphere® Institute. 2014. *World's most ethical companies*. The Ethisphere® Institute. [Online]. Available: http://ethisphere.com/worlds-most-ethical/. [Accessed 17 April 2014].

Thomson Reuters Governance, Risk and Compliance (GRC). 2013. *Cost of compliance survey 2013*. Thomson Reuters Accelus. [Online]. Available: http://accelus.thomsonreuters.com/sites/default/files/GRC00186.pdf. [Accessed 19 April 2014].

Tichy, NM & Sherman, S. 1994. *Control your destiny or someone else will*. New York, NY: HarperCollins Publishers.

Transparency International. 2013. *Corruption Perceptions Index 2013*. Transparency International. [Online]. Available: http://www.transparency.org/cpi2013/results. [Accessed 27 March 2014].

Tybout, AM & Roehm, M. 2009. Let the response fit the scandal. *Harvard Business Review*, 87(12):82–88, December.

Walshe, S. 2013. Mark Sanford's primary win demonstrates power of forgiveness after scandal. *ABC News*, 4 April. [Online]. Available: http://abcnews.go.com/Politics/mark-sanford-wages-political-comeback-political-redemption/story?id=18874019. [Accessed 20 April 2014].

Whitbourn, M. 2014. The tweet that cost $105,000. *The Sydney Morning Herald*, 4 March. [Online]. Available: http://www.smh.com.au/technology/technology-news/the-tweet-that-cost-105000-20140304-341kl.html. [Accessed 21 April 2014].

World Commission on Environment and Development (WECD). 1987. *Report: Our common future*. WECD. [Online]. Available: http://www.un-documents.net/our-common-future.pdf. [Accessed 1 April 2014].

World Economic Forum (WEF). 2012. *Global risks 2012*. 7th ed. World Economic Forum. [Online]. Available: http://www3.weforum.org/docs/WEF_GlobalRisks_Report_2012.pdf. [Accessed 21 April 2014].

World Economic Forum (WEF). 2014. *Global risks 2014*. 9th ed. World Economic Forum. [Online]. Available:. [Accessed 22 April 2014].

Wynn, C. 2014. Pinnacle CEO: Bribery charges a surprise. *Eye Witness News (EWN)*, 27 March. [Online]. Available: http://ewn.co.za/2014/03/27/pinnacle-ceo-says-bribe-claims-a-surprise. [Accessed 20 April 2014].

CHAPTER 5

Aljazeera America. 2014. Report: NSA kept tabs on 122 World Leaders. *Aljazeera*, 30 March. [Online]. Available: http://america.aljazeera.com/articles/2014/3/30/nsa-snowden-merkel.html. [Accessed 26 April 2014].

BBC. 2014. Garda commissioner Martin Callinan resigns over whistleblower row. *BBC News*, 25 March. [Online]. Available: http://www.bbc.com/news/world-europe-26730162. [Accessed 26 April 2014].

Blaine, S. 2012. Firms 'fail to advise' investors on social responsibility. *BDlive*, 23 August. [Online]. Available: http://www.bdlive.co.za/national/science/2012/08/23/firms-fail-to-advise-investors-on-social-responsibility. [Accessed 26 April 2014].

Deloitte & Compliance Week. 2013. *Compliance trends survey 2013*. August. Deloitte. [Online]. Available: http://deloitte.wsj.com/riskandcompliance/files/2013/09/us_aers_grr_final_deloitte_compliance_week_pdf_080813.pdf. [Accessed 19 April 2014].

Dinan, S. 2012. IRS pays $104 million to whistle-blower. *The Washington Times*, 11 September. [Online]. Available: http://www.washingtontimes.com/news/2012/sep/11/irs-pays-104-million-whistleblower/. [Accessed 26 April 2014].

ECR. 2014. Euromoney country risk, quarter 1. *Euromoney Country Risk*. [Online]. Available: http://www.euromoneycountryrisk.com/Default.aspx#. [Accessed 26 April 2014].

Ethics Resource Center. 2013. *2013 National ethics survey*. Ethics Resource Center. [Online]. Available: http://www.ethics.org/downloads/2013NBESFinalWeb.pdf. [Accessed 26 April 2014].

Garside, J. 2013. HP chairman quits as fallout over Autonomy sale rolls on. *The Guardian*, 5 April. [Online]. Available: http://www.theguardian.com/business/2013/apr/05/hewlett-packard-chairman-quits. [Accessed 26 April 2014].

Institute of Directors in Southern Africa (IoDSA). 2009. *King report on corporate governance in South Africa (King III)*. Johannesburg: IoDSA.

Institute of Directors in Southern Africa (IoDSA). 2011. *The code for responsible investing in South Africa*. IoDSA. [Online]. Available: http://c.ymcdn.com/sites/www.iodsa.co.za/resource/resmgr/crisa/crisa_19_july_2011.pdf. [Accessed 27 April 2014].

KPMG. 2014. *The 2014 M&A outlook survey*. KPMG LLP. [Online]. Available: https://www.kpmg.com/IE/en/IssuesAndInsights/ArticlesPublications/Documents/2014-m-a-outlook-survey-report.pdf. [Accessed 26 April 2014].

Melville-Ross, T. 2013. Ethical business: Companies need to earn our trust. *The Guardian*, 11 July. [Online]. Available: http://www.theguardian.com/sustainable-business/ethical-business-trust-values. [Accessed 26 April 2014].

NPR staff. 2012. 'The Ethicist' explains how to 'be good'. *National Public Radio (NPR)*, 21 August. [Online]. Available: http://www.npr.org/2012/08/26/159543077/the-ethicist-explains-how-to-be-good. [Accessed 22 April 2014].

PwC. 2014. *Global economic crime survey. Economic crime: A threat to business globally.* PwC. [Online]. Available: http://www.pwc.com/gx/en/economic-crime-survey/. [Accessed 18 April 2014].

Rosenoer, J & Scherlis, W. 2009. Risk gone wild. *Harvard Business Review*, May.

SAPA. 2014. Labour Court slams unfair police practice. *Fin24*, 22 April. [Online]. Available: http://www.fin24.com/Economy/Labour-Court-slams-unfair-police-practice-20140422. [Accessed 26 April 2014].

Schoeman. C. 2012. *Ethics: Giving a damn, making a difference.* Grahamstown: NISC.

SEC. 2013. *2013 Annual Report to Congress on the Dodd-Frank whistleblower program.* United States of America Securities and Exchange Commission (SEC). [Online]. Available: http://www.sec.gov/about/offices/owb/annual-report-2013.pdf. [Accessed 26 April 2014].

Sledge, M. 2013. Bradley Manning uncovered US torture, abuse: Soldiers laughing as they killed innocent civilians. *Huffington Post*, 21 August. [Online]. Available: http://www.huffingtonpost.com/2013/08/21/bradley-manning-leaks_n_3788126.html?utm_hp_ref=bradley-manning. [Accessed 26 April 2014].

South Africa. 2000. Protected Disclosures Act 26 of 2000. Pretoria: Government Printer. [Laws].

South Africa. 2009. Companies Act 71 of 2008. Pretoria: Government Printer. [Laws].

Tilley, A. 2014. Of (silver) bullets and whistleblowers. *Daily Maverick*, 16 April. [Online]. Available: http://www.dailymaverick.co.za/opinionista/2014-04-16-of-silver-bullets-and-whistle blowers/#.U1vBh_mSzYu. [Accessed 26 April 2014].

Transparency International. 2011. *Corruption perceptions index.* [Online]. Available: http://www.transparency.org/cpi2011/results. [Accessed 26 April 2014].

Transparency International. 2012. *Corruption perceptions index.* [Online]. Available: http://www.transparency.org/cpi2012/results. [Accessed 26 April 2014].

Transparency International. 2013. *Corruption perceptions index.* [Online]. Available: http://www.transparency.org/cpi2013/results. [Accessed 26 April 2014].

CHAPTER 6

Allié, M-P. 2011. Introduction: Acting at any price? In C Magone, M Neuman & F Weissman (eds.). *Humanitarian negotiations revealed: The MSF experience.* [Online]. Available: http://www.msf-crash.org/livres/en/acting-at-any-price/introduction-acting-at-any-price. [Accessed 28 April 2014].

Badaracco, JL. Jr. 1997. *Defining moments: When managers must choose between right and right.* Boston, MA: Harvard Business School Press.

Barton, D & Wiseman, M. 2014. Focusing capital on the long term. *Harvard Business Review*, January–February.

Bowie, NE & Schneider, M. 2011. *Business ethics for dummies.* Hoboken, NJ: Wiley Publishing, Inc.

Bridge Pictures. 2001. *The confession.* Bridge Entertainment Group BV.

Bronowski, J (writer & narrator), Malone, A, Gilling, D, Jackson, M & Kennard, DJ (directors). 1973. *The ascent of man, episode 11, Knowledge or certainty* [DVD]. London: BBC & Time-Life Films.

Executive Leadership. 2012. 3 signs of an ethical apocalypse. *Business Management Daily*, 19 October. [Online]. Available: http://www.businessmanagementdaily.com/32619/3-signs-of-an-ethical-apocalypse. [Accessed 27 April 2014].

Fuentes-Nieva, R & Galasso, N. 2014. *Working for the few: Political capture and economic inequality, Oxfam Briefing Paper.* Oxfam, 178, 20 January. [Online]. Available: http://www.oxfam.org/sites/www.oxfam.org/files/bp-working-for-few-political-capture-economic-inequality-200114-en.pdf. [Accessed 29 April 2014].

Galbraith, JK. 1958. The affluent society. Quoted in SD Levitt & SJ Dubner. 2005. *Freakonomics,* London: Penguin Books.

Goldman, SM. 2008. *Temptations in the office: Ethical choices and legal obligations.* Newport, CT: Preager Publishers.

Hardin, G. 1968. The tragedy of the commons. *Science,* 162.

Howes, B. 2008. *Review of 'Temptations in the office: Ethical choices and legal obligations' by SM Goldman (2008).* [Online]. Available: http://www.lpbr.net/2008/10/temptations-in-office-ethical-choices.html. [Accessed 30 April 2014].

Kandola, B. 2011. Is workplace loyalty an outmoded concept? *Financial Times,* 8 March. [Online]. Available: http://www.ft.com/intl/cms/s/0/85ec5d14-49d7-11e0-acf0-00144feab49a.html#axzz30IOgAMWT. [Accessed 29 April 2014].

Kidder, R.M. 1995. *How good people make tough choices: Resolving the dilemmas of ethical living.* New York, NY: Fireside.

Magone, C, Neuman, M & Weissman, F (eds.) 2012. *Humanitarian negotiations revealed: The MSF experience.* London: C Hurst & Co. (Publishers) Ltd. [Online]. Available: http://www.doctorswithoutborders.org/publications/article.cfm?id=5741&cat=books. [Accessed: 16 May 2012].

Rachels, J & Rachels, S. 2010. *The elements of moral philosophy.* Boston, MA: McGraw Hill.

Sagan, C. 1998. *Billions and billions: Thoughts on life and death at the brink of the millennium.* London: Headline Book Publishing.

Sartre, J-P. 1989. 'Dirty hands'. In *No exit and three other plays.* New York, NY: Vintage International.

South Africa. 1995. Promotion of National Unity and Reconciliation Act 34 of 1995. Pretoria: Government Printer. [Laws].

South Africa. 1996. Constitution of the Republic of South Africa, 1996, Chapter 2 Bill of Rights. Pretoria: Government Printer. [Laws]. [Online]. Available: http://www.gov.za/documents/constitution/1996/a108-96.pdf. [Accessed 27 April 2014].

South Africa. 1998. Employment Equity Act 55 of 1998. Pretoria: Government Printer. [Laws].

Strauss, L. 2008. Decision or choice: Is the difference stealing your focus and your time? *Successful Blog,* 28 February. [Online]. Available: http://www.successful-blog.com/1/decision-or-choice-is-the-difference-stealing-your-focus-and-your-time/. [Accessed 27 April 2014].

Terry, F. 2002. *Condemned to repeat? The paradox of humanitarian action.* London: Cornell University Press. [Online]. Available: http://graduateinstitute.ch/files/live/sites/iheid/files/sites/political_science/shared/political_science/3205/Terry-%20Condemned%20to%20Repeat_Ch%206-1.pdf. [Accessed 28 April 2014].

Thatcher, M. 1981. *The 1981 Sir Robert Menzies lecture.* Speech at Monash University, Melbourne. 6 October. Monash University. [Online]. Available: http://www.margaretthatcher.org/document/104712. [Accessed 28 April 2014].

TRC. 1995. Truth and reconciliation website [Online]. Available: http://www.justice.gov.za/Trc/. [Accessed 29 April 2014].

van Niekerk, AA. 2011. Chapter 3, 'Ethics theories and the principalist approach in bioethics'. In K Moodley (ed). *Medical ethics, law and human rights.* Pretoria: Van Schaik Publishers.

Webber, AM. 2000. Why can't we get anything done? *Fast Company,* 31 May. [Online]. Available: http://www.fastcompany.com/39841/why-cant-we-get-anything-done. [Accessed 28 April 2014].

World Economic Forum (WEF). 2013. *Outlook on the global agenda 2014.* November. World Economic Forum. [Online]. Available: http://www3.weforum.org/docs/WEF_GAC_GlobalAgendaOutlook_2014.pdf. [Accessed 29 April 2014].

CHAPTER 7

Burke, E. 1770. 'Thoughts on the cause of the present discontents and the two speeches on America'. In EJ Payne (ed). 1990. *Library of economics and liberty.* [Online]. Available: <http://www.econlib.org/library/LFBooks/Burke/brkSWv1c1.html>.. [Accessed 1 May 2014].

Gladwell, M. 2001. *The tipping point: How little things can make a big difference.* London: Abacus.

Piaget, J. 1932. 'The moral judgement of the child'. Quoted in HS Kushner. 1987. *When all you've ever wanted isn't enough.* London: Pan Books.

Transparency International. 2013. *Global Corruption barometer.* Transparency International. [Online]. Available: http://issuu.com/transparencyinternational/docs/2013_globalcorruption barometer_en/23?e=2496456/3903358. [Accessed 26 April 2014].

APPENDIX

South Africa. 1997. Basic Conditions of Employment Act 75 of 1997. Pretoria: Government Printer. [Laws].

South Africa. 2004. Prevention and Combating of Corrupt Activities Act 12 of 2004. Pretoria: Government Printer. [Laws].

INDEX

[Created with **TExtract** / www.Texyz.com]